Advanced Praise for *Awakening East*

It's likely you either have to be naive or crazy to drag your family to live a year in China. Maybe both. Johanna Garton fits the bill perfectly, with a wonderful optimism and willingness to try that ends up putting her family of four well outside the familiar confines of Denver, Colorado, and even outside the relatively comfortable expat outposts of Beijing and Shanghai. Framed through the stories of their two adopted children, Garton and her husband return with them to the land of their birth and try to trace the stories of their earliest days while diving headlong into the crazy and complex challenges that come with living as expats in the Middle Kingdom. It's a story filled with honesty and warmth, one well worth the time to read.

- Greg Rhodes, Author, Expat in China: A Family Adventure and Expat in China: The Chengdu Blues

In *Awakening East*, Johanna Garton's family embarks on an adventure: one year in China to allow her adopted children a chance to experience their birth-country. It's a year filled with hardships and humor, but most of all, with heart. If the year was Garton's gift to her children, then Awakening East is a gift to the reader, our chance to live with a vibrant family through all their ups and downs.

- Carolyn Wilson-Scott, Writer, Mother

D0121937

Awakening East is told in such an authentic and raw way that I cried several times, relating to the struggles with parenting, the balance between adventure and stability, and how to define one's own cultural identity amidst a sea of competing values. Garton has given us a gift with this story, as we are allowed a glimpse into a unique, cherished and inspiring experience.

- Carrie Esposito, Writer

I laughed and cried my way through *Awakening East*. Johanna Garton uses her personal and family journeys to capture the depth of emotion and meaning that accompany the various stages of growing a family through adoption. Garton will inspire all parents through her candid and humorous account of the love and endurance that carried her family through the ups and downs of living for a year in China. It's a must read for any parents challenged to think outside the box when dealing with issues unique to adoption.

- Eri Asano, Adoptive mother, Clinical Psychologist

If you're looking for a widely entertaining, richly written story that combines international travel, family, and inspiration for stepping outside of your comfort zone, *Awakening East* is your read. Johanna Garton takes us on a literary adventure through a series of life-changing experiences, all connected beautifully through humor and the deep love she has for her family. China itself is one of the major characters in this book, which you will meet in a richly personal way through a daring year of embracing life outside of America. While the conduit for this adventure is based on her children's adoption stories, anyone with a sense of awe for dashing into the unknown via travel will relish this ride.

- Melissa Yoder, Communications Manager, Writer, Mother

Some names and places have been changed to respect the privacy of individuals. With regard to those whose names were not changed, I wish to acknowledge that their portraits are based on my memories alone.
- Johanna Garton

Awakening East
Moving our Adopted Children Back to China

by Johanna Garton

Printed in the United States of America.
Published by Marcinson Press, Jacksonville, Florida.
© Copyright 2015 by Johanna Garton

Additional copies of this book may be purchased through most online book retailers and by request through major and independent bookstores. To purchase this book for your library or in bulk, please contact the publisher at www.marcinsonpress.com.

ISBN 978-0-9893732-9-6

Published by
Marcinson Press
10950-60 San Jose Blvd., Suite 136
Jacksonville, FL 32223 USA
http://www.marcinsonpress.com

awakening east

Moving our
Adopted
Children
Back to China

JOHANNA GARTON

For Will and Eden,
who've given me so much more than motherhood.

And for their birth parents,
whose gifts of two small lives gave me mine.

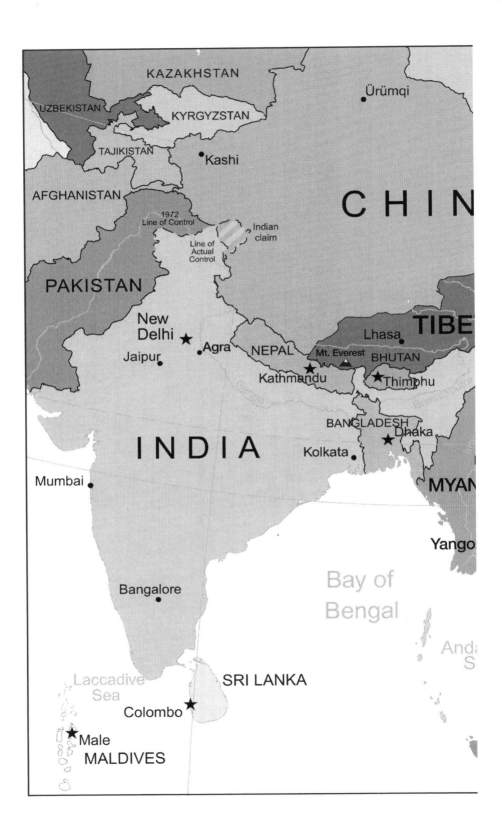

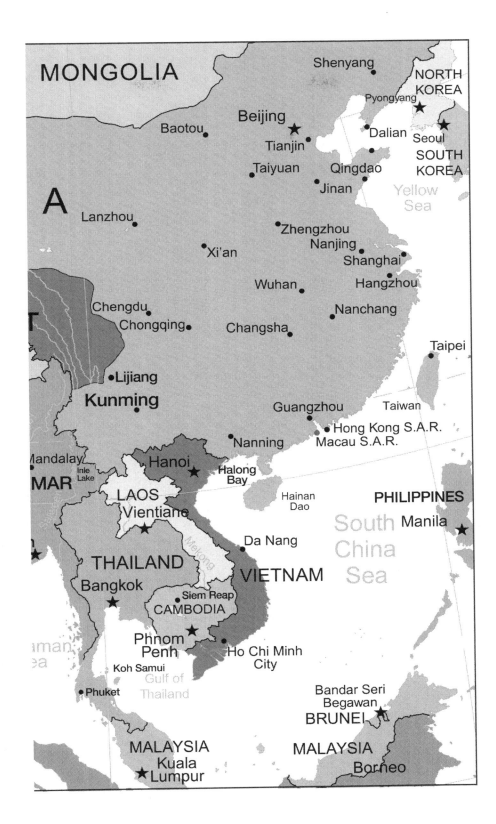

chapter one

The red dress stared out at me from the closet. Its weathered color was the result of too many tortured spin cycles in our cheap washing machine. *Damn. This looked so good in the Title Nine catalog a few years ago. Here in China, the life could be sucked out of everything so quickly.* I hear nine-year-old Will in the other room rummaging through his shirts, trying to decide what to wear.

"Mom, I think I'm gonna wear my blue shirt, cause it's my favorite. But also some nice school pants. I want to look good. Do you think I should wear my school jacket?"

"I think you should wear whatever you want," I answer. "Whatever makes you most comfortable."

The simple response echoed the same reassuring tone that mothers everywhere gave to children who were asking questions in moments of fear or anxiety. Or confusion. Or anticipation. Jumbled together, all of these emotions were heavy in the air this morning. This day was just like any other here in Kunming. It was a day that represented many of the reasons our family had left the United States. I hoped it would be a day that would provide richness and answers to Will's life story – his adoption story. It was, for our family, Orphanage Visiting Day.

I grabbed the dress and slipped it over my head. The washing machine was on the verge of breaking and our *āyí* would soon need to start washing our clothes by hand. Today, all that mattered was that it was clean and red, the color that symbolized happiness, good fortune and joy in China. Today we needed all three.

I walked past the children's bedroom where two large picture windows held cozy seats for both Will and our four-year-old daughter, Eden. The windows looked out over the busy street below. We had spent hours peering out the windows, fascinated by the movements of the locals – as if watching a movie. And there was always something dramatic happening. Live electric wires being cast down upon the street. Couples fighting. A scooter packed with a family of four and a basket of chickens heading to the market. My husband Ernie and I had a window seat in our bedroom, too. I'd found a pink shag rug and covered its base. I'd sit for hours watching the scenes on the street, planning my university lessons and Skyping friends at home. When we moved to China, I had promised the family that we would each have our own space, no matter how small. The children and I had ended up with these window spaces, while Ernie scored a small office in our tiny apartment.

As I headed to the kitchen, I noticed that Will was up to his eyeballs in Legos. He held a small creation in the palm of his hand, adding pieces meticulously. I knew the importance of what he was working on, so I continued walking. My mind churned with anticipation. Questions. Nerves.

The orphanage where Will had lived for the first eleven months of his life was only twenty minutes from our apartment. Still, it had taken us months to pull together the logistics needed to visit. We had run what felt like a hamster wheel as we tried to coordinate the visit in a way that felt comfortable for us. Heritage tours, designed to provide adoptees with a connection to the land of their birth, were becoming popular with adoptive families worldwide. Agencies specializing in such tours were flooding the American market, yet we lost the chance to work with an American agency when we hit Chinese soil and began to immerse ourselves in daily life.

We'd tried to organize a visit on our own, but reality hit us hard. Not only was it not possible to stroll up to the gates of the orphanage any time we wanted, but there were hoops even when using a very basic Chinese facilitator to help us navigate the process. Then there were the fees. A fee to the provincial authority, equivalent to $500, was required. When we pressed the facilitator about what the fee covered, we were given a long list of items, which we didn't need. Extra photos, snacks, a private town car. In the end, we graciously accepted all but a few things on the list, and negotiated a lower fee. Knowing what we knew of Chinese customs, pressing too hard would result in a loss of face for our hosts, jeopardizing what we hoped would be a meaningful experience for Will.

Please. Please let this not be a boondoggle. I ached for a transformative day, when in my heart, I knew those moments in life only came when unexpected. Defining our Asia experience here in one day was silly. The year could thus far have been summed up in one word: Unpredictable. I knew this meant that today would be no different.

In the kitchen, I scooped slices of mango into a bowl, placing it on the dining room table. Next to it, I served tiny cartons of yogurt with straws poked in the tops, Chinese style. Eden slipped into her chair as I poured her a glass of orange juice.

"I don't want to go to school. I want to stay with you."

Eden dove into her breakfast as she spoke. The sight of her full mouth trying to conquer both eating and talking made me grimace. Eating and talking were her two favorite activities, and here in China, both were welcome to live side by side. I gave her a look and asked her to please chew with her mouth closed.

"Will, are you up for eggs or cereal, bud?"

Ernie and I jostled for space in our galley kitchen as we prepared for another day. The iPad sat perched on top of the fridge and was streaming CNN. The live feed was *Anderson Cooper 360°*. Fourteen hours behind us in the United States.

"Not hungry. Can I eat later?"

I shot a glance at Ernie as he looked at me for direction. Food had been one of many struggles this year. Except for Eden, we had each lost weight. Keeping our bodies fed had become a goal I woke to every morning. Now on the back end of our year, it was apparent that we'd lived on the extremes. The tough. The gritty. The raw.

There was our daily life in China. Coordinating how to come here to live and work had exhausted us even before we'd left the United States. We had embraced this task without much help. There had been no American company sending us over with relocation services. Nobody to help us find a place to live. I had a teaching job providing visas, but little else in the way of communication before we'd left. People commented how lucky we were to be able to undertake such an adventure, but to me it felt nothing like luck. It felt like pure grit. A constant game of chicken with Chinese universities and the government as we scratched for every chance at jobs, visas, a place to live. I was wrung out before we'd even ordered our plane tickets. But the hope that life would be easy once we arrived buoyed me through months of packing and planning.

Easy was not in the cards. Life here was difficult for many reasons, at least the authentically Chinese way we'd chosen to undertake it. After nine months, my hair was grey. My nerves were frayed. I'd cried tears of frustration so often that I felt numb. Our family had gone to dark places that I'd never envisioned. Ernie and I had joked, half serious, that therapy for some – or all – of us was a given, once we got back to the States.

In an effort to escape daily life, we had traveled as often as possible, leaving China behind to see more of the world. In the process, we'd reached the highest peaks a family can reach together. We'd climbed the temples at Angkor Wat in Cambodia. Touched the pearly walls of the Taj Mahal. Crawled on hands and knees on the Great Wall. Our faces took in the sunlight on the Star Ferry crossing Hong Kong Harbor. We had stuffed our pockets with rocks from the pits of the Terra Cotta Warriors, gone on safari in Nepal and found wild rhinos in the jungle, snorkeled in Thailand, and gazed at giant pandas in Sichuan Province. A dizzy spin on the merry-go-round of Southeast Asia.

Yet with each short adventure, we ultimately returned to our quiet yet challenging life in Kunming. *What would today be about? Which extreme?*

"I want to go to the orphanage with you, Momma!" Eden looked up at me. A day off from her Chinese kindergarten would be much welcomed, I knew. But this day was just for Will. At four, she was too young to fully grasp the importance of our visit to Will's old home, and would be likely to whine and complain about being hungry on a day that such behavior would feel extra difficult.

"Honey, I think you'll have more fun at school. We aren't really sure what to expect today. And Wen Keh would miss you."

I used her best friend's name as bait to slip her school uniform on. The sweatshirt she was required to wear was too big, the pants too long. We had enrolled the children too late in the school year for them to get smart-fitting uniforms.

"This is a special day for Will, and we have your special weekend planned in a couple weeks."

Our son had lived his first year in an orphanage, but Eden had lived with a foster mother. We had gone through a totally different, but equally frustrating period of coordination in order to visit her foster mother. The visit was happening next month, the plane tickets purchased. Edie talked often and lovingly of this woman she could only remember from pictures.

"Okay. Can you bring me a treat then?" Eden countered.

"I'll see what I can do, Edie."

I made a mental note to pick up her favorite snack. She was a child who loved food. This meant living in Asia had been a blessing and a curse. Adventurous by nature, she would eat anything offered up from street vendors. And they loved to feed her, this little Chinese girl with the odd American parents. We'd become regulars at a tofu stand run by an old woman at the bottom of a footbridge near her school. Eden would deftly order a small carton of grilled tofu in her freshly acquired Mandarin skills. I'd taught her how to ask for it "not too spicy" and made sure to add in "No MSG please" so frequently that the woman now gave a little chuckle whenever I asked. She knew. It was just like a barista at any American coffee house. If you visited enough, they knew.

But the risky food choices brought occasional downfall. Eden's notorious stomach of steel was sometimes pushed to the brink as the result of poor food sanitation. She'd complain of tummy aches and vow to never eat from a street vendor again. But once the culprit passed, she was on to the next squid-on-a-stick or fried dough ball that was around the corner. She was riskier than the rest of us put together and I loved it.

I adored my daughter for her flexibility. She handled change like nobody else. As a baby, she had rarely cried. As a toddler, Will would brood for hours over a time out. Not Eden. She would bounce back and get on with her day. No time to waste. Especially now, her resiliency was an example to the rest of us.

I strapped Eden onto the bike seat as Ernie steadied the

bike. This lone ten-speed was our family's only mode of trans-portation this year, and it took Eden to school and back.

"Don't linger," I whispered to Ernie.

The guide and driver were picking us up in less than an hour.

"Bye, Sweetie! Have a great day at school. I'll pick you up in a few hours."

"Bye, Momma! Don't forget the treat!"

While Ernie took Eden to school, Will and I talked through the questions he had planned to ask today. There were no assurances that any of them would be answered, but Will felt certain about asking each one. Individually, the questions were monumental, representing hours of time spent thinking and daydreaming. On Will's part and my own.

What was Will's health when he was found?

Can we see the original police report filed after he was left?

Who was his primary caregiver?

Can we see where he slept and played as a baby?

Was he left with a note?

Do you have any knowledge of why he was abandoned?

"So buddy, when we get there, Dad and I aren't really sure, you know, who will be there to greet us or who we'll have a chance to speak with."

"I know. Gosh, Mom, you already told me that ten times. What the heck?" Will shook off my efforts to prepare for any scenario.

I'd spent the past few weeks immersed in literature about how to prepare for this visit. Ernie and I had talked about the questions we would all want to ask. We talked about how Will might feel when we arrived at the orphanage. There was a chance, we read, that he might panic and want to leave right away. Or perhaps he would arrive and want to stay well beyond what the orphanage was prepared to offer us. We had developed code words for him to use with us in either case. And we wanted to give back. Bags of clothes to donate to the children remaining in the orphanage were sitting at our front door. We had printed color copies of the photos we received when Will was a baby, before we came to pick him up. The photos were sent to us by the orphanage and we hoped they might spark a memory or two in staff still remaining after the eight-plus years it had been since we adopted Will.

"What about the sign, Will? Are you sure you don't want to bring a sign or a photo?"

I was pushing this issue, though I could sense his frustration.

"No way. Just the spaceship."

We'd also planned to visit his "finding spot" after we left the orphanage. This was the spot where he had been found as a newborn. We'd held the name of this apartment building for nine years, but had no idea where it was located in Kunming.

I had read stories of adoptees returning to their finding spots and leaving signs. Signs that included photos of them as babies and other pictures of them grown up. With brief blurbs about their happy lives and wonderful adoptive families. The thought was that if the birth parents remained in the area, there would be a slim chance that the sign would be seen and provide solace. But Will wasn't budging on this. Though he wanted to visit his finding spot, he preferred to remain anonymous. Instead, he had built a little spaceship out of Legos. He planned to leave this at his finding spot for another child to find and treasure.

"Okay, that's cool buddy. Just want to make sure."

"Mom, chill out. You're acting all weird."

"I just want to make sure we're all ready. Are you ready? Did you brush your teeth? Are you hungry? Is there anything else you want to bring?"

Will was ready. He didn't need my nagging, so I backed off. He sat down and began to work on origami at the dining room table. I wondered what he was thinking and how he was feeling. I couldn't imagine. At age nine, I was busy with my stuffed animals. The biggest stresses in my life were what songs or stories to add to the mixed cassette tapes I was making my cousins. Yet here I was, thirty-plus years later, expecting so much out of my own nine-year-old.

The transition to life in China had been more difficult for Will than any of us. While Eden had been a flexible and easy-going baby, Will always seemed to hold the weight of the world. As a toddler, one stern look from me and he would dissolve into tears, recovery sometimes taking hours. This provided an easy palette for me to teach right from wrong, but also had short-comings. He was a creature of habit and routine. New experiences were mostly unwelcome. Will was tiny as a baby and never broke out of the fifth percentile on the American growth chart. He was nine but looked seven and I feared this caused him insecurities. In the weeks leading up to our departure from the United States, he had announced "none of us could talk about China anymore." Ernie and I thus had to limit our discussions of packing and logistics to the hours the children were out of earshot or asleep.

He's going to be fine today. Ernie buzzed our front bell, signaling his return. We gathered the bags of donations and walked to the front gate of our apartment. The guard gave us a smile and a wave. All of our Mandarin skills were solid now, and it was the only language we used when speaking outside our apartment with the locals.

"Good morning," I said. "How are you?"

"Good," he replied. As usual, our conversation was minimal, though his eyes asked a thousand questions. Where are you going today? Why is your son not in school? I was sure he wanted to know. Though he would've directly asked any other resident of this massive Chinese apartment complex, we were one of only two foreign families here, and people provided distance. Whether it was out of respect or fear of foreigners, we weren't sure.

My cell phone rang to let us know that the car and guide were approaching. The guide we had been connected with used the English name Susan. We found her through Chinese adoption connections back home. There were introductions with the driver and then Susan began to speak quickly about our itinerary. Her pace jolted all three of us. Though friendly, she seemed most interested in knowing what our expectations were for the day. I started by telling her that we had many questions we wanted to ask the orphanage staff.

"What are they?" she asked.

"Pardon me?" I replied. The direct tone of the Chinese people was more familiar to me now, but still amusing at times. In China, we found there wasn't such a need to be polite or long-winded in your conversations or inquiries with others. In fact, we had learned that such dialogue was considered rude. Instead, the Chinese preferred to get straight to the point, an indication of respect for one's time.

"What are your questions? I will see if I can answer any of them."

"There are many questions about Will's life in the orphanage, and well..." I stopped. I remembered that this was to be my son's day, not mine. I was jumping into my usual role of manager, coordinator, and director. Not my place today.

"Will, are there any questions that you'd like to ask Susan right now, before we get there?"

"No, Mom. You go. You ask. And Mom, I'm kinda hungry."

I turned to Ernie and we both smiled a bit, relieved. The list of foods that Will would eat was slim. Any opportunity to expand that list was a blessing. Susan had offered us breakfast pastries when we'd gotten in the car, but they were made of beans and remained on the seat uneaten.

"Susan, could we ask the driver to stop for just a minute?"

"Sure." The driver pulled over and Susan jumped out, leading us to shop after shop of eateries that Will would never set foot in. As we passed each one, he would shake his head. No to the shop with pickled everythings. No to the icky muffin bakery. No to the stand with the boiled eggs. No to the nut vendor. I was reminded of the fact that we were in Kunming, a relatively traditional Chinese city. This was no Beijing or Shanghai. Though we had eaten many delicious meals at upscale restaurants in town, our daily meals were uninspiring. Our waistlines were smaller, and we began to refer to this phenomenon as The China Diet.

Finally, Will found a bag of dried peas and a bottle of sports drink. Satisfaction. We hopped back in the car and I killed time asking a few standard questions for which I already knew the answers.

"Are babies still abandoned in China?"

"Yes, but not as frequently," came her simple reply.

"Why has the process to adopt from China slowed down so much?"

"More domestic adoption, less abandonment."

"What does the average person think about China's One Child Policy?

"Some agree with it, some don't."

And then, "We're here," chirped Susan.

The van pulled around a corner and I gasped. "I remember the street, Ernie! This is it. I see the building." The monstrous, white building wore a tired look. But it was the same place

I had stood so many years ago. I grabbed for Will's hand. His eyes were cast upon the place that was once home. And he was smiling.

chapter two

It was just as I had pictured Scotland. The hillside was covered with lush, green grass. Rain came down in a steady drizzle, as I stood facing into it. There was a light wind and I felt cold walking with the soft ground absorbing my weight and the pattern of my hiking boots. *It's so peaceful*, I thought, as I stood alone. I was 20 years old during the spring of 1991, and had traveled here from Strasbourg, France, where I was in the middle of a semester abroad with Syracuse University. This was not a destination on anyone else's itinerary, so I had chosen to come by myself. I couldn't explain my need to be here, when all of Europe was calling. My friends and I had hopscotched all over the continent in the past few months. Sure, we were studying, but the more important learning came Friday through Sunday, when we traveled. Mid-week, we'd crack open our *Let's Go* guidebooks.

"How about Budapest?" Eileen offered.

"Too far," Holly replied. "let's save that for a school holiday."

"London? We have friends in the London program. I'm sure we could find a place to stay."

"Nah, they speak English. What's the point?" Holly countered.

"Lockerbie. Do either of you want to go to Lockerbie?" I was hesitant to bring it up, as we all knew what it meant. I'd brought it up before casually, and now I got the same reaction.

"Why exactly do you wanna go there? There's nothing there, Jo. Nothing. It's hard to get there, and for what? It's kinda morbid, if you ask me."

Eileen looked at Holly for confirmation of her opinion and received it. Alone. I was alone.

"I don't know, I don't know. It's weird," I mumbled. "I just feel I need to go there."

They would travel elsewhere that weekend, and I would take my silly little pilgrimage to Lockerbie alone. This meant a train to Paris, crossing the English Channel, then a train to London, and another one north to my endpoint.

The destination was well known to all of us studying in Strasbourg. It had been just over two years since Pan Am flight 103 had crashed on December 21, 1988, en route to JFK in New York, killing all passengers as well as eleven people on the ground in the little Scottish village of Lockerbie. On board were 35 students from Syracuse who were returning from a semester abroad in London. It was a senseless, crushing loss to our university. At the time of the disaster, we didn't know that it was an act of terrorism. Years later, it was established that the attack was ordered by Libyan leader Muammar Gaddafi. This was 13 years before 9/11, and up to this point it was one of the worst terrorist attacks in history. Americans had not experienced anything like this and two years later, my classmates and I were still deeply affected by the loss of our peers.

I had been at home in Wisconsin on winter break that December when I heard the news. Busy with Christmas shopping and catching up with high school friends had consumed me. I had just finished my first semester at Syracuse. I had gone there to study broadcast journalism and to run on the track team. At 18, I was full of drama and excited to be on my own. Homesickness had come in waves those first months, but by the time I was home for Christmas break, Syracuse had become my world.

Hearing the news that 35 of my classmates had been killed

was shattering. I nearly skipped Christmas with my family to immediately return to campus. When I did return in January, a heavy cloud had settled over the university. Memorials were held to honor individual students. There was a service in the Carrier Dome – the university's football and basketball stadium. Our track team tied small black bands on our competition jerseys, as did the basketball team that we shared practice space with.

I stumbled as I tried to come to grips with my reaction to the loss, which seemed more enormous for me than for some of my friends. I had not known any of the 35 students. They were at a point in their college careers that seemed so far away for me. As a freshman, I couldn't fathom what it would be like to be getting ready to graduate into the world. Yet, it was as if I had lost a piece of myself on that day. I began to dwell on what could happen to me in an instant. A car accident. Cancer. A tornado. The collapse of a building. A fire in the dormitory. We could all be taken away in an instant, and I was no exception. No longer immune from the problems of the world, I felt a shift within me to take more responsibility for my life.

I began to make small changes in order to fulfill the goals that my classmates had not been able to by their early deaths. It didn't matter to me that I had no knowledge what those goals might be. It only mattered that I walk the same path. This meant loading up on my course of study, adding French as a major so I could study abroad as a junior, just as they had done. It meant running with more purpose. Our coach led us in prayer before each of our cross-country races. My prayers said before each race had once been cluttered with thoughts about whether my laces were tied tightly enough, whether the spikes on my racing flats were screwed in far enough. Now the moments meant time to reflect and just be grateful that I could... run. I could run.

I began volunteering more, squeezing in weekly trips to a downtown childcare center. I made monthly visits with flowers to the Wall of Remembrance on campus, which had been erected to honor my classmates. The changes went unnoticed by even me, until I sat in Strasbourg with Holly and Eileen, completely insistent that it was time to go to Lockerbie. They didn't get it. Nor did I, for that matter. I just knew that it was time. Three days later, there I was. Standing alone on a hill in Lockerbie.

There wasn't a *Let's Go* chapter on this place, beautiful as it was. I had arrived by train the night before. Lockerbie's station was a two-track platform without a lobby or a gift shop. I got off the train, and not having made any plans about where to stay, I approached the stationmaster.

"Excuse me, sir. Can you recommend a place for me to stay?"

"Well, young lady, let me think. There's a bed and breakfast across the bridge. Let me give them a call."

He led me inside his small office and after confirming there was space for one that evening, he asked where I was from.

"I'm American."

"I guessed that," he chuckled. "I suppose I meant to ask you what you're doing here?"

"I'm studying in Strasbourg with Syracuse University."

"I see." I watched as he quickly downshifted his mood from jolly to resolved. "Then I know what you're doing here."

His reaction took my breath away. I let the emotions wash over me. Warmth. Emptiness. Uncertainty. Still confused as to what had brought me here, I nonetheless *knew* it was the right place to be. The people of Lockerbie and the students of Syracuse were bound.

The next morning I woke up well before my alarm. Lacing up my running shoes, I got directions to a nearby golf course. A run seemed a better start to the day than a trip to the cemetery.

"Just over the hill, Miss. You'll see it overlooking the village." The bed and breakfast owner sent me off, wishing me well.

I soon found myself on the golf course, close to the location where Pan Am 103 had come down. It had destroyed several houses, killing entire families, leaving a giant crater in the earth. It had been filled in and was no longer visible, leaving the village to return to a version of itself. I strode up the hill, which opened into miles and miles of Scottish countryside. Sheep grazed all around me, crossing footpaths and streams. In the silence, I picked up fallen leaves, and continued running, stopping when I started to cry. *I feel like I was meant to come here. What is wrong with me? Why am I crying?*

Turning around, I looked for something to give me an answer as to why I had come. There was only quiet. I relaxed into the countryside, sitting down. *A sign. A sign,* I thought. *I'll just sit here until I see or hear something.* I waited. Nothing. I sat longer. *Well, I'm just ridiculous. What do I expect is going to happen to me here? Good God, Johanna!* I stood and began to run, the hills carrying me back down into the village. I realized I had struggled on the climb up, but was now flying with the wind at my back.

My next destination was Dryfesdale Cemetery. The local community had devoted a portion of their space in the cemetery to create a memorial here called the Garden of Remembrance. It was beautiful, surrounded by little planted trees and pots of flowers. Leading to a stone wall, where each of the victim's names were etched, were the 35 stones I had read about. The nearby benches called to me to rest. Having been raised to use silence as a means to tranquility, I thought about how to move forward.

There's no way this was the end of their story. Not like this. I'm gonna have to pick up the pieces where they left off. I'll do better with my life. I'll be open-minded. I'll learn about the world and do what I can to help others. Oh my God, I have no idea what that means! Okay, well, must work on figuring that out.

I rose and walked to the wall, looking at each of the 279 names. I walked, tears streaming down my cheeks, and on each step of the 35 stones I whispered, "I promise." Thirty-five times. Thirty-five promises.

I was 20 and had no idea how to fulfill this vow to myself and my classmates. I only knew that I had come all this way for a reason, and the hills of Lockerbie had provided this calling. It would have to be enough to start my life.

chapter three

Graduation from college came and went, and with Syracuse in my rear view mirror, I made the decision to try getting work in Los Angeles where I had family. I was dedicated to doing something meaningful with my life and felt I could still do that as a journalist. It was 1992 and the job market was in the dumps. Driven by the sense that this was the right thing to be doing, I spent weeks networking in southern California. Nothing more than offers of unpaid internships fell into my lap. The end of summer came and I packed up my car and drove back to home base in Wisconsin. If I couldn't get a decent job, it was time to carry on with my plan to explore the world a bit more, I decided. The career office at Syracuse had posted a listing for teachers in Taiwan. *Taiwan?* I thought, *Is that part of China? Do they speak Mandarin?* It was a part of the world that I had no knowledge of. The thought seemed compelling, though. I had already done the whole Europe-with-a-backpack thing. Why not learn Mandarin? Surely it would be useful someday, right? I applied. Almost immediately, I heard back from a young American woman named Lindsey running an English language school in the south of Taiwan.

"You think you're up for it?" she asked over the phone. "It's a different part of the world, you realize? I know you have been to Europe, but Asia is, you know, nothing like Europe."

"I feel pretty confident that I could hack it." I really had absolutely no idea, but it seemed the appropriate response.

Summer turned to fall and I worked two jobs at home in

Wisconsin while I waited to hear about Taiwan. It was looking good, but there appeared to be a few paperwork hoops to jump through in order to obtain a visa. I could wait. I couldn't believe they weren't clamoring for my completely untested skills as an English teacher, but... whatever. One day as the holidays approached, the phone rang.

"May I speak with Johanna Garton, please?" the voice asked.

"This is she."

"Johanna, this is Craig Carpenter, *LA Times* Sports Department. We met a few months ago. Wondering if you're still interested in working for the *Times*? We've got an entry-level runner position open that's yours if you'd like it."

My heart jumped and sank all at the same time. I'd spent four years perfecting my writing, chasing news stories in Syracuse and hosting a sports radio show. A hard-earned journalism degree. The *LA Times* wasn't exactly the *Smallville News*, either. I would be a small fish. Big pond. Small fish. A thousand other candidates were no doubt lined up behind me to take the position should I pass on it. *What's my problem? I feel as though I should take the job. That's what's expected of me. It would be easier, wouldn't it, than moving to Asia?* Without really understanding why, I knew I had to decline. I told the *Times* I was planning to move to Taiwan.

"Taiwan? Really? That sounds like quite an adventure. I wish you the best, then, young lady. Hope it all turns out." Holy crow so did I.

Fall turned to winter and still problems persisted with obtaining a visa. *How hard could this be,* I wondered? While I waited, I struck up a friendship with another woman who'd also been crazy enough to take a job with the school. Her name was Ruby and she lived in New England. Unlike me, she actually spoke Mandarin already, and had been to Taiwan. We spent hours on the phone talking about what we were packing and why we had made the decision to go. Our contracts were for two years and the money was good. If we managed to save enough, we could come back to the States in two years with nest eggs at the young age of 24. Ruby hoped to attend medical school. It seemed like a thoughtful plan. I panicked, wondering what Craig Carpenter would be doing in two years, and if his offer would still stand.

Finally, the time came for us to leave. Visas obtained, Ruby and I spent the night before departure describing in detail what we'd be wearing when we met for the first time at LAX. We were scheduled on the same China Southern flight to Taipei, where Lindsey would meet us and drive us to our new home two hours south.

"I'm going to layer up," Ruby said. "Green shirt, Blue fleece top. Probably jeans. My hair is blonde and I am about five-feet-four. I will have a red Patagonia backpack." *Layer up. Nice. Practical. Very New England.* I smiled to myself.

"Got it. I think I'm gonna wear jeans, too. A red jacket. Probably a ponytail. My hair's kinda light brown. I'm five-feet-four, too."

The next day I walked towards the gate for our China Southern flight, mumbling to myself, *Green shirt, blue top, blonde hair, red backpack.* I turned into the waiting area and was swallowed into a sea of black-haired, brown-eyed Chinese passengers. I couldn't help but laugh out loud as I stared across the room at the one other Caucasian person on the flight. Green shirt, blue top, blonde hair, red backpack.

"If you aren't Ruby, I'm going to eat my hat," I laughed as we embraced, the journey underway.

As it turned out, Lindsey had been spot on. Asia was nothing like Europe. I *loved* it. Streets filled with bikes, food carts on every corner and people full of warmth, anxious to learn about America and the west. Whereas life in the USA had been routine and predictable, our days in Taiwan were filled with pure madness. The days were consumed with teaching English to children and running private lessons on the side to adults. I took classes in Mandarin and began working with a tutor to improve my tones and vocabulary.

Just as life took root, our school fell into crisis, along with our work status. Something about government officials and paperwork. Under the table payments, favors paid and favors owed. It was a new world to me, and much of it involved what the Taiwanese called "guānxi." It was a term that couldn't be translated into English, but meant something akin to the relationships and connections that people cultivate to get things done professionally. As I had come to understand it, you needed guānxi to get practically anything done in Taiwan. Without it, life became stagnant. And if you used your guānxi inappropriately, a price would be paid. In our case, this meant our school closed, forcing us to leave the apartment that had been provided. Without jobs, our visas were cancelled and we were told to leave the country.

"How can this happen?" I asked Ruby one day over the phone. She was racing around town trying to find a new place for us to live. "We didn't do anything wrong. We didn't do anything at ALL. Can't we just get new jobs at new schools?"

"Yes, but that would mean a boatload of paperwork for a new employer. Honestly, who would hire us for only a year?"

We'd been in Taiwan one year, and had planned for two. Click. Click. Click. In rapid succession, our phone was making noises I'd never heard.

"What is *that?*" I asked.

"It's our phones. I heard they've been tapped."

And sure enough, we were being watched. Our phones *had* been tapped, as we were now on deportation watch with the local government. In general, it had been hard to go unnoticed, as we were practically the only Caucasians in town. But this had taken things to a whole new level. We didn't want to risk being thrown into a Taiwanese jail, but weren't ready to come crawling home without fulfilling our desire to see more of Asia before we left. To avoid deportation, we resolved to continue teaching private lessons under the table while coming in and out of the country at two-month intervals, traveling on renewable tourist visas.

The plan proved a success. And when we finally had enough money socked away, we packed our backpacks and took flight to see Asia. Nepal, Cambodia, Vietnam, Indonesia, Malaysia, Thailand. Our passports filled as we jumped from planes to trains to overnight buses. The only country not on our itinerary was China. It was 1994, and China was still on the way to opening to the West. The One Child Policy was in full swing, restricting many Chinese to only one child in a society which largely preferred boys. As we traveled in surrounding countries, we began to hear about the abandonment of baby girls as a result of the policy. Families were leaving baby girls and trying again to have a boy, who would be more likely to earn money for the family and take care of parents as they aged. *Terrible*, I thought. *What a world!* I listened to the stories about an increase in international adoptions from China, made a mental note, and we continued our journey.

We traveled for months, calculating to the rupee how long we could continue until finances forced us home. Surviving months traveling in third world countries brought us a close-ness that could only come from that sort of test. We bickered and went days without speaking at times. I ran to the pharmacy when she was doubled over with the remnants of food poison-ing. She held me when I learned of my grandmother's death. I drove her batty with my goofy jokes and Midwestern naivety. I watched as her cool charm, beauty and intelligence melted hearts in every country we visited. Together we scratched our way to a version of what we'd planned for when we signed up for the stint in Taiwan long ago.

Eventually, the rupees ran dry and time came for a return to the U.S. Ruby was off to medical school out east and I'd taken a one-year position in Chicago as a member of the domestic Peace Corps, AmeriCorps VISTA.

"I can't believe it's over."

I stood in the driveway of Ruby's lake home in New Hamp-shire. She and I had continued our travels in the United States. Stopping in Wisconsin briefly to see my parents, and then car-rying on to her family. I was turning around to head back to the Midwest, with a stop in Syracuse planned.

"Kind of, you know, not what we expected, was it?" We both laughed at her observation and I tried not to tear up.

"After Taiwan, med school is gonna be a breeze."

"And Worchester and Chicago are basically the same dis-tance as Nepal to Thailand. No problem!"

We hugged and I drove down the bumpy road away from the lake. And away from Ruby.

This won't be end of our story, I told myself as I drove west.

chapter four

"So, wait. Are you telling me they won't speak with you because you're a guy?"

"Johanna, you've been here a month already. I'm male. Our clients have all been raped. They don't want to even *look* at me, much less have me take them to the doctor. You've gotta do it." My supervisor looked miffed by my need for clarification.

"Right. Okay. No problem, Jason. I'm on it. And a translator?"

"No translator available today, I'm afraid. You'll be fine. You're so... sunny." The appointments were simple medical checkups, but the patients – not so simple. My sunniness was going to need an added kick.

My family was full of do-gooders. Teachers. Social workers. Philanthropists. Therefore, my decision to join AmeriCorps was an easy one. The program had just been re-launched by President Clinton in the summer of 1994. I joined in the inaugural class in Chicago, and making use of my recent international experience, found placement with a treatment center for refugee survivors of torture. The work was difficult and emotionally draining. Our clients were from the countries with the worst human rights records. I poured myself into the work, helping coordinate mental health counseling for women raped during the genocide in Bosnia, art therapy for African women who had fled genital mutilation, managing dental appointments for Cambodian refugees who had seen their entire families tortured and killed, writing grants to the

United Nations to ask for more money, more resources, more help. Please, more help. Collapsing from emotional strain at the end of each day, I suffered from "secondary trauma." The world was hemorrhaging problems and I couldn't keep up fast enough to help.

"Honey, I think you need to start thinking ahead to your time after this is over," my mother pleaded on the phone.

"What about law school, Mom? There's a great program down here that focuses on international human rights law."

"An attorney? An attorney? You've never spoken of that as a career choice before."

"You don't HAVE to be a practicing attorney when you grad-uate, Mom. I think it might be a great way for me to learn how to be an advocate for, well, whatever I want." And so it was that I entered DePaul College of Law as a not-really-interest-ed-in-practicing-law student, and I hated almost every min-ute of the first two years. By the end of the second year, my GPA was in the dumps, but I was finally able to ditch contracts, torts and criminal law and take the courses I'd wanted since day one. I shifted from memorizing case law to working in the immigration clinic. I worked on an asylum case and won for a refugee from Sudan. I worked in legal services helping im-poverished clients seek justice. By the end of three years, I'd decided to at least consider practicing law. But not in Chicago – Colorado had been a frequent destination for me through-out my childhood. It was the one place in the country where I felt I could build a life and career. The mountains of Colorado were calling.

I drove a rental truck a thousand miles until the Rockies came into view. Colorado was home to two of my closest friends, my cousins Julie and Chris. I'd worked in Denver at the CBS affiliate after returning from Strasbourg. When law school graduation grew closer, it was the only place I wanted to end up. I'd registered to sit for the bar exam in July of 1998 and planned to travel a bit before preparing. I was itching to get back to Asia. Against the best advice of my cousins and my entire team of girlfriends, I opted to remain part of a trip with my now-ex boyfriend and his family.

"Who the hell goes on an international trip with an ex and family?" asked just about everyone.

"True. But they're going to Tibet, Nepal, Bhutan and India. How could I say to no to that?"

No matter that the boyfriend had broken my heart. The trip had been planned for a year and I was part of the plan. His family loved me, and insisted I join them. His sister suggested that we leave HIM at home. Even my ex seemed to genuinely want my company on the trip. Screw it. I'm going, I thought. In the name of an international travel fix, I got on a plane and spent a month reconnecting with Asia. By day we toured the streets of Lhasa and drank yak butter tea. The sound of Buddhist monks chanting in the monasteries we'd visited rang in my ears as I fell asleep at night. My Mandarin was still decent, my skills helping navigate in Tibet, now occupied by the Chinese.

We flew from Lhasa to Kathmandu and floated right past Mount Everest. I marveled at the size of the mountains. The Rockies looked like molehills in comparison. *Asia you rock! I feel at home here. I'm definitely coming back. I need whoever ends up in my life to see this. It's too incredible to miss!* In Nepal we wandered the back alleys of Kathmandu. We sat in tiny tour buses and drove for hours deep into the Himalayas. By night I lay in an uncomfortable double bed next to my ex cursing silently. *What a dumbass! You're going to regret dumping me, buddy.*

With jet lag still clouding my brain, the bar preparation class began. I studied in the morning and worked for an immigration attorney in the afternoons. It seemed to me that I should at least give this whole practicing law thing a shot. My plan came crashing down when the bar exam results came back and I had failed. Crap! The attorney politely dismissed me from his payroll and I began looking for a job. I found work at a refugee resettlement agency and sat for the bar a second time.

As fate would have it, Ruby and I had been reunited in Colorado. Her love for the mountains had been as strong as mine. When she graduated from medical school, she took a residency position in Denver. She now lived only a mile away from me. I was right. Our story hadn't been finished yet. She'd soon marry and we talked of how silly it was that we'd traveled the world over and ended up here in Colorado together.

The day my results from the second bar exam arrived, I drove in a fog to Ruby, who opened the door, took one look at me and said, "Oh, no. Really?" No words needed as she looked in my eyes. Though closer to passing, I'd failed again. My job with refugees was gratifying, but draining any energy I needed to concentrate on the bar exam. I was resettling Bosnians and the Sudanese Lost Boys by day and studying for the bar at night.

"Are you really going to take it again?" Ruby asked.

"Ruby, I just have to pass this thing," I lamented. "It's killing me. I'm so close. I want to try again. Just one more time."

"But Jo, you *never* actually had any interest in practicing law in the first place!" Ruby reminded me. She was right. Even now, I wasn't drawn to practice. Not in the way I should be for continuing the torturous process of bar exam prep.

"I know, I know, but I graduated law school and this is what people do. They pass the bar in order to – I don't know – give themselves options?" It was a statement, but it came out as a question.

"I can do this," I said. "It's just a stupid test. I'm not giving up."

"You can do this, Jo. We got through so much in Asia. Remember my blow out diarrhea in Vietnam? The altitude sickness in Nepal? Losing all your travelers checks in Jakarta?" Wrapping me in her embrace, we laughed over where we'd been. As she picked up the pieces for me, I realized we had been reunited for more adventures. Domestic ones, this time.

I sat a third time. I failed by mere single digits. And now I was – mad. It was enough to call it quits. Almost. I scoured the country for an easier bar exam, Colorado being notoriously tough. It didn't matter where I passed now, as long as I passed. Wyoming looked promising, though I would have to start entirely over and learn oil and gas law. I didn't care. I had completely lost sight of my goals, which were never to practice, but to stand up for good in the world. Blindly, I studied for my fourth bar exam, drinking coffee late into nights in order to stay awake and study. I could quote entire passages of tort litigation. Began to dream about provisions of obscure contract laws. I drove to Cheyenne, took the exam and felt good. If I passed, I wouldn't move to Wyoming. I wouldn't practice law. I would just know that... I had passed.

The hours of studying had helped, but not enough. I fell short by two points. Two damn little points! Even for me, that was enough. I was done.

chapter five

As I prepared for our first meeting in 2000, I pondered the meaning of "blind date." What did that mean, really? I knew this man named Ernie from emails and the description of my cousin Steph. To me, that was a step up from blind. I didn't know what he looked like, but I knew at least he wasn't an ax murderer. Other bits of knowledge were promising. A computer engineer meant stability. An interest in mountain biking meant a certain level of fitness. But the speed at which he always seemed to answer email was foreign to me, if not creepy. *At least it will be a free dinner.*

The doorbell rang, sending my dog, Nina, into a frenzy. He was silly punctual, too. As I opened the front door, it felt like I was looking at an old friend. Ernie was tall, with a bright smile, and a mouthful of braces. *Wait. He's 29 and has braces? Mental note to ask Steph why she left out that detail.* His hair was bushy and he had a thin beard that spoke of his commitment to mountain living in Boulder, Colorado. I was only twenty miles away in Denver, but he looked like he'd traveled much further to make our date.

We ate dinner at a small Italian place in my neighborhood. I had prepared for the usual round of first date questions.

"So, tell me about that party you had last month?" I inquired, picking at my salad.

"It was an election party, remember? I invited you, but you said you were having your own party."

"Right, right," I replied. I'd forgotten the circumstances, which had led me to turn down his invitation a month prior. Bottom line – it seemed too soon at the time.

"Sorry, yeah, I know that was lame to decline, but honestly I REALLY get into election coverage and I don't think you would've wanted me there. I am one of those people who needs to know exactly what's happening in every county in Ohio and how the exit polls look in Virginia and stuff." This part was true. I thought back to the election and remembered waking up on the couch the next morning. Results from the night before were still uncertain. Gore vs. Bush.

"Your party must've been small, then?"

"Yes, just my friend Ruby and our dogs."

Ernie needed clarification. "The party consisted of you, your best friend, and your dogs?" he repeated. I felt myself blushing at the ridiculousness of the concept. Could that even be considered a party?

"Yeah, I know. I'm kinda weird."

"No, no that's okay. Just interesting."

"Maybe next time. The next party you have, I'm there." My mind raced as I tried to determine if that had been too forward of me. Might I even be around if there were a next time?

Ernie chuckled. I could tell he was nervous, as he chatted in long gusts. I threw in a few unusual questions, journalism training from years ago still intact. He seemed warm. Cute in a nerdy way. And when he let me speak, I could tell he was busy composing himself, assessing where he stood.

"This is just a delicious Italian sausage. Would you like a bite?"

Oh my gosh! He doesn't know I am a vegetarian. I had stopped eating meat in Taiwan and never started again. This fact hadn't been disclosed yet. What would my grandmother do in this situation? *Mame, what should I do? Steph, you didn't tell him I was a vegetarian?*

And before I knew it, I was replying, "Yes, that would be divine. Thanks so much. But just a small piece, really."

I took a bite and tried to smile. The meat was the first I'd eaten in years, and as it slid down my throat, I calculated the worst-case scenarios. *Immediate throwing up? Just a bad stomach-ache and a poor night's sleep?* I eked out a smile and asked another question.

"What can I say, Ruby? He's a full-fledged Colorado nerd."

Ruby and I were in her kitchen. I'd pulled up a stool, sitting with a glass of wine as she sautéed vegetables.

"As in, he's a computer engineer who loves the mountains but can't make decent conversation?" She grinned. We both knew the type.

"No, not exactly. Leave out the conversation part. He's good at that. Add a bike. He has a bike."

"But he's not, you know, in LOVE with his bike, right?"

"Oh, no. He's not a bad boy, if that's what you're asking. He's solid."

"Good. Because we both know that you've had enough of those. The bad boys."

"Yeah, they're fun to date, but you don't wanna marry one."

"And he's fully aware of how ridiculous you are?"

I laughed and took a sip of wine.

"I don't think even *I'm* capable of understanding what kind of crazy ideas I could sprout next!"

Ernie was the kind of man you marry. Kind and patient. Steady when I shook. Open-minded, yet firm in his morals and convictions. The drama of my twenties had passed and I hap-pily turned forward to the future. We moved in together after just nine months of dating, were engaged six months later, and married seven after that. With babies happening all around us, we pondered how to approach creating a family. Adoption felt familiar to me, as our family was a multi-racial bunch. From the outside, it was never totally clear who belonged to whom, and I liked it that way. I always hoped, or shall I admit, *planned* to adopt. Though somehow in the months that Ernie and I dated, it appeared that I'd neglected to bring this up. Somewhere between the questions of, "What's your favorite beer?" and "What kind of computer do you use?" should have been wedged, "Oh, by the way, I really plan to adopt." I'd developed a horrible habit of planning ahead, even scheduling events, without telling or even taking into consideration what Ernie's expectations were.

It was what we now called a "See Ya Tuesday" moment in our house. The phrase arose from our early months of dating, when I was saying good night to him and had already projected that we could see each other on the following Tuesday. As he walked off I blurted, "Okay, I'll see you Tuesday!" He turned with an unknowing look and asked what in the world was happening on Tuesday.

When it came time to think about family, I simply wanted to be a mother. That was the end game for me. I wasn't scared of pregnancy or nervous about childbirth, but I lacked the craving to have a baby growing inside me that so many other women felt. And though I wanted a houseful of toddlers running around the house, they didn't need to look like me.

"I don't know, Johanna. Adoption seems so risky. I mean, you don't really know what you're getting." A friend tried to play devil's advocate as I bounced the idea off her at work one day.

"Huh? Don't know what you're getting? You lost me. How do you know what you're getting if you push a baby out of your vagina?"

"Well, you at least know what they'll look like, right?"

"Maybe. Does that matter? And also, there's a lot of crappy heart disease and cancer in our family. I'd rather not pass it on."

"Your genes? You don't want to pass them on?"

I laughed and said, "I'm certainly not convinced our gene pool is better than anyone else's! Ernie's losing his hair and I'm neurotic. Let's just leave it at that." Another friend took the financial approach with me.

"We'd love to adopt, but it's too expensive," she lamented.

"What part?" I asked.

"Well, you know, all those fees to the adoption agency."

"I get that. It's not totally free. But, is childbirth totally free?" As Ernie and I talked further about adoption, I bounced these conversations off of him at night.

"Ern, Sara said today she wouldn't consider adoption because it's too expensive."

"Some people don't have the resources to pay for the adoption fees, Jo."

"I get that there are some chunks up front, but you don't pay the whole fee at once, and it's damn expensive to have a baby, isn't it?"

"Go figure!"

"Are you KIDDING? Doctor visits, prenatal vitamins, maternity clothes, birthing classes, the cost of delivery. We probably wouldn't adopt a newborn, right? What about the cost of diapers and food and clothing for a year? Childcare for a year. Bouncy chairs. Toys!"

"If you're THAT curious, you should crunch the numbers, Jo."

"I'll do it. I'm gonna do it right now."

My numbers proved my theory correct. The cost of pregnancy and childbirth was at least as expensive as adopting, if not more. At least by my calculations. Not that it mattered to anyone but me.

Ernie remained open to both adoption and getting pregnant, though adoption was completely foreign to him. Like most other prospective parents, he had looked at adoption as a back up plan. As in the "If-we-don't-get-pregnant-we'll-adopt" approach. I felt differently, and encouraged him to avoid looking at adoption as second best. Where many other men would have dug in their macho heels, Ernie remained open to the possibility.

"What if we just started both processes at the same time?"

The two of us were on mountain bikes, a sport he'd gotten me hooked on. I'd tried to get him to start running, but he only managed one run before returning to his bike.

"Meaning what, exactly?"

"Well, we try to get pregnant and we also try to adopt, and just go with whichever one goes faster."

I stopped my bike and straddled the crossbar. Pulled out my water bottle. Took a glug. His idea seemed both odd and perfectly logical. Whichever one goes faster? Really? Hilarious. Unique. Letting nature take its intended course. It could be approached any number of ways. But his plan spoke to me and I jumped at it.

"Let's do it. It's perfect for us. Last one to the car is a rotten egg!" And off we sped.

We began to approach both the road to a biological child and an adoptive child at the same time. We piled over research on domestic versus international options, while at the same time I tracked my menstrual cycle. I found myself genuinely interested in both options. And like a sociology experiment,

I wondered which path would take us to the finish line.

After just a few months, it became clear that on the adoption front, China would be perfect for us. I had spent all that time in Taiwan after college, and Asia felt like home. Adoption from China in the early 2000's was straightforward, fast, and provided generous tax incentives from the federal government. Moreover, because of the One Child Policy, we would surely be matched with a baby girl, and the planner in me secretly enjoyed the idea of having certainty in this area. At the same time the road to China was becoming more exciting, the process of actually trying to get pregnant was becoming decidedly less and less romantic. I was spending more time reading about Chinese culture and less time looking at potential birthing centers. Our application with the adoption agency had sailed through the necessary channels and our documents were ready to be shipped to China, where they would sit until we were matched with a baby.

Ernie met me at the door as I arrived home from work, grocery list in hand.

"I'm off to the grocery store. Want me to pickup more folic acid? And the pregnancy vitamins, right?" I felt done with that road. The light had been shining on our China option. I tried to act nonchalant as I replied.

"Nah. I kinda think we should be done. What do you think? Maybe for number two?"

Ernie looked up from his list. His eyes seemed at peace.

"I think I'm down with that. Are we gonna do it?"

"We're doin' it!"

"It's done!"

Our families had a myriad of responses when we announced our plan. Elated. Surprised. Confused. Curious. Supportive.

I waited to tell my parents until we were in Wisconsin a few weeks after our decision. Ernie and I took them to dinner and told them the news. Their first grandchild would be adopted from China.

"WHAT!?! That's wonderful!" My mother shrieked and my father lit up. After the initial round of questions was answered – the when, the how, the why, I then delivered the kicker.

"And we'd like you to come with us. To pick her up."

"Come to China?"

"Yes. Would you be interested in that?" They were in. And just like that, my sister and I lost our star status. It was Grandchildren Time.

Our paperwork was completed, sent to China, and we began to wait for a match. In the meantime, we filled our days moving to a bigger house, painting the nursery, reading every conceivable book on adoption and juggling name choices. This process was made easier by the fact that there was close to a 95% chance that we would be receiving a baby girl, despite marking on our paperwork that we would be open to either gender. The Chinese had instituted the One Child Policy in 1980. The policy collided with a tradition of sons taking care of their parents in old age. The result was an abundance of baby girls being abandoned just after birth so the parents could try again for a boy. In another irony, abandonment was strictly forbidden in the country, so babies were typically left in the dark of night. Secretly. Many speculated that birth parents chose populated places such as markets or office complexes so that there was a higher likelihood of someone finding the newborn quickly. Still other stories we'd heard described birth parents waiting and watching in the shadows until their babies were found. It was a cultural phenomenon that we could barely wrap our heads around.

As we waited, I struggled with the contradictions our adoption had brought about. I'd studied international human rights in law school and my opinion on the One Child Policy was firmly in the opposition camp. Yet this policy would help us create our family. Though we felt the world was overpopulated and needed more families to adopt, we'd chosen to adopt from outside the United States, where there was also a clear need. The contradictions extended beyond our new family and I spent too much time reeling in my own shortcomings. I supported animal shelters, but I had bought my dog from a breeder. I believed in global warming, but I owned a gas-guzzling SUV. I knew that there was a drought in Colorado, but I longed for a green lawn and used a wasteful sprinkler system. I believed in philanthropy, but our annual tax return didn't indicate we were giving away close to what I felt we should be giving. Most of these struggles remained unresolved as time passed. My shortcomings were many and my moral achievements seemed miniature. The one struggle that smoothed out was our decision to adopt from China. We both now felt drawn to China and knew our baby was waiting for us.

The process to adopt a child was not an easy one. Though straightforward, China seemed to make parents go through an ungodly amount of hoop jumping. There were endless visits from social workers, multitudes of training sessions on baby care and attachment disorder, doctor exams and character references to submit. We were required to get documents signed and notarized multiple times, a nod to China's desire to see everything stamped and signed by the highest authorities. We obsessively followed the websites dedicated to tracking rumors coming out of China on when families would receive matches. I slowly amassed a closet full of baby dresses. My friends who had girls sent me hair ties, pink blankets and frilly diaper covers. I soon became so overwhelmed at all the pastel that I decided we would swing to the other direction and painted the baby's room blue. We knew it would be a girl, but surely girls liked blue, too, I decided. And, after much discussion, we picked a name. Piper.

As the day to our match grew closer, Ernie frequently marveled at the path we'd chosen. It was both so different and yet just as welcome as the one he'd anticipated before he'd met and married me. He joked that he was just along for the ride with me. The humor was well received, but one night I probed further.

The dinner table held the remnants of our meal as I stood up and headed for the kitchen. "You're still on board, aren't you, Ern? At any time you can try to knock me up again. You know that, right?"

I laughed, but was half serious. We both knew that I'd called most of the shots so far in the two years we'd been together. But I didn't want to be that bossy wife. I wanted a partnership. At least as long as it ended up in the results I was looking for.

"I'm totally on board. It just makes me wonder what ELSE you've hatched without my knowledge."

Here goes. Just that day I'd received word that I'd been accepted into a short term program to work for the United Nations in the Democratic Republic of Congo. It had been a dream of mine to work for the U.N. and my background in international human rights work plus my ability to speak French made me a perfect fit. But I'd also learned that spouses and families weren't welcome on the assignment. It was an area of war and multi-sided conflict involving both Rwanda and Uganda. It was clear that I would need to turn the offer down.

"There is just this one other thing. Or maybe two."

"Oh Lordy! Here we go. I'm ready. Hand me that glass of scotch, will you?"

"Remember when I told you I applied to the U.N. for that position a few months ago, right after the wedding?"

"I do. But I forget where it was. Did you get it?"

"I got it, Ernie."

"Amazing, Jo! Fantastic! Wait... where is it? And when? We're, you know, waiting for news on the baby."

"It's in the D.R.C. Ernie."

"The D.R.C? What's that, Denmark?"

"It's not Denmark, Ern. It's the Congo." I spoke in a whisper, nervous for the reaction.

"What? I didn't hear you. Where is it?"

"The Congo. It's the Democratic Republic of Congo, Ern."

"What the hell?! In Africa? Jo-HANNA! No way. We're not going to the Congo, Jo. With a baby? Are you freaking kidding me?"

"We're not going. I hear you."

He chuckled. "My parents would flip OUT!"

"They would? Why? They could come visit us. Also, you're an adult, last time I checked. You just turned 30, right? They'd be totally fine with it."

Ernie was full on laughing at me now. I was trying to laugh, too, though still a bit heartbroken that I'd have to turn it down.

"Jo, they already think we are a little – let's say – unconventional. Good GOD, woman!"

"I told you, we're not going. I turned it down."

"Finally. Some sanity. Thank goodness. Well tell me now if there's *anything else*?"

It was time to lay all my cards on the table.

"You should know that I plan to move our family abroad in a

few years," I announced.

"Gr-r-r-eat. Can't wait to see how you manage THAT one."

He smiled and turned back to the task of baby names.

After only six months from the time our paperwork arrived in Beijing, it became clear that the wait was nearly over. At the time, my work schedule was packed with travel, and I left our home in Denver on a flight to Kansas City just as the rumor mill went into overdrive. The baby matches – paperwork from the Chinese government revealing which child had been chosen for each awaiting couple – were in the air, crossing the Pacific Ocean on the way to adoption agencies all over the country. I scrambled to change my flight out of Kansas City so I could be there when our photo and match arrived. Part of our preparation with the adoption agency had been to submit a call list. Who would be contacted first, and at which phone number? Ernie received the first call on his cell phone. He declined their offer to tell him the baby's name, age and place of birth. As I landed in Denver, he drove to the agency, where he met me in the parking lot. We embraced. I had prepared all sorts of cheesy words about how much I loved him and how I knew he was going to be a great dad, but as I started in on my speech he shouted, "What the hell are you doing? Let's get in there!"

As we approached the front door of the agency, we noticed that it was decorated with "Welcome Baby" signs, crepe paper and a giant stork. In one corner there was a sign that said "It's a Girl!" and in another "It's a Boy!" We wondered if this was a joke, or if truly, some family had been matched with a baby boy. "What a shock THAT couple is going to have today!" I laughed out loud as we strode briskly up the stairs.

The conference room was filled with long tables, and couples looking at photos and details of their babies. At each table was a box of tissue and most of the parents had already made use of those, tears flowing. We sat and were approached by a young woman carrying a red file folder. She had a larger-than-expected smile on her face. She had seen our match already. I assumed her smile meant our baby was especially cute.

"Are you ready to see your baby?" she asked. We nodded.

She opened the folder, showed us a photo, and a moment of disbelief was followed by an elated scream. It came out of me, and it pierced the entire room, causing everyone else to look over at us. Looking up at us from a one-inch by one-inch photo was a round, adorable, content-looking, chubby, baby... boy. He was wearing a pink sweater and I could practically hear him bellowing, "Why am I dressed in PINK?" No doubt the orphanage had only pink clothes. As a nod to his gender, they had placed a small basketball in front of him. I looked at Ernie and he was staring at the photo, not saying a word and completely unable to look at me.

"OH. MY. GOD! WHAT??? ERNIE!" I shouted, as if he were suddenly hard of hearing.

"It's a boy! Ernie! A BOY! Say something! Holy crap, honey, it's a BOY!" We both began to laugh. Deep, long, and powerful laughs. The kind that you only experience when your life has taken an unexpected turn in a single instant. I remembered the closet full of pink dresses in the nursery at home. And a girl name, Piper, which would certainly not suit this little fellow.

It took a few moments for us to grasp the reality of... a boy. We clarified with the agency and were told that yes, every now and then it just happens. He had no special needs to speak of, other than the need for a family. The fact that we had ended up with a boy was beyond our comprehension. Beyond what it was like to feel certain, as a pregnant woman, that you are carrying a girl, and then be surprised by a boy. This was near certainty turned upside down.

I walked out into the hall and called my parents. They had known we were heading to the agency and my mother picked up on the first ring.

"We got the match! We're at the agency. Can you get Dad on the other line? Mom, you're NOT going to believe it!"

I heard my mom shouting, "Tony! Pick up the other line. She wants to talk to both of us! Tony! Tony!"

Her voice sounded desperate, and I was near bursting to tell them as I waited for my father to pick up the phone.

"I'm on. Johanna? What's the news?!"

"Well, I'm looking at a picture of a gorgeous, adorable, round-faced BOY!"

Silence. And then my mom squealed. Dad started laughing uncontrollably.

"A boy? How? Why? Where?" Their questions answered, Ernie and I got into our cars and began our round of calls. Ernie's parents. Our sisters. Ruby. With each call, the reality sinking in.

Fancy that. It's a boy!

chapter six

The next few weeks were filled with baby showers and packing and endless trips to swap the dresses I'd bought for more appropriate baby britches. I woke up in the middle of the night several times, laughing at the turn of fate. I saved a few of my favorite dresses just for kicks. We'd talked about trying to get pregnant a second time, and in that case the odds would surely be about even. Maybe the dresses would see the light after all!

Then there was the name. I'd kept my own last name upon our marriage, but I agreed to let the baby take Ernie's last name. A long, Italian name and it needed a first name short and strong. Noah. Reed. Cole. Liam. We batted them around but none stuck, and we were running up against the clock. We needed a name before we left. He had a name given to him by the orphanage based on the district in Kunming, China, where he'd been found. Wu Zhi Yong. It meant Brave Wisdom, we were told. In his eyes you could see the wisdom. *The brave part goes without saying.*

"What about Will?" I asked Ernie. He was engrossed in a Mandarin language CD, trying to learn basic phrases.

"You mean William?"

"What about just Will."

"Will has a nice ring to it with my last name. Will it is."

Tickets arrived for our trip, which we were making with my parents, to Kunming in Yunnan Province, China. I'd never heard of it, but was told over and over how beautiful it was by Chinese friends who had been there. How clean the air, how blue the sky. It was in far southwest China, bordering Burma, Laos, and Vietnam with perpetual spring-like weather, and the city had been coined The City of Eternal Spring for this reason.

I was working on Will's baby book, a silk-wrapped binder filled with notes of how we had come to adoption and what we'd done to prepare. There was a page about Will's birth parents that we were supposed to fill in. We knew nothing of his genetics or birth. The orphanage notes indicated he had come to them after he'd been abandoned at about one week of age. One week. What had he been doing for that week? Who had he been with? This was the last page of the book to fill out, and I felt stuck.

"Can you just make something up? Something positive?" Ernie naively wondered.

"NO!" I was getting frustrated, but I didn't know why. I didn't want to lie, but I agreed – wouldn't it be better to shield our child from the awful truth, that he'd been left outside, his birth parents thinking this option was better than a life with them?

"Okay, Johanna, you're going to have to get a grip and figure it out or leave it for another day."

I stared at the page. There had to be a middle ground. I wrote a draft on a piece of scratch paper and then, sure it was complete, I carefully copied the words into the baby book.

We only know that they loved you and put you in a safe place for someone to find you and help you get to us. We imagine they were unable to take care of you, and they knew we were out there somewhere waiting for you. We think of them a lot, and hope that they have peace and happiness in their lives. We are grateful to them for their gift, and we hope they know that you are happy and healthy and safe now.

And I closed the book.

chapter seven

Our arrival in Asia had gone well and after a couple days in Hong Kong, we boarded a flight to Kunming. A city of nearly seven million, it was still considered a "second-tier" city by Chinese standards. Kunming had served as an American air base during World War II, and old fighter planes still lay in grassy fields around the runways at the airport. We were greeted by Daphne, our Chinese facilitator who would walk us step-by-step through the next week. Daphne was well-versed in cross-cultural communication, adoption paperwork, and baby bottle temperatures.

"Welcome to Kunming!" she chirped. "I'm here to help you this week, so you can now turn off your brain and hand it to me."

The odd euphemism was music to my ears. I felt the weight of the past year of preparations releasing slowly from my body.

"Mom, I'm going to run to the bathroom," I called out as Ernie and my father filled out visa paperwork in the arrivals area.

I was incredibly grateful to have my parents with us on the trip. I wanted someone besides the two of us to remember the sights and sounds of this place. And to be able to share stories with Will when he grew. My parents were practical yet emotional as the day drew closer for us to receive Will.

Hello, squat potty, I said to myself as I entered the bathroom stall. *We are going to get along just fine for the next few weeks.* My comfort level in Asia was high. I spoke the language, knew the customs. I navigated the squat potties effortlessly. My mother – not so much.

"How was it in there?" she asked, as I exited the bathroom.

"We're in *real* China, now. This ain't exactly the Shangri-La in Hong Kong. It's a squat potty. We've talked about this, right? Do you need, I don't know... do you need... help?"

"Oh for goodness sake, how hard can it be?"

"Just be careful, Mom. I don't want you falling in or peeing on yourself or anything. We just got here." Mom shot me a glance and headed for the rest room.

Our hotel room at the Bank Hotel in Kunming was cluttered with baby gear. Though Ernie and I were seasoned travelers, we'd still amassed a pile of onesies and toys worthy of a king. As the sun rose on July 25, 2004, we busied ourselves by making sure the formula was on the right shelf, the toys aligned, and crib sheets tucked in just right. We'd barely slept the night before. Today was the day we were going to get our baby. Will was eleven months old now. We had been told he had limited mobility, and secretly hoped that meant he wasn't yet walking. There were many milestones that we'd missed, but this one we hoped to catch.

As we stood in the lobby, I began a downward spiral. Outwardly I looked composed, but inside, I was a puddle. On the edge of this life-changing moment, I was both completely ready, yet not ready in the slightest.

"Ernie, I don't know if I can handle this," I whispered. "I feel on the verge of a nervous breakdown. We don't know the first thing about taking care of a baby. What if he cries and doesn't stop? I'm freaking out. What if we're horrible parents?"

I was in full on labor now, with the pushing underway and my nerves were getting the best of me. The hotel lobby felt overwhelming. Sterile. I needed to get out of there and into a place that was warm and cozy. Preferably with a rocking chair. *Where the hell is my rocking chair?* Other parents-to-be had similar looks of panic. We'd read every conceivable book on the care and feeding of babies, had gone through months of required parenting training, discussing every possible reaction our baby might have on that first day. But still, just as with childbirth, nothing could prepare us for this moment.

"I'm totally clueless, too, Jo. What can I tell you? We're just gonna have to be clueless together." Some reassurance he was! I wanted to slap my husband for his honesty, but instead I just held him tighter.

We boarded the bus to the government office where we were to receive the babies. We were among a group of twelve other sets of adoptive parents and countless travel companions. The bus ride was quiet as Daphne explained what would happen over the next hour. While we listened, our eyes were glued to the scenes out the bus window. People went about their days selling potatoes from food carts. Sweeping their sidewalks with giant brooms made of bamboo. Occasionally someone would look up at our giant tour bus, point at the silly Westerners and giggle.

I knew that what had brought us here was simply a desire to create a family. Yet, we were taking children away from the land of their birth. Wait. Was I SURE this was the right thing to do? I looked out the window and began a silent conversation with the people on the street.

We are driving to an office where we will take twelve of your babies from you. We will take them from China and fly thousands of miles to America. We will raise them to speak English and celebrate the Fourth of July. Is that okay with you? How did it come to pass that you leave your babies on the street? I'm

*so sorry. We'll take good care of them. Thank you. I'm so very
sorry.*

It was now within thirty minutes of twelve families being
made. But there were no screams from labor rooms, no dou-
las coaching us. Silence. I began to cry, and my father's hand
reached up from between the seats and rested on my shoulder. Looking up and around at other families, I saw I wasn't
alone in my tears.

We piled into the tiny office of the government registration
building. Twelve sets of parents, travel companions, and all our
nerves. My hands were sweaty and shaking, barely able to grip
the stuffed toy I'd brought. A soft squeaky tiger with a small
mirror on its tummy. From a window we could see a little bus
pulled up outside and inside, twelve babies were held in the
arms of their nannies. The nannies were young and dressed in
uniforms. Some nannies were crying as they tried to calm the
babies, aware that something was about to change forever.

"Do you think we're gonna recognize him?" I asked Ernie.

"What?"

He couldn't hear me. The cries of the babies were beginning, as they slowly realized they were soon to be handed off
to strangers.

He's a boy, I thought. *The rest are girls. If I can't tell the difference between a girl and my own son, I'm in serious trouble.*

One by one the babies were brought inside. Parents were
told to stand in front of a Chinese flag for a photo with their
child at the moment each was handed over. What was intended to be a moment of joy wasn't fooling any of these babies.
This entire day sucked, and they were going to let their feelings

be known. Screams increased with each family unification. The first four families to receive their babies left the offices to sit outside on the grass. Daphne called out the name of each baby as they entered the room.

Wu Zhi Yong. Wu Zhi Yong. Where the hell is Wu Zhi Yong? And finally...

"Wu Zhi Yong! For Ernie and Johanna!" Daphne screamed above the wails.

And there he was. Dressed in the little red jumpsuit I had sent the orphanage after we'd received his information. He was looking absolutely, positively – petrified.

He was placed in my arms. Looked me squarely in the eyes. Paused for a moment. And began to scream.

I rocked him on my hip as he reached back for his nanny. She stood off to the side and thankfully didn't reach back for him as other nannies had done, the ones who'd been crying.

"It's okay, little guy. I've got you. I'm your mommy. Look at you. Look at how cute you are."

I was speaking to him in Mandarin. He stopped crying and looked at me with confusion. I could only imagine the thoughts running through his little head. The thoughts and the sadness. *Who IS this woman? Why does she smell and look different and why is she speaking Mandarin to me with such a dreadful accent?* I imagined him thinking.

Agonizing, this is truly agonizing, I thought. I was filled with joy and grief at the same time.

As I walked outside with Will on my hip, I whispered to him, this time in English, "I'm holding on. I'm never letting go of you. I'm never letting go. I love you. You're home. I'm never letting go."

Abandoned at only a few days old, he'd known little else in this world and likely transitioned easily to the orphanage. This was different. Everything about us was different. My attempts to look Will in the eyes were being rebuffed. It was one of the happiest days of our lives, and perhaps the saddest day of his.

Just hold on, I told myself. *We just have to hold on and not let go.*

I handed Will to Ernie so I could complete some paperwork before returning to the hotel. Magically, Will calmed down. Ernie had the touch. I suspected my husband was truly "father material" but in that instant, it became clear. Ernie walked Will over to a wall of ivy on the side of the building, spoke quietly to him, and the crying stopped. Will reached out his tiny fingers and grabbed at the ivy. He smiled the smile of a baby who quite possibly had never been in nature, had never touched a leaf. The ivy crawled up the side of a wall in huge masses, its dark green a brilliant contrast to his red jumpsuit. Will smiled – and then a giggle. Standing at a distance, I watched my husband become a father. My heart exploded with joy, but as I tried to approach and share their moment, Will caught a glimpse of me, gave me a scowl and clung tighter to Ernie.

And so this is how it's going to go down, huh, little guy? I chuckled to myself. Thankfully we'd been trained in attachment and bonding and I knew that it was possible for our son to initially prefer one parent over the other. I had hoped it would be me, but so it went. Seeing my husband transition to fatherhood was just as joyful.

We arrived back at the hotel and settled in, all of us exhausted from the emotions of the day. Will wasn't able to walk yet, but was crawling with full force. He explored the hotel room, then collapsed on the bed in tears. Worried about hunger, we tried to feed him a bottle, but he refused. He needed a diaper change, and a pair of clean pajamas for the evening. But we had been trained to leave on the clothes he'd arrived in for twenty-four hours, so as to prevent any further trauma. Ripping off clothes and washing Will, who we were unsure had ever experienced a bath – these were all tasks we'd been advised against taking on that first day. Instead we gingerly patted him clean with a washcloth. The zippered pouch I had brought to store the clothes he came in lay empty for another day. It would be filled soon enough with the red jumpsuit and the cheap Chinese shoes, the little socks and the tattered tag with his Chinese name that had been pinned to his cuff. The pouch would make its way into a box of treasures I would keep for him forever. The clothes on his back were all he had when he came to us, and I intended to treat them like gold. The only items we would possess from the first year of his life. I pictured Will holding them in his hands as a teenager. Running his fingers along the seams of the shoes. Imagining who'd put them on his feet first.

Ernie and I took turns pacing the floor of our hotel room with Will in our arms. I tried to feed him a bottle, but my movements were awkward and unfamiliar and he squirmed with unease.

Food was getting to be imperative. Will seem wholly uninterested in the formula we had prepared, and as night wore on, we got desperate. He hadn't eaten anything since we had received him some six hours ago.

"Mom, I have no idea what's going on. He's got to be hungry, but won't take a bottle."

My parents had left us alone for a few hours, but couldn't stand it any longer and had come to see how we were doing. Though anxious to hold their first grandchild, they knew the importance of letting me and Ernie hold him exclusively for a few days. I saw them shift and try to remain invisible as Will gave them a suspicious look.

We called Daphne.

"Daphne. This is Johanna. Zhi Yong isn't eating anything and we don't know what we're doing wrong. Do you think he's sick?"

"Have you tried congee?"

"No, just the formula."

"'I'll order the congee from room service and be right there."

She can't be serious. The congee was a watery mix of warm rice and pork, which to me sounded entirely inedible.

Daphne was at our room in less than two minutes.

"You've tried the bottle already?"

"Yes, and we used the exact mixture of formula that the orphanage recommended. I don't get it. He must be starving."

"Okay, let me see."

I gave Daphne the bottle and she shook her head.

"No, no. This won't work. The nipple isn't cut. And what about the temperature?"

"Warm."

"You Americans and your warm! These babies need HOT!"

She laughed and reached into her pocket for a small knife. In two small flicks of her wrist, she slit the bottle's nipple to create a large opening for the formula. Striding over to the hot pot, Daphne turned it on, added formula to the bottle and, when the pot whistled, poured in the boiling water.

I winced as she put Will on her lap and put the nipple to his lips. *It's too hot! She's going to hurt him!* I lunged forward but Ernie grabbed me as the nipple reached his tongue. Contentment crossed Will's face as he took mighty chugs of the bottle, barely breathing.

A knock at the door signaled the congee had arrived. The waiter brought in a small bowl filled with the rice/pork mix. As Will finished the bottle, his eyes tracked the bowl. As Daphne lifted the spoon to his mouth, he showed us for the first time one small tooth and a giant appetite. The congee was a hit. *Well, I'll be damned! We're on our way.*

One week later, our time in Kunming came to an end. We had finished the reams of paperwork required by China to take Will home. Pictures, stamped documents, four copies of everything. A naked medical exam, during which the doctors grabbed aggressively at Will's private parts and he struck back by peeing all over Ernie. A true baptism and welcome to fatherhood.

As our bus drove away from the hotel heading to the airport, I turned to Ernie and said, "I'd like to come back here someday. When we aren't picking up a baby. Maybe to live. I've always wanted to live abroad. You know that, right?"

"I know that, Johanna. We've got a full plate right now. Let's talk about it in a few years."

"I'm just letting you know. It's on my radar screen and I won't forget about it. So just, you know, be ready."

chapter eight

As the days, weeks and months passed, it became apparent that Will was the perfect baby. He slept well and ate like a champ. He was coordinated and began doing headstands with his tiny body. Though he grew, he was small and agile, always remaining in the 5th percentile on the growth charts. There were no outward signs of attachment disorder. As others around us struggled with potty training and discipline, we seemed to breeze through all of it. We felt so very blessed to have him in our lives. I transitioned easily into teaching at a private college at night so I could stay home during the day. Marathons, which I feared I would need to give up after children, were a reality again.

"So number two, then, Jo?" Ernie asked one day as we sat on the couch folding laundry.

Will, now two, was curled up with Nina on her dog pillow.

"What? What are you talking about?" I threw several socks his direction. I did the big folding tasks. He folded socks.

"We sort of have this whole parenting thing nailed, don't you think? I think we should start talking about another."

Yikes! He's totally Mr. Confident. Am I ready for two? I can't imagine loving another child as much as I love Will. Maybe we should hold off. No, that seems silly. Okay, here goes.

"I don't know, Ern. Things are pretty great right now. Not sure I want to mess it up. Plus, we never really decided about our approach for the second. Get pregnant? Adopt again?"

"I'm open to either. This was such a breeze. It only took, what, eleven months start to finish? Maybe we go for it again."

"I agree. I'm not exactly getting any younger, either."

I was thirty-five, the magic age where I was starting to hear that my eggs were rotting. I still had no particular desire to carry a baby. As I looked at Will, I realized why. It just didn't matter that he didn't look like me. He was my son, and I would dare anyone to tell me that I might love a baby from my womb more than him. Simply. Not. Possible.

We had the same view that most families had about childbirth. Sure there are ups and downs. Pregnancy can be tough. Delivery even worse. But at the end of the day, most couples chose to go down the same road again without regrets. Adoption was a backup for most people. For us, it was reversed. Our adoption had been so seamless that it only made sense to do it again. If it didn't work, there was always pregnancy. No regrets.

I had grown increasingly tired of people asking when we were going to have a baby "of your own." I felt insulted by the question, hurt that people didn't recognize that he *was* my own. I understood the question, but the insinuation stung. We had come to adoption by choice. Either way, our child was our own.

It seemed the only way to proceed was to adopt again from China. If the children wouldn't look like us, it would be nice if they could look like one another. We began the paper chase again. At first things progressed. Then, everything changed.

The signs began shortly after we'd sent our paperwork to China. This wouldn't be as easy as it had been with Will. For many reasons. For one thing, fewer babies were being matched with foreign families. It was a good problem, it seemed. In the two years since we'd adopted Will, fewer babies were being abandoned. And, we heard, more Chinese families were adopting. This presented a better picture of China to the outside world, eager to please as the 2008 Beijing Olympics were approaching in a couple of years.

For us, it meant waiting. A year passed. Will turned three. I started a consulting business, ran another marathon, we traveled to Italy and Costa Rica. Another year. We went to Mexico. My sister got married and I gained and lost the same five pounds. Twice. I joined a nonprofit board, taking the position of board chair to busy myself. Will turned four. We hosted an exchange student from China. I helped launch a charter school. Began cooking meals to freeze for when we had two children and dinnertime was more hectic. I felt as if I'd been nine months pregnant for an eternity. The wait got longer, as each month the Chinese government was only sending a small batch of baby matches.

Our friends and family constantly checked in with us. The questions made the wait both more bearable and more agonizing. People cared and wanted to help, but there was nothing to be done but wait and wait some more. There were no updates from China, only the statistics on the number of families being matched each month. We knew when our paperwork had been registered in China, so all we could do was watch the people in front of us "in line" and hope the pace picked up.

The SARS epidemic slowed the process, then the bird flu hit. Travel to and from Asia was ground to a halt, along with adoptions. I could no longer read the newspaper and began to turn off the radio as bird flu stories began. Then, in Sichuan Province, a magnitude 8.0 earthquake killed 69,000 people. The top story for days on end, it was impossible for me to hide from Will, now fully tuned in to the fact that "our baby was waiting in China."

"Is the baby okay, Mommy? Was the baby hurt in that earth-quake?"

He was questioning what I'd been thinking. *Was the baby okay? Was our baby hurt?*

"I think the baby is just fine, honey. We don't even know if the baby has been born yet." A hard fact to absorb, but the truth. We just didn't know. Anything. We didn't know a thing.

My patient husband was now exasperated and I was becoming a maniac. I slept poorly and every morning I rose to track the latest rumors out of China and calculate when we might possibly receive a baby match. And every month I was wrong. The wait was not remaining static, but getting slower. I spun my wheels with the options for adopting from other countries.

As our third year of waiting began, I grew more restless. I ran several miles longer than usual one day. Every few minutes I stopped to jot down the idea for another project I could start to occupy my time until the baby came home. The living room carpet held me as I stretched after my run and I downed an entire bag of gummy bears, negating the caloric effect of the run.

"I don't know if I can do this much longer, Ernie," I said.

We'd talked in circles about the options. I needed it. More talking. About the same thing. All over again. It had become routine for me to want to discuss our options. I needed to feel control over a process in which I had none.

Ernie detested these conversations. I knew that. The dialogue was circular. The conclusion the same one every time. Wait. Just keep waiting. My only real need when we talked was to see some emotion from him. The steadiness of his everyday demeanor bothered me. It had been an asset for so long, but at that moment, I just wanted someone equally miserable with our plight.

"Maybe we are good with one. Will wants a brother or sister, but really, he'd get so much more attention if it were just him. Maybe we're meant to have one." Even as he voiced this possibility, he sounded unsure and I was unconvinced.

"No. No way. I just don't feel that we're meant to have one. I think we're a family of four. But maybe China isn't the answer. What about getting pregnant? Let's talk about that again."

"I'm up for that, but it's really your call. You're 37. Is that something you want to put your body through?"

"Excuse me, but I run marathons, honey! I think I could do it, but I just feel like there's something else out there for us. Maybe our baby is just somewhere else." I began to list the countries where I knew adoption was still happening.

"Let's look at domestic adoption."

"For God's sake, Johanna! That's crazy talk. We both know that would take forever." He was getting frustrated. This was a conversation we'd had countless times in the past year. The answers never changed.

"Listen, I'm not ready to give up. It might take a long time to be matched with a Caucasian infant, but we've agreed we don't need that. We'd happily take a baby of any race. Agreed?"

Indeed, we had agreed on that, and we knew the likelihood of being matched with a baby of African American or mixed race was higher than with a Caucasian baby.

"But the adoption would be an open adoption, and we don't want that. Agreed?"

"Agreed. What about other countries? And why the hell don't you seem more upset by all this? We've been waiting for over two years! I feel like I'm doing it all. I did all the research and all the paperwork and you just sit back and wait for me to present the options. It's like you don't even care. What's your problem?"

"Know what? I don't want to talk about this anymore. I don't know what you want me to do. I'm sick of having this *same damn conversation* every month and I'm sick of waiting, too. This sucks for me, too! Stop being so self-absorbed. What's happened to you?"

He left the room, just as frustrated as I, but with more capacity to step away. Our marriage wasn't in danger, but we sure weren't enjoying one another as we once had.

There were no quick solutions. Will was four-and-a-half now. I dreaded the thought of having my days alone while he was at school. I'd forgotten about him in the moment. He'd been listening to our entire conversation from the corner of the room where he was working on his toy train set. His eyes were wide, as he'd heard a swear word and knew it conveyed stress between his parents.

"Mommy, I dream about my baby sister every night," he said sweetly as he rolled the caboose along the track. He could sense that his father and I were struggling with something bigger than our nightly dinner plan.

"Me, too, honey. Me, too." I drew him into my arms and pasted a smile on my face. He was so young and untarnished by the world and all its challenges. But he saw right through me.

As our wait continued, others around us carried on with the baby making. One afternoon Ruby's husband, Philip, showed up to take our crib. It was apparent that we would not be needing it any time in the next year and we'd offered it to them. Their baby was expected any day. Ernie had dismantled it, and pieces lay in a pile in the finished nursery, unnoticed by Will until it started coming down the stairs. Will snapped.

"What are you doing with the baby's crib?!" Will seemed confused.

"Honey, Ruby and Philip need the crib for their new baby. We won't need it for awhile."

"No! What if the baby comes tomorrow? We need the crib, Mommy. Don't give away the baby's crib!"

I continued to try to explain, but Will wasn't having it.

"Philip, don't take the crib. We need that crib for our baby." He was pleading now.

Philip looked at me with concern and whispered, "Jo, we can get another one if this is going to be a big deal."

"No, no, take it. We won't need it for a while. You do. We'll get it back when you're done with it. It's fine. Will is going to be fine."

I felt my hands shaking a bit. The curtains in the living room brushed my cheek as I stood holding Will and watched Ernie and Philip finish packing the crib into Philip's truck.

"But the baby. Where will the baby sleep?" Will's whispered concerns sent a stab through my heart. I bit my lip and felt the taste of blood. I closed the curtains as the truck pulled away.

I stood in the shower, the steam fogging the glass door. I ended up here every month on the morning that matches arrived from China. Calculating on the steamed shower glass. How much longer we would need to wait. Will had started kindergarten now, and I was alone during the day. Having started a consulting practice, I had the appearance of being busy, but my mind was elsewhere. We'd taken on a Chinese high school exchange student for a few months. The baby's room, which had been finished when we'd started the adoption process, was now completely undone, and replaced with a bunk bed and dresser set. The room had life again, albeit the teenage version.

We passed the three-year mark and finally, there was a little bit of light. The progression of adoptions was slow, but steady. People just ahead of us were finally getting matched. The stories of families who'd waited nearly as long as us who were matched were joyful. Inspiring. Our time was approaching, though that meant anything from one month to six months. Still, it was clear that we would not be waiting another year. We broke open the baby names book. This time, we made sure to pick a boy name AND a girl name. The list of boy names was short. I wanted Elias. Eli. The girl list was long, Claire. Amelia. Charlotte. Scarlett. Eden. Maeve. Bay. Liesel.

Our exchange student left. The crib returned, and with it, our hopes. But another month came and went without a match. Every day now was like walking through molasses. I was putting one foot in front of the other, barely able to smile. My pregnancy was at the nine-month stage for three-and-a-half years and counting.

"Mommy look!" Will said, "It's a ladybug! It means our baby is on the way."

We were at the school playground and it was March 2009. I could barely contain myself, swallowed up by my son's contagious optimism. I was shopping, baking and working like a madwoman. Every minute felt like an hour. Ernie was as affected as me. We spent our nights in silence, not discussing the baby or when we might or might not hear. I turned to Ruby once again. One happy by product of the wait was that it appeared Ruby's 18-month-old daughter Hayley, and our baby would be roughly the same age.

"I know you can do this, Johanna. You've already been through so much. You just have to make it through a few more weeks. Days, perhaps." Ruby said. I had taken the phone up-stairs and closed the bathroom door so that Ernie and Will wouldn't hear me crying.

"We don't know. We just don't know when we'll hear. We are so close. We've waited for so long. I hate China. I hate that en-tire country and their ludicrous policies and red tape and their communism. I just hate them all, Ruby. Why didn't I learn my lesson when we were in Taiwan. I just don't GET the Chinese."

"I know, I know. It's not fair. The wait has been terrible but you are so close. I know you can do this."

And, as she always was, Ruby was right.

chapter nine

April 3, 2008. I returned home from the school drop-off and got on our landline for a conference call. It was interrupted by the ringing of my cell phone. I looked down and saw it was the adoption agency. And with that, the end to our wait. The conference call was put to a quick finish. I sent a text message to Ernie, who was also in a meeting. My text message appeared on his laptop screen and he promptly closed the cover, stood up, and announced to his staff, "I have to leave. I just had a baby."

We had decided to take Will with us to see the baby's photo, so I drove to his school to pull him from kindergarten for the rest of the day. Will's teacher knew. She'd seen me all year, starting from optimistic and full of life in September to these days in April, when the light had gone out of my eyes. I no longer volunteered in class. The sight of other families with babies made my heart ache. As I walked into the classroom that day, she could tell that we'd received our call.

"It's here, isn't it? The match is here. I can tell!"

"It's here, yes, it's here! I need to take Will out of class for the rest of the day."

I was crying now, and so was she. She stood from the reading circle and came to me, wrapping her arms around me. The children looked at us, shocked to see a mommy and their teacher crying in the middle of the story.

"Go! Go! And bring the photo tomorrow!"

Ernie and I sat down in the agency conference room. Will sat on my lap. The red folder was opened and inside was a photo of a baby girl. This time, a girl. She was a chubby little baby sitting in a red car. A second picture of her showed her seated in a bouncy chair. She had heart-shaped lips and a perfectly round face. Her name was Fu Yan Zhu, which meant Beautiful Pearl. We would call her Eden. She was about to turn one and was living in foster care in Jiangxi Province. Already a completely different experience than Will. A girl. Living in foster care.

Will looked at Eden's photo. "She's kinda chubby."

"Yeah, babies are chubby. That's a good thing," Ern said. "What do you think? Isn't she beautiful?"

"She's cute, yeah."

What the heck? Where was the enthusiasm? Somewhere between ages four and five-and-a-half, Will had become a little less thrilled with the idea of having a sister. As a matter of fact, today he seemed downright nonplussed.

"Can I play with your phone, Dad?" Will asked.

Is that boredom? Ernie looked at me and I shrugged. *I suppose he must process this at age five-and-a-half differently than I do. Whatever.*

Ernie and I looked at the map of China and found where we'd be traveling. We studied the photos sent to us. They looked identical. Her face, clothing and poses were the same in both.

"What the hell? Has she been PHOTOSHOPPED?"

Incredulous, I asked for a magnifying glass to see if there was a difference between the two pictures. None. The first photos of our daughter had been doctored. *What the hell, China?* We giggled and shook it off.

We made the round of calls to parents, friends. Posted on

our blog. When we got home I pulled out my journal and looked at the entry on Eden's birthdate, nearly one year ago.

April 10, 2008: Here's today's quote: "Mommy, we had a lovely day today!" It was snowy today. Walked Nina. Went to Mandarin class with Will. Then to REI and out for pizza. It was a lovely day.

It had been an agonizing year, this last year of waiting. But our daughter had been alive, growing, laughing, and learning to experience the world. And soon we would experience her, too. I closed the journal and began packing.

After waiting so many years for a tiny photo of our baby, we now had to wait for approval to travel to China. The Chinese government alone was the authority on this, and until they gave us the green light, we could do nothing more than stare at Eden's photo. Bird flu was running circles all over Asia, and China was no exception. The pace of travel approvals slowed and we were stuck again. The crib, now returned from Ruby and Philip, sat in the nursery. Books filled the shelves. I entered the room daily to sit in the cozy glider. I tried to imagine what it would be like to have a house with two children. A full house. A family complete. The images were there, but the feeling was out of reach as I rocked, rocked, rocked.

On Eden's first birthday, we invited Ruby, Philip, and their kids over for cupcakes and champagne. It felt odd, gathering around the dining room table to sing Happy Birthday. But sing we did. Eden's photo was the centerpiece. I'd wrapped a few gifts for her that would be torn open in a few weeks when she came home. Both Will and Theo, Ruby and Philip's three-year-old, were bemused by the idea of singing to a photo instead of a chubby baby with a face full of chocolate cake.

"I don't get it, Mom," Will laughed. "Eden's not even here!"

"I just want us to stop for a moment and realize that your sister is somewhere far away, celebrating her first birthday today. "

In reality I knew that it was *me* who needed the moment. Along with the realization that the celebration happening in China was likely not nearly the production it was here in Denver.

"Can I eat her cupcake then?" he inquired.

And so he did.

chapter ten

At last, it was time. We'd decided to leave Will at home with my parents. A hard decision, as many other families had chosen to bring their younger children with the hopes that sibling bonding could begin immediately. We opted to focus on our own bonding, and decided to bring my aunt Deirdre as a travel companion. Deirdre was energetic, well traveled and an adoptive mother herself. My cousins were all grown now, but she remembered the routine of creating a family by adoption. She knew that on this trip she wouldn't get to hold Eden. It was a practical decision, as we felt it critical, just as we had with Will, that Eden know immediately who Mom and Dad were, and not get bounced around from person to person. Deirdre understood this twist, and happily volunteered to join us, serving the role of dinner fetcher and backpack hauler.

Our suitcases were loaded with the essentials of adoption travel: Cheerios, baby ibuprofen, headlamps for late night reading in bed, a laundry line, baby toys, American diapers. Before meeting Deirdre in Hong Kong, Ernie and I flew first to Beijing, doing the usual two-day, super speed tourist thing. We climbed on the Great Wall and toured the Forbidden City, but our thoughts were elsewhere. On our last afternoon, we straddled rickety Chinese one-speed bikes and rode through *hútòngs*, ancient alleyways that surrounded the area around the Forbidden City. Each pedal stroke moving us forward. Out of the United States now, and inch-by-inch, closer to Eden.

We met Deirdre in Hong Kong, spending a couple days

there, recovering from jet lag and meeting the other families in our travel group. The Star Ferry shuttled us back and forth across Hong Kong Bay, where we hopped on a bus up to Stanley Market on Hong Kong Island. At the market, we fawned over traditional Chinese baby outfits and began to purchase the 16 gifts we would give Eden over the next 16 years. Just as we'd done with Will, we purchased small gifts to give her every year on the anniversary of the day we received her. In the adoptive world, this day was known as "Gotcha Day" but we called it Family Day. Our gifts to her would include a box of fancy chopsticks, a stuffed panda and a Chinese name stamp with her name engraved on the bottom side. I made a list of the age-appropriate gifts I was buying for each year from now until she was 18. And because her name meant "Beautiful Pearl," we bought a string of pearls to be given to her when she turned 18.

The bird flu buzz was still loud, and as we made our way through the airports in both Beijing and Hong Kong, there were constant reminders. Pamphlets were passed out with information about the disease and its transmission. Announcements were made by flight attendants. Anyone sick or feverish should opt out of flying. People dressed in hazmat suits came on board to spray some sort of decontaminant from a can while the passengers sat, perplexed, if not amused.

Our flight to Nanchang was on time and we landed on May 24, 2009. We were bouncing off the walls, as this was the day we'd get Eden. Our bus would take us to the hotel. We would have a chance to change, get the room prepared and meet in the lobby where the babies would be presented to us. All at once we were excited, nervous, exhausted. And healthy.

But meanwhile, we were stuck in the immigration line in the Nanchang airport and it barely budged.

"What the hell? Is this about the bird flu? Why is it taking so long?" My irritation grew as the minutes passed and we got nowhere.

"I'm sure we'll get through this in no time, sweetie. Hang on."

My aunt Deirdre spoke calmly. She was the voice of reason on this trip, balancing my impatience. Wisdom radiated from every bit of her, and I hoped to capture it as we moved through our trip. Soft curls fell around her face as she strained to assess what was happening in front of us. It appeared that people were having their temperatures taken as they approached the front of the line. This had been protocol at several points during our travel. I wasn't concerned about that. Just concerned that any delay would mean one more minute without my baby.

Ernie approached the front of the line. A temperature gauge was waved over his head by a doctor, then a look between the doctor and the immigration police. Ernie was taken by the arm and led to a small room off the immigration area. My heart sank. His temperature had been elevated, indicating a risk of bird flu.

"What's going ON? Deirdre, he's not sick. Oh my God! This cannot be happening."

My tone shifted from irritation to worry as I weighed the possibilities. Could he be kept another hour? Two? My watch indicated we had only a few hours to go before the babies arrived.

Another adoptive father behind us was led into the same room as Ernie. His name was Jay, and his wife, Mary Beth, seemed bothered but calm as she watched her husband being taken. Our travel group had now decreased by two – Ernie and Jay. Panic. Full-on panic set in for me. We'd waited too long, come too far, for this to be happening now.

I looked over at the Chinese policeman sitting behind the metal desk outside the room that held Ernie and Jay. The desk looked worn and I knew it had been perched upon by Red Guards in its time. The desk had a history, and now it was the only thing standing between me and the possibility of being with my husband for the delivery of our baby. The policeman looked up at me and I said, in my best Mandarin, "Excuse me for the bother, but my husband is not sick. There's no need for this má fan." This was one of those words in Mandarin that I adored, as there was no real translation into English. The nearest translation was something close to "pain in the ass." Predictably, it was the not the best choice of words for the communist police. He grunted and looked back at his paperwork.

This cannot be happening! I repeated to myself.

Deirdre and I cleared immigration. Forward movement would have meant proceeding through the sliding doors into the arrivals area. I didn't move. My feet remained stuck in the area of limbo between immigration and arrivals. The police were having none of it. I was pushed forward with the rest of our group until we were on the other side of sliding doors. Our luggage had been collected, the bus pulled up, parents began piling on. I didn't move. Deirdre and I stood in the foyer of the airport. My hands were shaking. I walked as close as I could to the sliding doors before a policeman gave me a look of warning.

"It's going to be fine, Johanna. They'll let them out. They're just making a show of the whole thing." Deirdre's voice was soothing, but unconvincing.

"Deirdre, I can't do this. I'm so, so tired." I felt myself biting the inside of my cheek. I didn't want to cry. Not for this reason. Not on this day. I was not going to give China the satisfaction of seeing me cry. And then, *I'm totally going to cry, aren't I?*

She took me into her arms as the tears began to flow. We watched the sliding doors that separated us from Ernie for any sign of movement.

"Why is this happening? This cannot be happening. We've waited too long. We have come too far. Do they realize what today IS? Why? There's no reason for this. The bird flu? Are they &#%!@?! kidding me? I need my husband today. He cannot miss this. This is our baby. I don't want to do this alone! Oh my God! Oh my God!"

People began to stare at me. The weird Western woman was having a total breakdown. The rest of the travel group was on the bus. Deirdre and I were the only holdouts.

"It's time to go. Johanna, you need to get on the bus now. It's time to go." Our Chinese facilitator this time around was named Ellen, and she approached me, pulling me forward towards the bus.

"I'm not going. I refuse. I'm not going anywhere until they let Ernie and Jay go. Let me go talk to them again. I can be charming. I can be Chinese charming. They have to listen to me."

"I spoke to them. They told me that Jay and Ernie need to stay here until their temperatures return to normal. And maybe go to the hospital."

"Normal! Are they serious? He's not sick. He is fine. We don't even eat chicken or birds of any sort! I'm a vegetarian!" I was grasping at straws. Ellen gave me a sympathetic look.

"I'm sorry, Johanna, you'll just have to leave your husband here. Fu Yan Zhu needs you." Ellen used Eden's Chinese name, a name I knew as well as the one we'd picked for her.

I moved. My daughter needed me. More than my husband needed me, here, in a full on panic. In the Nanchang airport. I didn't need that. Nobody needed that. The world didn't need that. And Eden certainly didn't. So I moved. One foot in front of the other, moving towards the bus. I got on, sat down next to Deirdre, and closed my eyes.

What the heck is wrong with this place? There's no possible way that this is even remotely how things should be conducted. I need to write a letter. I'm good at letter writing. That's it. I'll start a letter-writing campaign when I get home. To do something. About this. Deep breaths, Johanna. You're about to become a mother for the second time.

I took deep inhales. The kind that women learn in labor classes and then practice in real life. The kind that are overtaken by the real pain, the real emotions of the day. And so it was with me. The bus sat. Ellen raced a few times back and forth to the airport. I watched through the windows and looked back at Jay's wife, Mary Beth, the picture of composure.

Why can't I be more like Mary Beth? How is she doing that? I'm strong. I can do it, too.

The bus engine hummed to life. And then from a distance, I saw Ernie's lean, 6'2" body stride forward out of the airport. Practically running from the place. Out of the bus I leaped and across the parking lot I ran. We embraced and I heard him laughing. While I was decidedly NOT laughing. I was still mad as hell. But he was – bemused.

"That was sure a scene. I got to practice my Mandarin a little. I think I amused them with that part. They took my temperature five or six times and finally let me go. And that's that," he shrugged. "I think the whole thing was just a show of force, personally. Whatever. It's done."

"I'm mad as hell, Ern. I'm gonna write a letter to someone."

"I'm fine. We're fine. No need for a letter. Let's go get our baby." We climbed back onto the bus and tried to refocus.

The bus rolled away, leaving Jay behind. He was predictably untouched by bird flu but quarantined nonetheless. Mary Beth remained the picture of confidence – and she received their baby girl alone that day.

chapter eleven

We crammed into a hotel conference room to await our babies. I had put on a strapless black sundress. I knew that skin-to-skin contact was beneficial in the bonding process. If I'd been able to receive Eden naked, I probably would've done it.

We'd seen the babies for a just a moment as they gathered in the hotel lobby. All were dressed in matching light green jumpsuits. They looked, predictably, terrified. Our facilitator, Ellen, shuffled us into the conference room and gave us the standard speech about how we would all be great parents. I fiddled with our video camera, handing it over to Deirdre to manage.

The babies began to appear outside the doors of the conference room, and parents were called forward. I strained to see Eden for the first time.

"Is that her over there, Ern? Could she have gotten that big?"

"I don't think that's her. What about that one there?"

"Ernie and Johanna!"

Ellen bellowed over the wails of the babies. This time, we were fourth in line. Seven families behind us, their babies still in the arms of caretakers. Infants and toddlers, eyes wide and terrified, as they watched the other babies slowly being handed over to unknown foreigners.

We stepped forward and a man approached with Eden on his hip. Her hair had been shaved in the back, no doubt because of an exposure to lice or possibly to fend off the summer temperatures. The look on her face was stoic. I could tell that I was going to need to reach out, take her and Just. Hold. On. This time around I was confident I knew what I was doing. I reached forward and took Eden in my arms, thanking the man.

"Hi, honey. How are you? Ohmygosh! I love you so much." I whispered to her, looking into her eyes with disbelief. Here she was. The weight of the many years began to melt. Eden gave me the same blank stare that Will had given me at this moment. It was the what-in-the-hell-just-happened stare.

"We've waited so long, Eden. What a story, little girl. Look at you. Look how cute you are."

She continued to stare at me with a totally deadpan look. I felt my heart begin to brace itself for the onslaught of tears that I knew were just around the corner. Once again, I was frozen in that moment in time, which represented pure agony for my child and pure bliss for me. My only job was to hold on and not let go. Certain I could do this, I smiled and continued talking to her sweetly, turning her towards Ernie, who was bending over so that his height didn't overwhelm her.

Ernie began cooing at her, holding out the toy we'd brought. She didn't crack a smile nor a frown. Her scent was musty. She had a sturdy little body that felt heavier than Will had. I could see thick legs, the cuffs of her green sweatpants pulled too tightly around her calves. As I held her, her body stiffened, turning away from me and back to the man who'd just let her go. I had no idea what his connection was to her, but in this moment, in her eyes, he trumped me. Needing to break whatever ties remained, I turned towards the door.

"Johanna! Where are you going?" called Deirdre.

I'd walked the wrong direction upon exiting the conference room, heading right into the dining room where dinner was being served to hotel guests. My head was simply unable to focus on anything but holding onto my daughter and putting one foot in front of the other. I turned towards Deirdre, who was holding the camera as she walked backwards towards the elevator.

"There you are. I'm Mommy. I'm your mommy." I spoke soft Mandarin as we walked, as I had with Will. I could see Eden's bottom lip begin to reveal her true feelings about being handed over to a stranger. Her eyes looked watery. I took a deep breath and stepped onto the elevator as she began to whimper. I grasped her around her shoulders and pulled her into me. She pulled away and began to cry.

Here we go. I'm ready. Here it comes. This is it. It only gets easier from here. Hold on, now, Johanna. Sound happy. So very happy. Smile, now.

"This is Daddy. Look at your daddy. You're so cute. I love you. Don't cry."

By the time we reached our hotel room, Eden was in a full on meltdown and there wasn't a darn thing we could do about it but hold on. Ernie and I alternated holding her, and she seemed more comfortable with him, just as Will had. I busied myself by ordering rice congee from room service. The crib next to our bed looked straight out of the 1940s. I fluffed pillows, sticking them in crib corners to make it appear a little less institutional.

Eden's cries turned loud. Will's had sounded almost animalistic, but hers were just plain horrified. I began running through the checklist in my head to see if I could pin her tears on anything other than mourning. Hungry? Earache? Skin infection? Teething? Rash? Tummy ache?

"Let's try changing her diaper, Ern."

I could smell the hours of panic in the air, and suspected I'd find a sopping wet diaper to match her mood. We gently removed her bottoms. Her diaper was a cloth version, and it was held together by a tiny bungee cord.

"Good God!" I gasped. "Her diaper is tied on with a cord, Ern. Check it out."

I threw away the diaper, cleaned her up and put on an American disposable version. The process took all of 90 seconds, but wasn't the elixir. Eden's tears continued. I held her, walking over to the window and looking down fifteen floors to the ground below. Bouncing her gently on my hip, I continued talking to her through her wails. She was mourning. Pure and simple.

I bounced some more. Almost an imperceptible bounce, but movement. Soothing, I hoped. Then I tried swaying with her. Closing my eyes, I tried to envision her at age six, playing dress up with her cousin Penelope. I thought of her sitting at our dining room table coloring with Ruby's daughter Hayley. I knew from experience that this moment would pass, but right then and there, the pain couldn't be denied. Hers. Mine. Ernie's, who stared at us helplessly from across the room.

Bounce. Sway. Bounce. Sway.

I looked at Ernie, my eyes screaming that I was going to crack. All the years. All the delays. The airport fiasco. Everything had led to this moment. Eden didn't know me, and I suspected she'd never seen an adult cry. In an instant, she got both. We stood, bouncing, both of us with tears streaming down our faces.

"It's awful, honey. It's just so... awful. I can't believe she has to go through this. I can't believe someone left her. Why would someone leave her?" I cried as I looked at Ernie. He sat on the bed, rolling a stuffed bear through his hands.

"I know, Jo. I know. Just hold on. Just keep holding. She won't remember this moment. You will. Don't let it crush you."

I stopped my tears after a few minutes, but continued to rock her until exhaustion took hold. We removed the green jumpsuit and put it in a sealable bag with the urine-soaked diaper cord. I added the little shoes she had on, and the nametag that had been attached to her top with a clip. Fu Yan Zhu, it said. Beautiful Pearl was now ours.

chapter twelve

A scream on the first night woke me from a restless sleep. Eden's scream. I looked over to see every parent's worst nightmare.

"Oh my God! Ernie! Ernie! I think her head is stuck between two of the crib slats!"

Ernie fumbled for his glasses while I flipped on the light. I was right. Eden's little head was wedged between two of the metal crib slats. A look of pure panic was on her face.

"Get her out! Get her out!" I was shaking, having gone from sleep to fully wired in about ten seconds.

Ernie gently twisted her head. Her ears bent a bit as he pushed her head back through the slats and freed her. Once free, I lifted her out of the crib and held her as she screamed.

"It's okay. It's okay sweetie."

I sat in bed with her in my arms, rocking her while my heart-beat returned to normal. My fingers stroked her hair as Ernie's stroked mine. I lay Eden between us and we watched her slowly fall back asleep. As she slept, I explored her face with my fingers. Her ears were prominent, a contrast to her brother's. I ran my finger along the ridges and then I noticed it. A freckle. Behind her left ear. I looked over at Ernie, but he'd fallen back to sleep.

I giggled to myself. She had a single freckle behind her left ear. I knew one other child who had the same single freckle behind the same ear. It was 2 a.m. here, but noon in Denver, where he lived. Will would love it. A matching freckle with his baby sister.

Eden survived the first night, proving she was resilient. Each day with her revealed another amazing characteristic. After her very first day of tears, she rarely cried. It was as if she put it aside and decided to try us on. See what we had to offer.

On our second full day, we noticed that her diaper was still dry hours after we'd changed it.

"What in the world, Deirdre? This is just plain bizarre. She's been drinking all day. What's with the dry diaper?"

"I'm not sure. Wonder if we should be concerned. Maybe she's trying to hold it for some reason?"

"We could try to hold her over the toilet. I've heard that sometimes babies here are toilet trained. Who knows? I find it hard to believe, but what the heck? Let's give it a go."

I brought Eden into the bathroom, removing her pants and diaper. I held my forearms bent at a ninety-degree angle and sat her upon them facing away from me and toward the toilet. I had only a vague recollection of how to do this from one of our adoption trainings and it felt incredibly silly. Nothing happened. Deirdre stood by for support and I rolled my eyes at her.

"This is just crazy. She's only twelve months old and her foster mom was like 75. There's no way. My arms are getting tired."

Ernie poked his head in and saw what was going on.

"Isn't there something you're supposed to say?"

"Oh right, you're supposed to make some sort of peeing sound. Uh, I'm dying here."

My forearms were burning from holding twenty pounds.

"Pssss... Pssss... " I made a sound that mimicked urinating, and tried not to laugh in the process.

The sound of Eden's pee hitting the toilet water made me jump.

"Holy crow! Good job, Sweetie! She's doing it!" Deirdre's yelp alarmed Ernie, who ran back into the bathroom.

"Well, I'll be damned. Twelve months old and she's already potty trained."

She was a shover. That's what Deirdre dubbed her. A shover. Some kids were pickers. Picked at their food. Some threw it. Others spit it out. Eden seemed to have a love affair with food of all sorts. It hit us like a tidal wave. We'd been experiencing the opposite at home. Carefully measured tablespoons of peas and pasta made up Will's plate at dinner.

And now here we were, 10,000 miles away. With a shover. Meals would start slowly. Then the torrent would be unleashed. Plate after plate of food placed in front of us. Eden's eyes widening at each one. Laughter filled the restaurant as we watched her take handful after handful of noodles and shove them into her little mouth. And apple juice by the liter. Fearful of constipation, I was liberal with juice. More than I should have been. With each nibble and sip, Eden seemed in heaven. I wondered whether she'd simply never tasted these foods, sipped these liquids.

Our distraction with her eating got the better of us one evening at dinner. We sat eating Indian curry. It was delicious, and I began eating with my fingers. Bread soaking up the yellow curry. A wonderful change from the Chinese food we'd been served. I was ravenous. Licking my fingers, I looked over at Eden. Slumped in her chair, she had a look of contentment. We'd put her in a diaper for mealtimes, just to be safe.

At the table next to us, a glass tipped over and fell underneath

Eden's high chair, shattering. Instinctively, I reached down to feel her exposed legs to make sure she wasn't cut. I felt something wet on my fingers.

"I think she's cut her leg. I feel blood!"

I pulled up my fingers, expecting to see the red of my daughter's blood on my hands. Instead, it was yellow. *Thank goodness, just my curry.* Relieved, I put my fingers in my mouth, licking it off. A wave of shock washed over me as my taste buds identified the flavor not as my delicious curry. I glanced over at Eden, still happily poised in her high chair. Another glass of empty juice sat on her tray. I realized with horror that I'd just ingested a bite of my daughter's blown out diaper. The combination of the broken glass, the fear of a cut on her leg, the yellow curry and the over indulgence on apple juice had resulted in a shocking twist of fate for my taste buds.

Oh shit! I thought. Literally. *Johanna, you've just eaten your daughter's diarrhea. I would like to crawl into a hole now.* I stood straight up, trying to use as few words as possible as I grabbed a napkin and began spitting into it.

"Don't panic, but I need some help! I think I just ate some of Edie's poop."

Ernie and Deirdre jumped up, unsure what to do.

I raced to the bathroom, but even that was of little help. We'd been instructed not to drink the tap water for fear of disease, so as I swished and spit out mouthful after mouthful, I had alternating visions of giardia and worms crawling through my intestines. I couldn't believe this was happening. Who the hell eats their child's crap? I looked up into the cracked mirror. I had a horrified look on my face but I couldn't help laughing. Though this fiasco was the product of my own idiocy, it still had a distinctly Chinese stamp on it. I would only accidently eat shit in a place like rural China where anything was possible. I looked at myself, humbled by this country. With all the ways China had made me tear out my hair year after year, there was always something like this to keep me on my toes. Unpredictable. Unimaginable. This place was beyond my comprehension. I hated it. And part of me loved every bit of it. I felt China sink more and more into my being as I swished and spit, swished and spit, swished and spit.

chapter thirteen

We sailed through the rest of our time in China. The medical appointments. The endless signatures needed on ten copies of every document. Eden continued to eat well and clearly loved Ernie. If she wasn't in his arms, she had to have one of her hands on him at all times. And if I touched him, she'd scowl at me. We made a little game of it and laughed our way through the final days.

We boarded our plane in Hong Kong and flew through the night. Arriving in Denver, we were met by my parents and Will at the airport. I'd fixated on this moment for years. This was not a sibling who'd arrive swaddled. She'd be mobile. Require constant attention. Be after Will's toys within minutes. Ernie and I realized this, and we each held our breath as they laid eyes upon each other for the first time.

He gave us quick hugs and then gazed at her, almost in disbelief.

"Hi, Eden!" Will's greeting caused Eden to look straight at her brother. A stare that didn't break. Expressionless. Not even a blink. I'd come to know Eden's stare well as she grew. Merely an assessment of her situation, nothing more or less.

She sized him up and then looked at my parents who were as emotional as they'd been in Kunming four years ago when they traveled with us to get Will.

"I brought her a giraffe, Mom," Will announced.

"That's so sweet, honey. I'm sure she'll adore it."

"She's really fat, Mom!" Will laughed and poked at one of her chubby thighs.

"Will. Let's not use the word "fat" okay? Little girls can be sensitive about that word."

"Oh for God's sake, Johanna, she's a baby," Ernie cackled.

"Also, Mom! She doesn't speak English."

"Fair enough. She speaks baby. That's it at the moment. I'm just saying, we've got a girl in the house now. Could we pick another word besides 'fat' to use? How about 'well fed?' That works, right? I officially coin 'well fed' as our new word and banish 'fat' from our family vocabulary."

"Oh my gosh, Mom!"

We collected our bags and walked out into the Colorado sunshine. Our car was parked in a nearby lot. Mom and Dad got us settled and then hopped in a taxi to meet us at home.

The scenes of parents leaving the hospital with their newborns raced through my mind. Tentatively strapping in their babies into rear-facing car seats. Checking and double-checking the buckles. This was the same moment, albeit the forward-facing version. I strapped Eden into the car seat and she looked at me with confusion. This was new. *What is THIS thing?* I imagined her wondering. Quickly, she was distracted by Will, who'd taken the liberty of unwrapping the giraffe for his sister.

"Toss it to me, Eden! Toss it to me!" Will giggled as he taught her how to throw. He had a playmate in the back seat at last. We drove away from the airport and I soaked in the sound of two children in the backseat. Their laughter was the most beautiful sound I'd ever heard. I turned and saw them there, smiling at one another. I'd spent years with only one child in the backseat. And now there were two. Suddenly two. Looking at each other. And then up at the road ahead. Playing. Smiling. We'd finally finished creating our family. And on we drove, into the sunlight. China in the rearview mirror.

chapter fourteen

Our lives unfolded as they do for families everywhere. Play dates and preschool for Eden. First grade, then second for Will. Though different ages and genders, the children seemed drawn to each other. Now that we had a full nest, we marveled in their differences.

Will had always been a deep thinker. He needed explanations of how things worked and why decisions were made. This often resulted in protracted arguments in meaningless topics. Meaningless in the eyes of his parents, that is. He carried the weight of a young adult in turmoil on his shoulders and often looked at the glass as half empty. Yet his ability to reason was also useful, as he seemed to take in data in boatloads. We never needed to explain more than once how something worked. In fact, he vividly recalled conversations that we'd had with him at ages three and four. While my memory was lapsing, his was just firing up for the decades ahead.

Eden was a contrast to her brother. She rarely made a fuss if she was asked to do something she didn't agree with. Instead of dwelling on the meaning, she just got over it as soon as possible so she could move on with her little life. She asked questions, but they were about feelings and the humanity of issues, not the mechanics. Her days started with smiles. One morning I described to her why her brother was having a difficult time getting rolling. She was three years old and life at 6 a.m. seemed as exciting as it was at noon.

"You know, honey, some people wake up sometimes with

just a little cloud over their heads. It happens to me sometimes. And to Daddy, too."

"Rainbows," she replied.

"Rainbows?" I asked.

"I wake up with rainbows over my head, right Momma?"

Indeed she did.

We'd enrolled the kids in basic Mandarin lessons from the age of two. We trekked down to the adoption agency, whose wise language instructors guided the kids through the basics: colors, greetings, animals. My language skills were still superior to theirs, but slowly we were able to have very basic conversations in Mandarin at home. I watched as the months passed and thought about how good we had it. A comfortable home. Dear friends. Enough money in the bank. Our health. But for some reason, I wanted more. And it wasn't more in a material sense. It was more of the world. I desired experiences with different cultures, other people, and new languages. And I wanted to do that with my family. To literally give them the world.

I made good on my promise to not let my husband forget my desire to live abroad someday. Ernie, who'd never been to a third world country, already knew I was crazy about exploring the world. He listened patiently as every six months I would bring it up. The conversation was typically one-sided and went something like this:

"So Ern, I am bringing up that thing that you think is crazy."

"Right. It's looney, Jo. Complete looney tunes. But go ahead. What do you need to tell me about this time?"

And then I would launch into my latest news. Often the pieces were mere subtexts for the actual overseas move. Such as, how difficult it would be to bring, Nina, our dog. And best to wait till she had moved to dog heaven. I'd quietly crunched the numbers on the average age Weimaraners lived, and calculated how much longer she'd be with us. Letting her live out her life with us dictated almost everything.

Or maybe I would talk about where we'd be moving, as China was not fully on the radar yet. Beaches seemed a good option. Somewhere in Central America, perhaps? That would mean we'd need to learn Spanish, but that was a minor inconvenience.

Very rarely was there a discussion of career. As in, what the hell are we going to live on for a year? I had assumed we'd live a life of poverty. Poor but happy, as I'd lived in Asia when I was young and single. When this topic arose, Ernie called my bluff.

"Johanna, we have children now. This isn't exactly the same thing as teaching English and bouncing in and out of the country to maintain your immigration status."

"I know that, but I feel like things will work out. We're resourceful. We'll find a way to make money. Come on, believe in it with me! Where is your sense of adventure, you old fuddy duddy?"

"Check back with me in six more months, honey. I want a better plan with fewer holes."

I'd return to the drawing board. In between play dates and consulting gigs, I'd sketch out new and flexible plans. I stood in the shower, hot water running over me, writing on the glass shower door once again. The years ahead and how each coordinated to the age of the children. 2010: Eden 2, Will 7, and so forth. It was beginning to dawn on me that 2012 would be our year. Eden would be just a year away from entering kindergarten. Old enough to have some independence, but young enough to adapt well. Will would be in fourth grade. Nine years old. *That's halfway to leaving our nest*, I thought. Not fully involved in sports or friends every waking moment. Perfect.

As for jobs, I reached out to an organization in Boulder that I'd heard about called Colorado China Council. CCC was run by a woman named Alice, an energetic one-woman show who had decades of experience placing Americans in China to work as college professors. I had known Alice for years. I'd been eyeing her program for at least as long as we had Will. Five years prior, the demand for American professors to teach English was high. I wasn't certain if that was still the case. And China didn't exactly suit our desire to be someplace warm and tropical. Still, if I was to get this plan off the ground, I was starting to realize I needed more than blind faith. Ernie was right. Better plan. Fewer holes. I called Alice to talk about the possibilities.

"Johanna, I gotta be honest. It is getting harder and harder to place families. The demand was high a few years ago, but now everyone and their mother wants to go to China. Standards are getting higher and placing families poses some challenges."

"I get that. I do. More paperwork. Bigger housing. But come on. I've already taught in Taiwan, I speak Mandarin and I've got a doctorate. The Chinese love higher degrees."

"True. I think we could make a good case for you, but I just want you to be aware that if you decide to proceed, it might not be as rosy as you think."

"Alice, you're talking to someone who just went through the China ringer for years trying to push through the adoption of our two kids. What could be worse?"

"I hear you. Let me know if you want to move forward. And if so, I should meet Ernie. He's on board with this?"

"Well, to be honest, I haven't filled him in on this particular piece of the plan yet. I wanted to talk to you first."

"Johanna, he NEEDS to be on board with this. We're not talking about moving you to France, here. This is serious business."

"I got it, I got it. Don't worry. It's cool. I think he'll be into it."

Crap. I had NO IDEA if he'd be into it. China had squeezed every drop of energy from us with Eden's adoption. And to be honest, the thought of proposing China to Ernie made me a bit nauseous. But it seemed like such a logical choice on paper. The kids and I spoke Chinese, the kids *were* Chinese. We were planning to enroll them in a Mandarin immersion elementary school. I loved Asia. There were so many incredible places to visit. Wonders of the world. And the food. My mind began to swirl with visions of phad thai on the streets of Bangkok. Picnicking on the Great Wall of China. Wandering the temples at Angkor Wat in Cambodia.

I brought it up again. This time with a target date in mind. Departing in 2012 for a year. Or two. The kids were occupied with a cave made of pillows and blankets as I pitched my plan over a glass of wine one night.

"So Ernie, remember that crazy idea? I want to talk about it again."

"Right. Have six months already passed? Whatcha got for me, Jo?"

"I have a plan... 2012, that's our year. China. I think I can get a teaching gig there."

"China? *You must be joking.* They've already sucked the life out of us once. You'd really consider *living* there?"

"That may be, but for the kids. It would be amazing for the kids. You know, to live in the land of their birth. We could visit Will's orphanage. Eden's foster mother."

"And the job part? You think you could find one easily?"

"I talked to this woman, Alice, at that organization in Boulder that places Americans in teaching jobs. She seemed to think it was doable." I had totally skipped over the entire piece about families being hard to place. Oops.

"And what about me? What would I do there?" In the expat community there was a name for what Ernie would be. "The trailing spouse." He'd be the trailing spouse and I loved the thought of it. Handing over the duties I usually took care of to him. Nice. But I didn't let on, proposing another plan instead.

"Well, you know, if the company values you enough they'll just put you on sabbatical and take you back to your old job when we come home. Easy peasy."

Ernie worked for a large cable company. He managed a group of software engineers. Not work that could be done re-motely.

"You're serious about this, aren't you? Oh my God, you're se-rious!"

"Deadly. Watch me do this. I'm moving this family to China and I'm not leaving you behind. Get ready."

"And our mortgage? The rental properties? The cars?"

"It's all noise, Ern. We'll figure it out. I just need to hear that you're open to the idea. I know it totally freaks you out, but so did a bunch of other things I've convinced you to do."

As I continued to spell out my reasons for wanting to up-root our family and move overseas, Ernie's eyes clouded over. I could tell I'd lost him.

"Ernie. Honey. Are you WITH me?"

"Wait, what? I don't get it, Johanna. Why do we have to do this?"

"I'm not saying we have to, I just want to, you know, live a little. Just because we've had children doesn't mean we can't have a bit of wanderlust."

I thought about the fact that Ernie and I had only dated for a year before we'd gotten married. And then Will's adoption only a year after that. *Holy crap, maybe he didn't really know me at all.*

"Okay, you know how you thought you'd get married in a church but I convinced you it was better to get married outside at my parent's house?"

"Yes, my family still won't forgive me for not standing in front of an altar, but yeah, I remember."

"And you liked it, right? Our wedding?"

"I did. It was awesome. Remember those baby turtles that hatched and kept walking through the reception on the way to the pond?"

"Totally. THAT wouldn't have happened if we'd had a church wedding, honey. And remember the time you wanted to go to Florida on vacation and I convinced you we should go to Tanzania instead?"

"Ah, how could I forget? We took an awful, fourteen-hour bus ride and I got a nasty case of the runs."

"Right, but it was fun, wasn't it?"

"Yeah. Where are you going with this, Jo?"

"Bear with me. Remember how I proposed that instead of trying to get pregnant, we should adopt? Adopt first. We can always get pregnant later, I said, right?"

"That was all you, yes."

"And look at our kids, honey. You wouldn't change a single thing, would you? If I'd gotten pregnant we'd have a couple of pasty white kids with both of our genes and we BOTH know that spells trouble. Instead we have Will and Eden and every day is a... it's a beautiful mystery."

"I'm catching on, but China, really?"

"Trust me, Ern, you're gonna love it. It's gonna be great. It'll be like hitting a giant reset button on our life, honey. Doesn't everyone need to do that every now and then?"

"A reset button, huh? That makes it sound like something's wrong with our life. When, in fact, everything is sailing along perfectly. Why mess with a good thing, Jo? If we want adventure, couldn't we just talk about something a little less intimidating like a big camping trip or remodeling the kitchen?"

chapter fifteen

To achieve a higher likelihood of buy-in from Ernie, I launched an operation familiar to many wives. It goes a little like this: Come up with a great idea and subtly make your husband think that it is actually HIS idea. This makes HIM feel powerful and creative, while allowing you to still retain the knowledge that it's really YOU driving the family train. This usually worked well when I'd tried it with small house projects, where to go skiing, which restaurant to dine at. Minutiae. This endeavor posed greater challenges. By the time the middle of 2011 rolled around, it was clear that I was one year out from what I hoped would be wheels up. A 747 lifting off, bound for Asia with all four of us, a bushel of suitcases and bottomless optimism for the future. I kicked my plan into overdrive, cornering Ernie on the couch late one night after the kids had gone to bed.

"Ern. We're about one year away from our departure. I might want to talk about this more than once every six months."

This was step one. Discuss the plan as if it's already a foregone conclusion.

"You still haven't told me how this will work. What do you expect from me at this point?"

"Well, perhaps you can approach your boss and just tell him that you need to leave for a year to follow your wife's career."

"You've lost it. You don't even have a job!"

"That doesn't matter. Because he doesn't need to know any details at this point, and anyway, I WILL get a job."

"And you expect that we can survive on your salary?"

"That's not completely certain, but you could always teach private English lessons if we needed more money. And if the company's really serious about keeping you, maybe they'd let you do a little contract work remotely."

"I doubt it. The logistics alone would be too much for them."

"I don't know, Ern. I think you should just put it out there in the world and see where it goes. Make them believe that it's their idea to have you work remotely. Ask them to brainstorm with you. You know, give them some ownership over the thing."

This was step number two. Pass the make-them-think-it's-their-idea plan on to a third party.

I actually had zero confidence that the company would let Ernie telecommute. I'd heard of it happening domestically, but from Asia? With a fourteen hour time difference. It sounded outlandish. Nonetheless, Ernie was a brilliant and valued engineer and I knew that losing him as an employee would sting. And the fact was, I truly believed in putting ideas out into the open forum. Letting others take the credit for bold strategies. Forging connections in China for Ernie's company – that was bold. I crossed my fingers that someone would nibble. It would mean the difference between life as a poor expatriate family and life as a very comfortable expatriate family. I knew myself. I wanted comfort.

Then, a nibble. Ernie spoke to his boss and people began to speculate on the possibilities. Word came from above that someone had heard of Ernie's plan to take a leave while his wife worked in China. By chance, a joint venture was in the works with a Chinese company. Ernie sat back quietly while the details were hammered out. The chatter continued, the company plan taking hold even as I was still entirely without a teaching job.

Six months away from our target 'wheels up' date, Ernie came home with a bouquet of flowers. He had a grin on his face walking in the back door, and took me into his arms.

"You're not going to believe it."

"Oh. My. God! They're going for it, aren't they?"

"Yup. I've been cleared to work remotely, up to forty hours a week. From China. At the standard U.S. contract rate."

"What?! Holy crap, Ern! You realize the cost of living is like a tiny portion of what it is here? I thought if anything, they'd put you on par with Chinese salaries."

"Nope. I'm going through a U.S. contracting house based in Beijing. They have to pay me in U.S. dollars. At a U.S. rate."

"Holy smokes! And the job, no managing people for a year?"

"Nope. Just gonna be an individual contributor for a year, and they said when we come back I'll probably just go back to a version of my existing job."

I yelped. The children walked in and wondered what the fuss was about.

"Guys, we're really going to do it. We're going back to China. Daddy got a job and we're gonna do it!"

"Can I bring my dress up clothes?" Eden wondered.

"I don't know. I'm not sure how this is going to go," said Will.

"Your mom has the whole thing mapped out, guys. Don't worry. It's gonna be great. She's got this," their father reassured them.

The kids shrugged as Ernie and I stood in the kitchen, incredulous. We cracked a fresh bottle of wine. Ernie had the glow of a strong, creative man. After all, it was his idea. Wasn't it?

I sipped my glass of wine that night, making sure that all four of us were enrolled in frequent flyer programs with appropriate Asian partners. I printed a small map of Southeast Asia, marked the spots I wanted us to travel, and stuck it on the bathroom mirror. Things were about to get interesting.

Our year looked different now. Instead of living on a shoestring, we'd have enough funds to get a decent apartment, travel a bit and perhaps even sock a little away. Ernie would be able to come home to a job when our year was finished. Uncertainty about life after our year abroad disappeared. Still there was the matter of MY job. Alice sent my credentials to all parts of China, but focused on Kunming and Lijiang in Yunnan Province. Located in southwest China, it was the province where Will was from and the weather was warm year-round. Even better news was that its location was only two hours by plane to Bangkok, the jumping off point for many adventures I was already salivating about. It was time to tell our families. I called my parents, curious to hear their reaction.

"You're moving *where*?" My mother sounded excited and dumbfounded. "Tony! Pick up the phone. Good god, they're moving to China!"

"Johanna, I don't know about this one. Hasn't that country already taken enough from you?" Dad was with Mom on this one, and I understood why.

"Remember the tapped phones in Taiwan, honey? Didn't you and Ruby go into hiding for awhile there?"

Had we? *My mother remembered everything.* I suddenly had a flashback of me and Ruby riding our bicycles very fast late one evening down dark alleys. Were we trying to escape the Taiwanese police? Or just being silly 23-year-olds?

"Mom, that was twenty years ago. Things are different now."

"How will we communicate with you? We'll have to have some sort of secret language. You know it's a communist country, don't you?" Dad asked.

"Of course! It's gonna be great. You guys can come visit us."

"Been there. Done that. We could meet you halfway for vacation, though. What's half way? Guam? Fiji?" My father's wheels had already begun turning, as he was ever the traveler to exotic locations. Mom wasn't letting up.

"What about all that international human rights work you've done? What if they follow you? What about the kids? You've got a Chinese boy. What if someone tries to kidnap him? I've heard that happens, you know." That was a new one. I made a mental note to Google "kidnapping of Chinese boys."

"Mom, I've got this under control. I promise to do my due diligence before we make any final decisions."

Ernie's call to his parents had a similar tone of disbelief. Super that Ernie had some guarantee of employment, they concurred, but what about help with the actual move? Where would the kids attend school? Where would we live? How would we communicate and what if one of us got sick? The number of answers we had for them to any of these questions was roughly – zero.

A few hours later, Ernie's sister called. I heard him chuckling, though I couldn't make out the context. He hung up and walked into the living room, flopping on the couch next to me.

"She heard, didn't she? Your mother called her, didn't she?"

"Yup." Ernie's grin grew at the mention of his mom.

"Oh my gosh, Ern, what did your mom say to her?"

"Beth said she answered the phone and all my mom said was, 'Guess what Ernie and Johanna are doing NOW!?'"

There was work to do. On several fronts.

University after university expressed hesitation, and it became clear that the family was an anchor. Jobs were becoming more scarce as Western migration to China increased. The jobs that did exist were going to fresh college grads with Mandarin skills and no appendages in the form of a husband and children. My experience in Asia, my doctoral degree and my Mandarin language skills meant next to nothing. Three tagalongs was enough to bring in rejection after rejection.

"Johanna, a school in Nanjing is interested in you, but I know you aren't interested in living that far east."

Alice and I were putting our heads together. It was May, and we hoped to leave the United States in August.

"Alice, I seriously don't think we could hack it in Nanjing. The pollution is awful. The weather is so far from ideal. And honestly, we just want to be closer to Southeast Asia."

"My dear, at this point, you cannot afford to be picky. We're down to our final few options."

"Let's keep trying. Let's focus more on Kunming."

While I was struggling to get a job, Ernie's stock was rising at work, and he was being sent to China in advance to lay the groundwork for his project. I felt a mix of jealously and joy for him.

"Have faith, Jo. This is going to work."

"Don't throw that 'have faith' crap around with me! I don't know why we thought China was going to work for us. Why am I surprised? And, that 'have faith' line is mine." I grumbled the last line under my breath, as if telling myself to take my own advice.

My friends and cousins propped me up. Again. As she had with the 40-hour bus rides in Asia, the failed bar exams, and the adoption drama, Ruby was there. My cousin, Chris, spent hours boosting my morale as rejections piled one on top of the next.

June arrived and with it another lead. This one was in Kunming, and it was at a university right in downtown Kunming, not far from the part of town where we hoped to live. Perfection. The pay was terrible, but the program seemed solid and it was our last offer. I signed a contract and sent it back before they could reconsider. Two days later, we bought four one-way tickets to China. It was the end of June. Five weeks until wheels up.

chapter sixteen

Anyone who's ever moved with children can imagine the emotions involved in preparing to relocate to China. I'd adopted the method of packing one room at a time. In theory, this was supposed to make me feel as though I were breaking the task into smaller pieces. Instead, it simply created many small scraps of paper with checklists of things for me to do once we returned from China. I uncovered projects big and small that would need addressing. Reorganize the photo albums, buy new pots, sew new curtains. The task of boxing our belongings was also therapeutic. I fast forwarded one year and began to realize what toys and clothes would be outgrown when we returned. Week after week I called the Salvation Army to come pick up another load of possessions I felt we could live without.

"Think the kids are going to notice that you just donated their sandbox?" Ernie wondered out loud. They didn't.

"What will Eden do when she sees that she only has three dolls, not ten?" he asked. It didn't draw attention.

My purge didn't go completely unnoticed. A pile appeared in Will's room of things he wanted to bring overseas. It seemed too big. One night I checked with Ernie, feeling lost in expectations.

"Too big? What do you mean?" he asked.

"Well, I mean, he's got like three Nerf shooter things, and his collapsible basketball hoop and all of his Pokémon cards. It's too much. We can't possibly bring all of that with us, can we?"

"I don't know, Jo. Can we bring the 15 boxes of vitamin C powder or the twelve packages of bandages you bought yesterday?"

"That's not fair! Those things are important!"

"So are his Pokémon cards to him. Take a moment and realize what you've gotten us into here. What you've gotten THEM into."

"It's going to be priceless. They just don't know it yet."

"Bingo. They don't know. All they know is that their mother is furiously putting together piles of stuff that SHE wants to bring. And so they're mimicking you. They're just doing their part, Johanna." I took his comments to heart. Tried to behave a little less harried. And hide my piles.

The weather was warming and I began pushing the kids outside so that the quickly dwindling supply of "stuff" wouldn't be apparent. We packed up the car at the end of June. The kids said goodbye to their friends. And we went to the one place in the world that would bring us the love and support we'd need before undertaking a year of unknowns. We went to the lake.

Elkhart Lake is in central Wisconsin. I'd grown up on the lake in the summers as a child, surrounded by dozens of cousins. Elkhart was home to a few of my first cousins, and those of us who didn't live there year-round came for long periods in the summer. At first, we came as children, and now, with children of our own. We were a loud, happy, loving bunch. Needing nothing more than each other, visitors to the lake were often transfixed by our numbers. That we knew who our second and third cousins were. And that we could hang endlessly with one another, week after week. My generation had been packed with girls, and now the litmus test for all newly minted husbands was that they could simply sit on the beach with us and not be overwhelmed by our strong personalities or the constant activity surrounding lake life. Our extended family was so tight that one of the most recent men to marry into the family compared it, lovingly, to a commune.

Ernie didn't have the benefit of two months of vacation, but my teaching schedule allowed it, and I took full advantage. I liked to joke that all we had to pack for our two months at the lake was a pair of pajamas and several swimsuits. Our days consisted of swimming or being outside in some capacity that required nothing more. This summer was both the same and entirely different as it had been for the past 40 years.

Our car had been filled with more than swimsuits this time. We'd decided to depart from Chicago, meaning we'd brought our China load to the lake. I'd stored five of our big China suitcases in the hallway, and to the kids they were a daily reminder of what lay ahead. Not to mention a burden in our small condo.

"Mom, these suitcases are in my way." Will's voice carried an irritated hum. He stumbled into the kitchen where I was fixing breakfast one morning just after our arrival.

"I don't want to see them and I don't even want to talk about China. Don't talk about it." Then I did what every mom does when her child says he doesn't want to talk about something.

"Why not, honey? What's up? Let's talk."

"Mom, I don't want to talk about it. I just don't want to go. Why are we doing this? You're taking me away from my friends." Will leaned back on the counter stool he was perched on, bringing him precariously onto only two of its legs. My arm began to reach out to grab him, but I stopped myself. The conversation being more important than the correction.

"I know. It's super tough. Dad and I are leaving all of our friends, too, and we're scared and excited. Both. At the same time."

"Why, Mom? I don't want to go. Why did you make this stupid plan?"

"I totally hear you, buddy. I just want you to try to let go of some of that worry and let me hold onto it. Worrying is my job, not yours."

It was a catchphrase for the kids my cousin Chris had taught me, repeated so often now that I feared its effectiveness was waning.

Will hated change and I had known that he was struggling with the move in theory, but now here we were. Four weeks out. The floodgates opening. A card catalog of correct parenting phrases spun in my head. *Was this when I was supposed to validate or stand firm and push him to stay strong? Should I cry with him so he could see my emotions, or change the subject? Crap. I'd remembered to pack the probiotics and enough dental floss to last the entire year. Why could I not remember what to say in THIS moment? How had I overlooked this piece?*

"Let's talk about the things we're going to and not what we're leaving. How about that?"

"Like what?"

"Think about it. You're going to get to travel to places that you've read about in books. You'll get an entire year of our attention. We're gonna be like a band of superheroes."

"Mom, that's babyish. Come up with something better."

"Well, are you excited about being in Kunming? It's where you were born. We'll get to visit the orphanage this year."

"Yeah. I don't know. Kinda." Eden raced through the kitchen, swimsuit in hand, begging to go to the water. My conversation with Will ended abruptly, allowing me time to gather my thoughts.

It hadn't occurred to me that Will would be anything less than thrilled about our choice of Kunming as home base. My naivety slowly began to dawn on me at that moment, and as the next few weeks spilled ahead of us. *This particular component of our impending life in Kunming must be scary*, I thought. Even if he couldn't articulate why. It made sense. We had no way of knowing if his birth parents even resided in Kunming. Perhaps they'd come from the countryside and abandoned Will in the city. But such speculation was a technicality to Will, who'd come to believe that Kunming represented his first home, and home to his birth parents. They could be walking the same sidewalks as us. What a scary and mind-boggling thought for an eight-year-old.

Will's apprehension consumed me for the rest of the day. Ernie and I had nerves about the move, but they were of the logistical sort. Housing, language barriers we'd face, health scares that might befall us. Eden appeared to have zero concern about moving and her flexibility and excitement lifted my spirits. But in Will, I now saw what I should have seen months before. What I should have addressed months before. Will was going to have a bear of a time adjusting to our life.

At the lake that day, Will looked like a regular kid. He practiced dives with his cousins while I sat on the beach, letting Eden bury my feet while I bounced ideas off my cousins, Julie and Chris. I trusted the two of them to guide me with the concerns I was having with Will. Julie, with her social work background and Chris with experience in elementary education. They'd surely see things that I couldn't.

"Here's the thing, you guys. I don't regret our decision to do this, but I'm slowly realizing that I'm in deeper than I thought

I was with Will. We're just bringing to the surface all those issues that other adopted kids have years to wrestle with." I rolled my fingers around the handle of a bucket and gave it to Eden, who walked to the water's edge to fill it.

"That's rough. What about having him write his feelings down?" Chris' suggestion was a good one. Journals for all four of us went on my mental shopping list.

"What about Eden? How's she handling it?" Julie asked.

"Edie? She just cares about where her next meal is coming from. How she'll eat without a fork, that sort of stuff." Julie and Chris knew her well and laughed with me as Eden returned with the water.

"Is anyone planning to visit you? To break up the year a bit and make it easier for him to manage?" Julie wondered.

"Yeah, Liz and Kirk are planning to come over. At Christmas," Chris responded.

The Christmas visit from my cousin Liz and her family was one that we'd already talked about a little bit as a family. It needed to be front and center for Will, I realized. Desperate for him to have small milestones to hang onto, I affirmed Julie's suggestion.

"Their visit is going to be critical. I should talk about that more, Jules. Good idea."

Eternally grateful for the help from my cousins, I went home that night with fresh ideas. Given that there wasn't exactly a solution to Will's difficulties, ideas would suffice. It was a start, anyway, until I had a better handle on what he was going through, or whether it was just my imagination.

The sounds of people enjoying late night cocktails on their

deck below us muffled cries coming from the bedroom.

"Buddy, what's up? Are you crying about leaving?"

"I don't know," Will said. I'm just feeling weird. I don't even know my China parents, but I'm missing them."

There it was. I knew there was more beneath the surface. I grappled for something profound to say in the moment, but in truth all I could think was, *Oh, crap, I left the adoption books at home in Colorado.* The perfect scenarios that they laid out for dealing with moments like this. Moments when your adopted child starts to have an identity crisis.

We'd been so busy with the logistics of getting ready to leave that I'd overlooked the emotional toll it might take on the kids. In many ways. Will's growing identity crisis was the first casualty of the move. How could I have not been more sensitive to that? We were basically throwing his emotions to the forefront with the decision to not only move to China, but to the city of his birth.

Feeling like a selfish, irresponsible mother, I stumbled through the conversation with him before he fell back asleep. And then, putting aside the checklists of things to pack, I launched into all I could read. About Asian American boys, pre-adolescent behavior, managing stress for children, cross-cultural identity challenges for children. It helped me feel better that what we were experiencing was normal, but as I tried to decide which technique to use, they seemed a jumbled mess. His anxiety didn't fit into one box, but several boxes. I felt like I was playing a child's matching game as I tried to figure out which tool to use to help ease his worries.

The path around the lake wove its way from our home to

the beach where we gathered every day to swim with our cousins. My arms were weighed down with our beach bag, towels, snacks and sunscreen in every possible SPF. I tried to act nonchalant as I brought up Will's struggle again.

"You know that thing we were talking about earlier, Will?"

"The problem. My adoption problem."

Will had come to characterize all the challenges he faced as an adopted child as "problems." We'd tried to reclassify them as "challenges." Similar to the challenges faced by any other child –one who's gifted in math, a child who's a twin, or one who has an extraordinary talent in music. So far, our tactics hadn't worked. He still called it a "problem" and I ached every time I heard it.

"You know I don't like it when you call it a 'problem,' sweetie. But yes. That."

"Whatever. I'm just worried about my friends. How I'm gonna make new ones. What about my old ones? What if they forget me?"

I'd been so ready to dish out all the advice I'd read on identity issues over the past 24 hours that his response took me by surprise. This was just regular moving anxiety stuff. I switched gears.

"You're super friendly and funny, Will. I'm sure you'll make friends in no time."

"Mom, my Chinese isn't that good. What if they don't understand me? What if I only have Eden to play with – she's only four years old!" The thought of Will and Eden having only each other to play with was a secret, minor motivation for our move, though I didn't tell him that. I liked the idea of narrowing their four year age difference by manufacturing closeness through an overseas move. It seemed genius to me.

"These are worries that are only for Mom and Dad. Not

things that a child your age should worry about. It's going to be our job to find playmates for you who are able to understand you. Both Chinese kids and kids who speak English. We'll find both."

"First of all, Mom, you can stop using that thing that Aunt Chris told you. I get it. I should hand over my worries to you. It's hard. So hard. I just made all these friends and now I have to say goodbye."

"I know, honey. But you'll see them again. I promise. We'll be back before you know it. The year will be so full of excitement and your friends will still be there. It's hard to believe, but true."

My words seemed little consolation to Will. He cried again that night as I held him, unsure what to say. I didn't question our decision to leave, but I questioned my preparedness to handle the emotional toll it would take on him. His Mandarin was strong, having several years of immersion education under his belt. But I knew that would be no match for the other eight-year-olds in China. We hoped to put the children into regular Chinese public schools. There was an international school in Kunming, but it seemed pointless to enroll the kids in a school where English was the target language if one of the major objectives in moving to China was to improve our Mandarin skills.

I tucked both kids into bed, then headed for the phone to recap the past couple days of emotion with Ernie. My worries about Will's looming questions of self, the possibility that friends at school might not come about as easily as I hoped.

"You've got to be flexible about this school thing, Johanna."

I rambled on about options, even though everything depended on where we ended up living, which wouldn't be determined until we arrived. Uncertainty was not my forte, I told

Ernie.

"You don't like uncertainty? Then why, pray tell, are we moving to China?"

chapter seventeen

I left the kids in Wisconsin with my parents and boarded a plane back to Denver. One week left until we departed the United States, and I hesitated leaving Will, in particular. My parents would notice his fragile emotions and cause them worry in turn. Yet the job remained of packing the rest of our house in Colorado. I needed to finish filling a dumpster with accumulated nonsense as I boxed up the rest of the house. I needed to sell the car. I needed to collect Ernie. I needed to meet with the family who would live in our house. We'd found a young couple moving from Seattle who wanted to rent for just a year. In negotiating the lease, we realized we'd be able to secure a rent that would allow us to cover our monthly mortgage. The wife and I seemed in sync – she was Type A and so was I. She had a baby, Willa, and I had a Will. She spoke Mandarin, ran marathons, and grew up in upstate New York, home to my beloved Syracuse. I was at peace turning over the keys to the family, and wished them a happy year in our home.

With the keys turned over, it was time to leave Colorado. Ruby loaded us into her minivan for the trip back to Denver International Airport. As we drove, I wondered if we'd form friendships like this where we landed in a few weeks. Community and friendship were pivotal to our lives in Denver. We didn't live near family members and depended on friends for love, advice and comfort. What would we do in China?

"I can't believe you're leaving for a whole year," said Ruby.

Ernie was unloading our bags onto the curb at the airport,

Ruby and I oblivious to his need for help. We were saying our goodbyes and it was harder than I had expected. Everything we'd been planning for was leading to this point, but I hadn't wrapped my head around how it would feel.

"It's going to go by in a flash," I reassured her. "Plus, you have all your other friends. Me, well, I'm just stuck with Ernie for a year!" I was trying to lighten the mood, but as I said it, the weight of my words felt heavy. *Wait a second! I only have my HUS-BAND to talk with for a whole year? What in God's name was I thinking? Furthermore, the kids and I drive each other batty after a weekend at home together without play dates or activities planned. Oh no! We aren't going to have play dates for MONTHS.* My anxiety was rising, so I redirected my attention and took off my wedding ring.

"Here," I said, handing Ruby the ring. I only wore one ring, not the combination of an engagement ring and a wedding band that most women favored. When I took it off, I felt naked, and as I stared at my finger, it was hard to get used to the way it looked. The ring was simple, but held five diamonds. And like the old television commercial encouraged, it cost Ernie a month's salary. Though one of my most treasured possessions, I wasn't planning to take it with me. The countries we'd be visiting were impoverished, and wearing a diamond wedding ring would seem ostentatious.

"What's this?" she asked.

"I'm certain that I won't want to be wearing this in the places we'll be going," I replied.

"So what... do you want me to lock it up, wear it, or what?"

She was trying to be serious but we both laughed. The thought of wearing a diamond had never crossed her mind. Where I was girlie and sentimental, she was practical and uninterested in expensive jewelry. I loved the contrast in our personalities.

"Lock it up and give it back to me when I'm home," I directed.

Leaving the ring at home made sense to me for more than just practical reasons. Our hope was to show the children how little was needed to be happy. We were lucky enough to have friends, family, and plenty of stuff right here in America. I wanted us to discover that we could be happy without that. And prove that, really, all we needed was each other.

Ruby and I were crying now. Ernie pretended he didn't see.

"Time's going to fly, Ruby, I promise. You have so many other friends to lean on."

"It's not the same. It's not the same."

She was right. Nothing was going to be the same here. Or there. Or even upon our return, for that matter. She and Philip had moved across town to be closer to the kids' school and their orbit was changing. Time would tell where we would land.

Ernie and I flew back to Wisconsin and to the children. We had a few more days before leaving the United States and priority one was to finalize our packing. The luggage scale indicated that we had room to spare. To me, our bags looked as if they were groaning with the treasures buried inside.

-Vitamins
-Protein powder
-Ten boxes of electrolyte supplements
-Extra running shoes
-Five tubes of my favorite toothpaste
-Twenty rolls of dental floss
-Ten tubes of sunscreen
-My favorite pillowcase

-The children's prized art supplies
-A giant jar of peanut butter that would be the first casualty
 in our final hours of packing

Our small condo on the lake was positively exploding with life. We'd decided to leave from the lake because it offered the chance to board a plane in Chicago and get all the way to Asia in one flight. The plan was a good one, but the signs of China were now everywhere, scattered in piles around our condo. The life that we intended to cram into seven suitcases. The topic of my packing was now a running joke among my cousins. The chatter at our family beach would go into overdrive at the mention of my latest addition to our packing piles.

"Johanna, do you REALLY need five tubes of toothpaste?" Chris chuckled.

"I do! That stuff they have in China is nasty and the American brands are off-the-hook expensive." I was right.

"Peanut butter? A six-pound jar? Get real, Jo!" Steph laughed.

"But, I'm worried we won't be able to get it there and what then?" I was wrong.

"A thousand bandages? Seriously?" Liz agreed with the rest of my cousins – I was batty to the tenth degree with the packing.

"I just don't think you can get quality bandages there." The jury remained out on that one for the entire year. My bandages came and we used plenty.

"Did you guys hear she's bringing two hundred tampons?" Julie chirped.

"T.M.I. you guys! Johanna, you've gone off the deep end." My cousin, Ben, was having a coronary as he listened to the list of my stockpile continue to grow.

"Bite me, you guys. I'll have you know that they don't use 'pons in China and I'm not leaving home without them. I'll leave the protein powder if I have to."

For all their teasing, I knew we'd made the right decision to stay at the lake until it was time to leave. My cousins had always provided me with the strength I needed in any situation. A laugh at just the right moment. We'd grown up together, and if they thought I could pull this off, I knew there was hope.

Our last afternoon at the lake was just right. The jokes about my packing stopped. My family knew that I'd zipped our bags and they transitioned to a full blown cheering squad. Liz and Chris brought a bottle of champagne and lemonade to the beach, passing out small plastic cups to the twenty-five of us who were there.

"To Ernie and Johanna and Will and Eden, may you have an amazing year and come home with many memorable stories!" Chris held up her cup, and we downed the champagne as the kids played a final game of water tag.

That night, a calm came over Will. He focused on the flight, the toys in his carry-on, the goodie bags that I'd pulled together for the journey. I held my prepared pep talk, hoping his current mood would sustain us for the trip over. Eden knew that we'd be getting on an airplane, and that the trip would be longer than a flight to Denver, but whether she really understood what it meant beyond that was anyone's guess. My best assumption was that she planned to capitalize on the entire thing. Coloring books, new stickers, lollipops. I'd seen her digging in my purse and even at age four, she knew how to play her mom and dad in just the right ways.

We'd hired a private shuttle to take us to an airport hotel in Chicago where we'd spend a night before boarding an early morning flight. And so, after a final swim early on departure day, we left the lake, hanging our wet swimsuits in the closet, where they'd remain until we opened it twelve months later.

Standing on the sidewalk outside our condo, the shuttle driver took a look at our luggage and grimaced.

"I told the person who took our reservation that we had a lot of bags. I think I told her seven, to be exact." I felt defensive, having spent so many months considering how to pack as minimally, but smartly as possible.

"Yea, well that didn't exactly get conveyed to me. This must be SOME trip you're taking!"

"Well it's not a trip. We're moving."

"Where to?"

"To China."

"Moving to China? Oh! Well, that explains it then, I guess."

Having said goodbye to my parents the night before, I turned to Chris and Liz, who'd come to see us off. Chris and her family had recently moved back from many years living in Tanzania. She knew the drill of packing for an international move, and she knew me better than almost anyone.

"Holy crow, Chrissy, what the heck are we doing? Please tell me this isn't the dumbest thing I've ever come up with?" I said, through tears.

"No, no. It's going to be wonderful. You're going to do fantastic. Jo, you're so strong. I can't wait to watch you do it." She grabbed my hand and looked me square in the eye.

"All things worth doing require a little struggle. You know that, Johanna. You can do this."

Next it was Liz's turn. She and her family were planning to come to visit us at Christmas. They were the only ones with a stated plan to do so, and I was incredibly grateful. Their visit would be a godsend.

"We'll see you in a few months then, Jo?"

"For sure, Liz. We'll be the ones at the Kunming airport who look different and the only ones screaming English."

Ernie helped the driver cram the final bags into the back, closing the hatch with a thump. I piled Eden and Will inside. They began digging through the treat bags their cousins had given them. Their preoccupation was welcome. Their mother was falling apart at the moment her dream was beginning. What. The. Hell?

As we pulled away, Will asked, "Mom, can I watch a movie on the iPad on our way to the hotel?"

I hesitated and began silently running through the litany of rules and exceptions we'd devised about screen time over the years. Only on weekends, unless it's summer. Then weekdays okay, but not anything over an hour, and the content must be edited... and then I stopped. They would be denied so much in the next year. Their friends, their favorite foods, their school. I caught a glimpse of our family standing on the sidewalk waving, their faces getting smaller as the distance between us grew. I softened, changing my tune.

"Yes. Yes, you may. Will, your moment of YES is now here!"

We arrived at the airport hotel, stored our bags and watched the Olympics. The London Olympics had started and we'd begin by cheering for American teams and end two weeks later cheering the Chinese participants.

"Mom? I know I've been stressed out the past month," Will said.

Were we about to have another meltdown? Will was perched on top of a suitcase watching the U.S. dive team perform.

"Just a little," I lied.

"Well, I'm thinking that now that we are actually going, you know, I think I'm kind of getting excited."

Sweet mother of God! I'd never heard better words. I knew the emotions would change a million times in the course of the year, but for the moment, this was enough. Just enough.

The next day, our trek through the airport was smooth. Once we arrived at the gate, I began pacing. I walked up and down the hallway with my phone attached to my ear. I packed in every last word I could manage with Chris. She sat on the beach at Elkhart. I could hear the noise of kids jumping off the diving board. But I concentrated on her string of relentless pep talk and reassurance until the last call for boarding the 747 that would carry our family and our dreams. Then I turned off my phone and stuffed it away into a crevice of my carry-on.

We boarded and Will and I sat together, him at the window, me in the middle seat. Eden and Ernie were across from us and I could see that Eden was going to tear through the activity book I'd packed for her by the time we took off. The plane took its final turn, lining up for takeoff. I felt the engine power up as we began to roll down the runway. I'd never been a good flier, and my hands became sweaty. I wrapped Will in my arms and we stared out the window together. We were flying into a complete unknown. No idea where we would live, who our friends would be, what we would eat, or what we might experience in the next twelve months. As the plane lifted off, I heard Will whisper to himself...

"Bye bye, America. Bye bye."

chapter eighteen

Our plane landed in Chengdu in Sichuan Province. We were late beyond late. Exhausted and ravenous. Giant bowls of ramen noodles in the Seoul airport had been our last meal more than eight hours ago.

"Ernie! Johanna! We're here!"

In a sea of people outside the immigration stand, we spotted Tim and his fiancé Yifan. They would be our instructors for my two weeks at the Summer Institute; a program part crash course in teaching English in China, part crash course in living in China. We all attended to ensure the family had a little transition time before we flew on to Kunming.

"The kids must be exhausted! Let's get you out of here fast, shall we?" Tim helped us manage our suitcases, quickly filling the minivan that picked us up. Small bags of snacks on our seats were devoured within minutes. We sped through the night and arrived at our hotel in a small village an hour away from the big city. The kids were zombies as we piled into the two hotel rooms assigned to us.

"Mom, I'm cold. I need a blanket." Will was shivering in the excessively air conditioned room. I could not for the life of me figure out how to adjust it.

"Just go get him a blanket," said Ernie.

Blanket, blanket... oh my gosh, how do I say 'blanket?' I remembered the word for pillow, bed, sleep, tired. But 'blanket?' No way. I made my way down to the lobby and began explaining to the front desk staff what I needed. My Mandarin was limited to speaking. I could neither read nor write characters. The best my brain could do in that moment was the equivalent of "My children need a sleeping thing. A thing for a bed." I was both horrified and amused thinking about what I must sound like.

The first desk clerk looked desperate to understand and repeatedly asked if I wanted more pillows. *Could the kids just pile ten pillows on top of themselves and call it good?* I wondered.

Multiple hotel staff members gathered as I played charades. Pretending I was sleeping, waking up shivering, pulling something over my chest. After several minutes of pantomime and three desk clerks, they figured it out. It felt like a major triumph.

The next morning I felt the dizziness that comes with crossing the international dateline with two small children and seven stuffed suitcases. *All we need is food,* I speculated. Our hotel was billed as a "Western" hotel, so I expected we'd get at least some coffee and something resembling cereal for the kids. We let Ernie sleep while we rolled downstairs, following the signs reading "Restaurant." As we turned the last corner, I was practically drooling with desire for sustenance. Yet all that lay in front of us were a few metal tables with plastic chairs. Breakfast was plates of pickled something-or-other, steamed buns and a bowl of hard-boiled eggs. And congee. Congee. There it was again.

"Mom! I can't eat this. Do they have any cereal or pancakes?" Eden looked at me with desperation. I felt like I might either laugh or cry. But then again, congee was ALL that Will ate when we'd picked him up as a baby. Could I work this angle somehow?

"Look at the fun congee! This is what you ate when you were babies. Yummy! Let's try it."

"Mom. You've lost it. I don't wanna eat that stuff. Gross."

"This might be it for your choices, guys. I'll see what I can do about getting some peanut butter tomorrow so we can put that on the buns. But for now, try them without. Come on, this'll be fun! It's our first morning in China. Be adventurous!"

The children reached for the buns. They were a light tan in color, and clearly made of white flour. I'd been eating gluten free by choice for years, and these didn't fit the bill. I'd need to let go of my neurotic food choices – starting now. My hand slid forward and touched the soft crevices of the bun. Unexpected warmth hit my fingertips, and then, "Mom! Mom! They're yummy!" As I took my first bite, I knew that we'd make it. At least through the day. Gluten, be damned.

With a free day before my training was to start, I was determined to find the peanut butter that would add protein to the one meal I knew that Will and Eden could tolerate for the first few days. Like a lioness, I needed to feed my children. We hopped on a public bus with directions from Tim and made our way to a grocery store.

"I'm not seeing anything that looks like peanut butter, Jo," Ernie called from one aisle over. I held in my hand something that looked like jelly, but the label displayed a photo of a squid. Eden wandered up and down each aisle, grabbing things off shelves and fingering packages of odd-looking chips.

"I can't read any of these labels, Jo, but I'm pretty sure we're gonna have to do without peanut butter for the moment."

Ernie's conclusion was spot on. The grocery store held nothing that looked familiar. The shelves were overcrowded, but the occupants were foods that looked like they would take time to get used to. Once we got to Kunming, I imagined more choices.

In this small village, we'd have to jump head first into the adjustment phase. Peanut butter or no peanut butter.

I began my training, leaving Ernie to hang with the children all day. With only minimal language skills, he didn't venture far. The kids made forts in the room. They unloaded the one suitcase full of toys and exhausted every one within two days.

We made a small path every night to a noodle and dumpling place near our hotel. We'd branched out from the buns and the cooks at the restaurant had memorized our dumpling preferences. The kids floated around the small dining area and spilled out onto the sidewalk to play while we awaited our food.

"I don't know, Jo, the kids did okay today, but they're going a little stir crazy."

"Well, sure. Because here's the thing – they only have each other to play with, right? How rough must that be?"

"It's not like we can just drum up some play dates with English-speaking children. Any suggestions?"

"Who said anything about English-speaking kids? Isn't the point for them to branch out and mix with the local kids?"

"Sure, but are they bold enough to just start hanging around with random kids they can't communicate with?"

"I don't know. We'll just have to wing it for now. We're only going to be here another week and then we'll get to Kunming and settle into a routine. They'll meet other kids eventually."

Laughter from the street turned our attention outside. Two of the cook's children had wandered outside with a ball and were kicking it to Will and Eden. The game didn't require much conversation, though Will would have handled the basic Mandarin well.

"Dad! Mom! Look! This little guy's pretty good with a ball!" Will shouted and smiled, the first genuine smile I'd seen since we'd landed in China. Eden tried to keep up but missed every kick, laughing at herself and then chasing down the errant ball. The children were a step ahead of us. At age four and eight they were perfectly capable of socializing themselves.

Our server came over with steaming bowls of beef noodles and vegetarian dumplings. Protein... check. Vegetables... check. *Gluten... well, you can't win 'em all,* I thought to myself. I wasn't going to be winning any competitions for the healthiest year. Ernie and I ate our dinner alone that night. The kids played beyond their bedtime, forgetting their jet lag, the noodles on the table, and the language barrier.

chapter nineteen

My two weeks of teacher training passed. The jet lag eased and we now slept and woke at the proper times. We were back in the Chengdu airport, this time on the way to Kunming, about two hours south. We hadn't been back to Kunming since we'd adopted Will, and though Ernie and I were excited, we continued to worry about him.

Traveling anywhere outside our hotel had become a lesson in adjusting to one thing in particular. Staring. The cultural taboo of staring being a bad thing was seemingly absent in China. In any situation. But our family drew a particular kind of gawk. Western parents with Chinese children, and a boy child, at that. At first it was amusing, but the staring grew old fast. By the time we headed to Kunming, we'd each developed our own methods of handling it. Ernie stared back. Will and Eden ignored. I tried to smile back at the stare, but sometimes, depending on my mood, I lowered my eyes and looked away. Our coping methods were kicking in, ugly as they may be at the moment.

As we landed in Kunming, it was clear that we were far from big city life. Red, terraced fields covered the landscape. Low mountains surrounded us on all sides. Small villages with dirt roads poked between long stretches of countryside. The haze we'd experienced in Chengdu disappeared and blue skies with a setting sun greeted us.

We were met at the airport by Mr. Zhang who was essentially my "handler" for the year. His real title was International Affairs Liaison, or "wàibàn." Everything I'd heard about him indicated that he held all the cards for our family. He would help us arrange schooling for the children and help me get adjusted at the university. It felt good to have someone in our corner, though the communication prior to departure had been spotty. Mr. Zhang found us without a problem as we rolled our luggage through doors that led from baggage claim to the arrivals area.

"Johanna!" He called out to me and I felt instantly relieved to have someone take charge. Mr. Zhang was a smartly dressed man with a pair of glasses. I loved glasses. I loved nerds. This guy looked like a nerd. We'd be totally fine. After introductions, he spoke as we walked towards the waiting minivan.

"Johanna. We have prepared an apartment for you. I think you will find it most suitable."

We had heard that the university had an apartment ready for us, but the description was a bit cloudy. I felt myself tense at his optimism. The accommodations provided to teachers typically sounded atrocious. Tiny, dingy, and completely not workable for a Western family of four. I would try to be flexible, of course. I mean, could it really be THAT bad? We were adventurous and were coming here in part to get away from the conveniences of our cushy American life. And to decline an offer of housing would be incredibly offensive on many levels. It would be a loss of face in the worst way. Embarrassing the university might result in less help for our family. And boy, did we need help. At worst, I speculated we could live there temporarily until we found something suitable.

"Mr. Zhang, thank you for preparing a place for us to stay. Our children need a lot of space to run and play." I began to set up an out in case we needed it. Mr. Zhang's English was excellent and I was sure he could understand my meaning.

"Yes, but we've bought you new rice bowls and a pot to

cook with."

"Thank you so much. We are so grateful. You are very kind."

"Also, there will be students there to greet you and help you with luggage."

With our luggage loaded into the minivan, we raced towards Kunming, Mr. Zhang behind the wheel. I sat in the front passenger seat of the minivan, the spot I'd occupy on all taxi rides for the rest of the year. Bridging the communication gap between the local Chinese and my family was in the front of my mind. I needed to be in the passenger seat at all times.

The sun had set over Kunming, though activity remained high on the streets. Vendors were out in front of their tiny storefronts. Children in school uniforms carrying violins and piles of books. I looked out and thought, *This is our home. This is our home now.* And I was absolutely petrified.

"You must begin teaching the day after tomorrow," Mr. Zhang said. He accelerated beyond a speed I thought acceptable, given that here in China, seat belts were often buried below the seat cushions, completely unusable. The news that I'd start teaching so quickly took my breath away. I'd assumed there would be an adjustment period of at least a few days to allow us to get settled.

"Oh, wow! I wasn't told about this. Do I have a regular schedule yet?"

"I'm not sure. I just know that there is another teacher gone and you will need to teach his classes for a few weeks. And also, you will not be teaching here on the main campus. You'll need to take a bus to a different campus to teach. The ride is one hour each way. It's no problem."

No problem, my ass! This would need to be addressed. Soon. A little pre-planning would be nice, but it appeared that I'd start teaching without a lick of prep time. Ugh.

"We'll stop so you can buy some food," Mr. Zhang reported.

I had no idea what this meant. *Was there nothing in the cupboards at our apartment? What should we buy?* Stopping at a local convenience store, we bought a loaf of bread, some cereal and milk. Then it was on to the apartment. My heart raced. The children were wilting, their heads resting on Ernie's shoulders. Ernie looked tired. I knew he was just as anxious as I was to see what we'd be offered for housing.

The van pulled up to a drab-looking building. A group of college students was waiting for us. They swarmed the van and unloaded our bags. Multiple students carried each one. We were herded to the staircase and walked three flights up. With each floor, my anxiety grew. The building displayed the look of Chinese communism. Gray. Concrete. Bars on the windows. A layer of dust covering everything. I knew what we were about to encounter was not going to be what we'd hoped it might be. I held my breath as Mr. Zhang turned the key and opened the door to our apartment.

My heart sank. It was worse than I thought. A miniature apartment greeted us. The kitchen floor held a puddle of water, a testament to the leak dripping from the ceiling. The bathroom was barely big enough for one person to sit on the toilet. Bugs raced around the living room floor. The room where the children would sleep was busting at the seams to hold two twin beds. The bed Ernie and I had been given would never fit his long-limbed frame. *And the smell!* Everything about the place smelled old, musty, and dirty. I couldn't see our family surviving here for more than a few days. I looked at Ernie. His stoic façade had cracked. His entire face shouted, "What the HELL have we gotten ourselves into?"

As the students carried up bag after bag, it was clear that our luggage alone would cause a problem. It filled the entire

JOHANNA GARTON / 141

living room. What in the world would we do when they were unpacked? Where would we even unpack them?

This was the moment of truth. So many of our logistics had been ridiculously unclear prior to our arrival. The one thing we knew we needed in our year was a safe, clean, warm environment for the children to flourish. Or at least not crumble. This was not it. The problems with this place were insurmountable. But refusing the housing provided to us would set a course in motion from which we might not extract ourselves. Offending in this way was about the least culturally proper thing we could ever do. I knew this.

"Mr. Zhang, thank you so much for picking us up at the airport. The children are very tired and we'd love to get some rest. Could we talk to you in the morning?"

"Yes... tomorrow I may not be available, but you can speak to one of our students. Her name is Jenny and she will help you."

We thanked the students, gently pushing them out the door as they fawned over Eden and Will. Ernie closed the door, locked it and turned to me. His eyes searched mine for an answer and I knew there was only one.

"We'll start looking tomorrow, Ern. First thing. I promise."

chapter twenty

The bus to Yunnan Nationalities University rolled past the outskirts of Kunming and into the countryside. As in much of China, downtown universities were overcrowded, and satellite campuses were being built as fast as students could sit in the seats. My first day teaching English had come just as Mr. Zhang had announced it would. And in those 36 hours we'd managed to move all of our luggage out of the dorm we'd been offered and into a hotel. The students who'd moved everything up three flights of stairs had dutifully come to move it all back down. I had no idea what they thought of this. I just knew that we needed somewhere clean and warm to stay until we could figure out Plan B. And it was apparent that Plan B would need to be implemented on our own. In turning down the apartment, even as gently as I'd tried, we'd sealed our fate for the year. Mr. Zhang didn't return my phone calls. It wasn't a good sign. I had no idea what it would mean for our year, but like everything else, I hoped we would just figure it out.

Safely secured in a hotel our first night, I'd wandered out to find dinner. A noodle shop across the street had been my destination. I managed to order four bowls of soup noodles, each brimming with hot broth and mystery vegetables. The server loaded each down with MSG and I made another one of my famous mental notes: *Learn how to say, "No MSG, please."* Despite the MSG, I walked out of the restaurant with a deep sense of satisfaction. I was back to the task of feeding my family. It was instinctive, primal and the only thing I could think of to prove to each of them that I would take care of us this year.

The move to the hotel had taken the entire day, and before we knew it, we'd had a night of sleep and were on the bus to the university. All four of us. Without me, the children and Ernie were virtually helpless. Will hadn't gained enough confidence to use his Mandarin on the street, so for the time being, I was the provider in every way. And so they came with me. Relief washed over me when we made this decision, as I realized I needed them just as much as they needed me.

We were met by Benjamin Shen, the Chair of the English Department. Thick glasses hung on his face. He had decent English and seemed genuinely interested in the children. Things were looking up. We walked to my first class and as I walked in, there was silence. I came with a crew of three. Two of them children. Siblings. Chinese. And a boy. The class was a group of 30 sophomores, mostly young women. They stared at the kids as Benjamin introduced us.

"We welcome Professor Garton here to our university. This is her husband and her two children. She'll be your teacher."

Ernie and the kids found seats in the back of the room. I hadn't had time to prepare a lesson plan. I'd managed to dig out a dress from my suitcase for the first class, but the sneakers from moving up and down three flights of stairs with our luggage were the only footwear I'd found. I felt unkempt. Unprofessional. The students looked at me, waiting for the first word. Benjamin smiled at me, nerves apparent in his eyes. No doubt thinking, *this woman BETTER be as good as her résumé looks.* A pang of inadequacy rose within me until I started to speak. And then I remembered. *I'm a teacher. I can do this. I'm actually good at this part. This is my den. Hear me roar, one and all.*

The first part of our year in China had fallen into place.

chapter twenty one

As predicted, we were alone. Apartment hunting and trying to entertain the kids by day. The school year for the kids had started, but we had no earthly idea how to get them into Chinese public schools. Mr. Zhang had dropped us completely. His effort to welcome us to Kunming had stopped when he'd left us at the place Ernie and I now lovingly referred to as "The Squalor" every time we walked past it. We were sure the lack of contact was a direct result of how we'd offended him by refusing the apartment.

We were going on one week in the hotel and the noodle place across the street was no longer holding the appeal it had held on day one. Finding a proper home was priority one. A friend in Colorado had given me the name of a real estate agent in Kunming. He's a miracle worker, the friend had told me.

"What's his name?"

"China Lee."

"No, seriously, his real name is 'China'?"

"Well, you know, that's his American name. It fits. Trust me. You'll get it when you see him."

China Lee was now on speed dial. And sure enough, he fit all the typical Western stereotypes of a real estate agent. He was outgoing, boisterous, and well-dressed. And he carried many pens, which sealed the deal. I loved a man with a good pen. China Lee was our guy. He'd helped us navigate the area of town we hoped to live in and at the one-week mark we were nearing decision time.

The kids were going crazy climbing the walls of our hotel room. Our origami paper supply was dwindling, as was our patience with each other. We couldn't give the kids our undivided attention all day, as we were focused solely on finding a place to live, feeding ourselves, and for me, teaching was in full swing.

The four of us were walking the grounds of a park that bordered our hotel. Pond after pond of koi drew the attention of Will and Eden. We stopped to buy fish food being sold by a vendor when my phone rang.

"China Lee! Nǐhǎo, what do you have for us today?"

"Johanna. Good day. I think there is not much more and you must decide today. We will go back to see the apartment near Green Lake."

The place that China Lee referred to turned out to be perfect. A 500-square-foot apartment on the ground level of a complex with close to 400 occupants. Two bedrooms, a galley kitchen and two bathrooms, which made it just about the nicest place in town. Our front door opened onto a courtyard that was filled with trees to climb. Lush bushes provided the perfect place for the kids to make forts and play hide and seek. There was a pond full of fish, space to run, play soccer and make friends with the neighborhood children. Guards were situated at three different entrances. Elderly Chinese couples gathered in the morning sunshine on benches, looking adorable. There was the matter of the 500 square feet, roughly the size of some master bedrooms in Denver. But oh well... we took it.

Move-in day was on Will's ninth birthday. We found our way to a New Zealand café called Slice of Heaven that was run by a fellow teacher. The pastries rivaled the versions at home, and we stocked up on brownies, the closest thing we could find to a birthday cake. The dining room of our apartment echoed as we sat down that night, indicative of the relative lack of furniture.

"This is the worst birthday ever." Will looked crushed. The only present he was receiving was the promise of a visit to the local shopping center. Once we figured out where that was.

"It's not so bad, buddy." Ernie tried to put a positive spin on it.

"We have each other, and we have this nice apartment. You aren't going to school yet. I mean, come ON. All your other friends are practically halfway through their year!"

"This isn't fun, Dad. I don't like China. Why are we doing this?"

Ernie shot me a look of desperation. The canned answers were my specialty.

"We're doing this to spend time together. Away from everyone else. Everything else. To realize how blessed we are to have the life we have in America. To explore, to travel, and see different parts of the world. We are doing this to... to... "

There was a word on the tip of my tongue. What was it? I'd used it a few months ago with Ernie. Reset. Was it a crappy word or a perfect word? I couldn't remember. Will glared at me, awaiting the end of my sentence.

"Reset. To hit the reset button."

"That's good, I like that." Ernie, who'd previously ridiculed my word choice, drank the Kool Aid. His compliment was intended to help melt the ice coming from Will's corner of the table.

"I don't wanna hit the reset button. We don't need to reset anything. Nothing's wrong with our family. I just want a regular birthday and some cake."

Will's words crushed my newly-coined phrase. A reset button may not have been the perfect string of words. I'd have to do better than that. I changed the subject.

"How about a blessing? Our birthday blessing. It'll be different here, won't it? More special."

"No, it won't. This sucks."

"Will Garton!" Ernie used our son's middle name to underline the obvious. That wasn't a word allowed in our house. In America. Or China.

"I've got something to say, but let's do this first." I felt an idea brewing to smooth over the grief of an absent ninth birthday.

I grasped Will and Eden's small hands on either side of me, with Ernie doing the same. Our family connected, I repeated a version of what we said for each of their birthdays, every year.

"Thank you to Will's birth parents. We're thinking of you today. We hope you're at peace and somehow know he has a good life."

It was meant to be a sweet toast, and in normal years, I got choked up. I believed in our tradition to acknowledge the people who gave the children life. It was the least we could do, to honor them out loud, once per year.

I glanced at my son out of the corner of my eye. His life certainly didn't seem all that good at the moment. At least to him.

"Momma, if he's not going to eat his brownie, could I eat his?" Eden's comments sounded familiar, and then I remembered Will's request to undertake the same task for her on her first birthday years ago, before she was with us.

"I understand you're hurting, Will. And that this isn't the best birthday. Here's my proposal. This year, let's celebrate half birthdays, too, okay? By the time your half birthday rolls around, we'll know exactly where to go for dinner. Where to get better gifts. Which bakery has the best cake. Deal?"

Tremendous, I thought. *Half birthday celebrations. I'm so good under pressure. I'm a rock star!*

"Mom, my birthday is August 29. I don't HAVE a half birthday this year."

A quick calculation affirmed the obvious. *Damn. Leap year.* The score rose in Will's favor. China's favor. And I was struggling to hit the ball.

chapter twenty two

Despite the bumps, small pieces fell into place. My class schedule was hammered out. We struggled with an Internet connection at home, but it was finally resolved and Ernie began telecommuting. To facilitate this, we purchased a virtual private network system to bypass the Chinese censors that monitored Internet traffic. I needed to have open conversations with my mother and Ernie needed to be able to speak freely about his experiences here with his co-workers back home. It bought us the peace of mind that we wouldn't have the Chinese police knocking on our door to pull down our Internet connection.

We spent a small fortune on a soft mattress to replace the thin version we were provided with. The children were accepted into local Chinese schools and were scheduled to start in a few weeks. The schools weren't in the same location, sadly, but both close to home. We bought a bicycle, which would serve as our only source of transportation for the year.

Though we thought our family size was four, we then brought in two people who were invaluable. Our meals and cleaning were made easier with the hire of a housekeeper named Xiaocui. A luxury we could never afford at home, but at $50 for 20 hours a week, it was impossible not to enjoy. Xiao spoke not a word of English, but had been recommended by another expat family. Her skills were wide-ranging and she soon fit the role of cook, cleaner, laundry lady, and occasional babysitter. Her home was in a different part of town, and we learned later that it was nothing more than a mud hut with a dirt floor. The money we paid her each week sustained her family of three, along with the salary of her husband who worked in the local market.

Xiao's scheduling proved challenging, as the only days she could come were days that I was teaching classes. That left Ernie at home with her, trying to communicate our daily needs. The first few weeks brought call after call from Ernie, as he humorously tried to communicate this or that.

"Jo, can you tell Xiao that we need to buy a better frying pan? I keep showing her the pan we have, but she thinks I'm trying to tell her that she needs to cook today."

"Jo, can you tell Xiao that she shouldn't buy the blue chickens at the market? Or the ones that still have the heads on them? Eden freaked when she brought that home the other day."

"Jo, can you tell her that I'm actually working here in the office? She thinks I'm just playing games all day. I don't think she understands that people get paid to work on the computer."

The second addition to our clan was a young Chinese woman who went by "Helen." Anticipating Will's need for help in school, we hired her as a tutor. She was a bright, energetic 23-year-old college grad, with aspirations of going to America and outstanding English skills to back up her hopes. Her language skills allowed us to ask her for help with many daily challenges. Ordering jugs of drinking water. Securing a plumber. Finding the local post office. The work of overseeing Will's homework would kick in soon, but for the first few weeks she helped all of us get established with life in China.

Our family felt like six now. Both women were in our home several days a week for many hours at a time. At home it would have felt like an intrusion. Here, we felt comforted surrounding ourselves with people who could help us in our daily lives.

When it came to matters related to our immigration paperwork in particular, Helen became our lifeline. Our status was murky, as the children and I had entered the country on tourist visas. I knew that I needed to get a proper work visa, but the university had stopped helping me navigate the immigration maze and I had no idea how to handle its complexities.

One afternoon, Mr. Zhang called to tell me we needed to leave China to get new visas and re-enter the country on those. I clarified the dates with him and made plans for the four of us to travel to Hong Kong on the way home from our previously planned fall break in Thailand. He also said we needed to register with the local police.

"Register for what?"

"You need to tell them who you are and where you live."

The entire operation seemed very creepy and entirely communist. Ernie and I cleaned up the dinner dishes that night as I recounted the conversation, stating the obvious.

"Well they surely know us. The police station is right below our apartment and there's zero chance they could miss us, right? But of course we'll register. Anything to get this process finished. I don't like being here on a tourist visa."

"At least one of us is here legally," he joked. After all his efforts to carve a career niche for himself here in China, Ernie was now being treated like a king by the contracting house in Beijing that was handling his paperwork. He'd been flown to Beijing for a simple medical appointment, and was to return in a few days to finalize his status. He was bringing Eden with him. I'd follow with Will a few days later for a long weekend.

Life was beginning to shape up, but the daily struggles weighed heavily on us. The children had slowly made friends in the apartment complex, but the language barrier was ever-present. Mealtimes were made difficult as we were still managing to navigate the new tastes at the local markets. The apartment needed everything from trashcans to bed sheets, resulting in

endless trips to the local shopping mall with Helen. My meticu-
lous packing had been beneficial, but there were some things
that I now realized I'd left behind. More American snacks. Hand
sanitizer. English books for the children. We'd thought only about
the books Will might read, knowing they could be accessed on
the iPad. But I was planning to teach Eden how to read this year,
and I'd failed to bring a stack of easy readers. We resolved to call
home in a few days, asking my parents to send a few. Along with
some more t-shirts for Will. In a baffling error in my packing, I'd
only packed shirts that were red and orange.

At the end of every day we sat for dinner and talked of gratitude. Our hearts were full of things we missed, yet the small
victories were apparent. One night our conversation went something like this:

Dad: I'm grateful that we found a place to buy a bunk bed so
you two don't have to share a bed anymore.

Will: I'm grateful that Mom let me buy gum today.

Eden: I'm grateful that we're going to see Grams on Skype
tomorrow.

Mom: I'm grateful that we were able to find salt to buy today.

Eden: We got mail today!

Despite our small victories, exhaustion was apparent on our
faces, in our body language, and in our lack of appetite. Bedtime for Ernie and me became 8 p.m. At this time in America, I
was just settling in with a cup of tea and a good book. Here, it
was time for rest. We crawled into bed completely spent at the
end of every day. Ernie and I were overwhelmed, with no desire to touch each other, lying as far apart as possible, the day
running through our heads. The sights. The sounds. The smells.
Everything new.

As we fell asleep one night, I heard him mumbling to himself, "Oh my God, we're living in China. China. Oh my God."

chapter twenty three

I held the phone away from my ear. Eden's shouts of happiness were loud enough to echo through the apartment. She and Ernie were calling from Beijing.

"Mom, we went to the aquarium and Julia bought me a hot dog! And we're staying in a nice hotel with a swimming pool."

Eden sounded elated and was enjoying being spoiled rotten by Julia, Ernie's handler at the contracting company. I was jealous of her daddy/daughter trip to Beijing, even though Will and I planned to follow in a few days. For now, we were in Kunming. Both still acclimating to life here, while I finished a week of teaching. Desperate for a vacation, when an opportunity came up for us to join Ernie in Beijing, I grabbed it. In reality, it hadn't really "come up" as much as been created. By me. Leaving Kunming often on such mini-vacations thus became a theme that stuck with us all year.

"It's pretty incredible, Jo. We're in a Marriott on the executive level and there's an actual bed with a real, down comforter."

"I bet it's amazing, honey."

"Can't wait for you two to get here."

"We're so ready. You have no idea."

A few days later, Will and I sat at the gate in the Kunming airport awaiting our flight. The flight attendants announced a delay. One hour, then two. This was typical, and so we settled in. Three hours. Four.

"Let's get something to eat, buddy."

The choices were limited here at the airport. Outside of the standard ramen noodles and wrapped meat sticks, there was junk food. At this hour, all I needed was to get something in Will's body to pass the time. Junk food it was.

I handed the cashier my Chinese debit card and got a receipt.

"*Ní yóu méiyóu beitze?*" English translation: Do you have a pen?

I was asking for a pen to sign the receipt, but I'd butchered my tones. The cashier and Will were giggling as they looked at each other and back at me. I quickly ran through my tones and realized my mistake. *Nose* and *pen* were very similar in their sounds. I'd asked the poor guy if he had a nose. Even in this frazzled state, I could laugh at myself.

Will ribbed me as we returned to the gate and at long last, boarded our plane. It felt like we'd been in Kunming a year, though only three weeks had passed.

For the first time in Beijing we were finally surrounded with Western food and language. I let my guard down as soon as we hit the Marriott. Every emotion that I'd been suppressing came to the surface. And it wasn't pretty. Instead of being happy to see Ernie, I was grumpy and critical.

He took our bags as we walked into the room, a beautiful suite overlooking the streets of Beijing. The living room was stocked with a huge, gorgeous desk, a comfortable couch and a massive bathroom. The bed was as Ernie had described. Piled with pillows and calling to me to rest my weary mind and body.

"So glad to see you guys. We've missed you!" Ernie lit up at the sight of Will and me, haggard as we were.

"Oh my gosh, we had the worst delay EVER! What's wrong

with Chinese airlines?" I gave Eden a hug, then flopped on the couch, bypassing the hug and kiss that Ernie reached out for.

"Bummer, Jo. That must've been rough. But you're here now. So why don't you eat? I ordered food like you wanted me to." I looked over at the room service cart and saw a spread of food, which, though lovely, didn't match my custom order.

"I said he wanted ramen noodles and you ordered chicken," I ranted. We were arriving at midnight and the spectacular room service Ernie had ordered was soured by my mood. Will began to cry with exhaustion.

"I wanted ramen noodles, Mom."

"*Gēge, Gēge,*" Eden chirped, using the Mandarin word for older brother. "Why's he crying, Mom?"

"He's just tired, Edie. Just give him some space."

"Jo, I'm sorry. Trust me, though, the food I ordered will be delicious. The chicken is real. Not Kunming blue."

"I'm sure it will. It's just... he's tired. I'm tired. Everything about this day has been tiring. It's fine. Whatever. Chicken is fine. I'm just grumpy because I'm exhausted."

Ernie's deflated look made me pause slightly. What was going ON with me? I didn't like this snippy side of myself, though I felt like I couldn't control my temperament.

The bed was as glorious as Ernie had described. Cushy, warm, and absolutely heaven. I tucked the kids in, sank into bed next to Ernie, stuck in earplugs, and had the best sleep I'd had since the States.

The next morning I awoke refreshed, but still on edge. The immediate apology to Ernie that should have crossed my mind was replaced by a passive version. I curled into him in bed, my small, warm body completely engulfed by his towering frame.

"I can't believe you married me, Ern."

He chuckled. This was a comment I made often, usually in

the midst of some ridiculous plan I was launching.

"I can't believe you convinced me to put my job on hold, sell my truck, and move our family to China for a year. You're spectacular, Jo."

"I'm a hot, spectacular mess. And thank you very much for putting up with me. I love you."

"My life would be a complete bore without you, and we both know it."

"That's true. You'd just be a single guy in Boulder who mountain biked every weekend and only ate mac and cheese."

It didn't feel like an apology because I felt more inside me waiting to explode. So, for today, this was all I could muster.

We carried on with our day, visiting Tiananmen Square and the Forbidden City. Ernie's handler Julia had hired a private SUV for us and we were treated like royalty.

The walls of the Forbidden City rose up around the children. Scampering from room to room, the children delighted in being able to run and touch history. Each part of the complex held a different story of a different emperor. Each tree contained a legend. Ernie and I were fascinated by the stories of the way each Chinese dynasty fell into the next. The children had little patience for the details, preferring to run in and out of the maze of rooms. Chinese tourists stared as we spoke to them in English, trying to figure out what the relationship was between the children and between them and us. The stares and pointing fingers had accompanied us to Beijing. With polite smiles, we nodded at those who persisted.

Over the next few days, we took rickshaws through the ancient alleyways of Beijing. Climbed the Great Wall of China. Each experience standing on its own was enough to talk about for a lifetime. And in the moment, happiness prevailed. The children climbed to each lookout tower on the Wall with excitement. Ernie and I delighted in their smiles. I laid out a picnic lunch on the Great Wall of China, just as I'd dreamed. As we ate, the children peeked over the Wall, looking forward as it stretched over mountaintops into the distance.

"How long can we stay here, Dad?" Will begged.

"We can stay as long as we want to, guys. Just gotta get back down before sunset."

"Let's climb that harder section. The section that you have to climb with your hands," Will suggested.

"I want to do that, too, Mom! Climb with my hands!" Eden laughed at the thought.

The hands and knees climb happened just as they wished. Ernie and I boosting them up by their bottoms to reach each of the following steps higher onto the Wall.

The day drained us in the best of ways. Back at the hotel we scarfed down plate after plate of Western food. Burgers and fries. Pizza. Ice cream. Genuine laughs infused our dinners. The comforts of home brought me peace, but also left me face-to-face with the reality of our year. Released from Kunming, I felt clearly my disappointment with how things had unfolded so far. The expectations that we had – unmet. The help that we anticipated having from the university – not there. My visa situation was still murky, leaving me with a feeling of unease about how things would look as we returned to Kunming.

As we prepared to go home, I became more rigid, blind to the good that was happening all around us. Ernie absorbed the weight of my negativity. We went shopping for a few items of clothing for the kids on our last day, and I had trouble finding anything positive to say about the food, the clothing, the cab drivers, and the prices. After an hour of standing on a street corner trying to get a cab back to the hotel, we decided to walk. I continued my complaints as we walked the crowded sidewalks of Beijing.

"This country doesn't make any sense. Why did those two cabs stop and talk to us if they weren't going to pick us up? What the hell? Do we look scary?" I held bags of our purchases, and swung them around to make my point, nearly hitting Eden in the back of the head. She scampered over to Ernie, who shot me an irritated glance.

"And what's with the stupid rule about cabs not taking passengers at five o'clock so they can all go on break? Have you HEARD a more ridiculous concept?"

"Mom, don't say 'stupid!' That's a bad word."

Ernie had hit his limit with me. He exploded in a way that I'd never experienced. Weeks and weeks of helplessness pouring out in a tirade. With a raised voice, he stood inches from me while the children looked on silently. Seeing their father in a way that was foreign and frightening.

"Pull yourself together, Johanna! Jesus! This whole thing was your idea, and now you're miserable. You're the only one who can speak halfway decent Mandarin, and you're not making an effort to help us. Get over yourself and stop being such a god-damn ugly American! You pride yourself on being so worldly and keen to travel, but you've turned into this inflexible woman. I don't even know who you are anymore. You're all talk."

He turned and walked away. *Oh. My. God.*

The kids stared at us, as did people walking by on the sidewalks we shared. I didn't move.

"Daddy, you said a bad word, too. You owe me six yuan," whispered Will. Our goal to not curse in front of our children was backed up by a promise to pay them a dollar every time we misstepped. And sadly, we'd already done so here in China. They had done the math. The exchange rate was six yuan to a dollar. They were on top of it. I cringed.

Ashamed, I felt like a ton of bricks had fallen on my shoulders. His words hit right where they were meant to. Who had I become? Someone stubborn. Judgmental. An over-privileged American. Everything I despised. The singular contrast of the moment grabbed me. This had, after all, been MY dream, hadn't it? I'd pushed my children and husband beyond places that perhaps they were capable of going. The truth screamed at me with an intensity that I wasn't prepared for. I'd been selfish at first for pushing all of us to undertake the journey, and now I was miserable while in it. Furthermore, there was no turning back. What a mess. The moments in my life that had led me here were being squandered, and I knew something needed to change or I'd ruin the year for all of us. I took hold of the children's hands and walked forward.

chapter twenty four

The Beijing blowout jolted me back into a place of quiet unease. The loud version disappeared. The version that was accompanied by thoughtless comments and loud complaints that I knew the children would likely internalize. It took an act of husband hysteria on an Asian street corner to convince me that I'd been off-kilter for far too long.

Returning from Beijing, we were confident that Ernie's immigration status was on solid ground. For the rest of us, there was still work to be done. A trip to Hong Kong to finalize paperwork would happen in a few weeks, along with a week on a beach in Thailand. For now, our goal was to get the children into a good routine at school.

Eden had been accepted into a special kindergarten for the children of university professors. Will's local school would be the primary school up the road from our apartment. Each school was lined with steel gates and guards at the entrance. There were fees to pay at each, and I doubted that they were applied to the locals. Nonetheless, we'd vowed to at least attempt to get them acclimated to regular Chinese schools and not automatically stick them in the fancy international school where English was the primary language.

Eden's kindergarten felt warm. Chinese families positively lavished attention on their children until the age of six when the real work began. Her classroom would have about thirty students and two teachers, neither of whom spoke any English. The day was scheduled to run from 8:30-5:30, five days a week.

My head spun at the thought of being away from her for such a long period of time, but we agreed to try. Eden started school a few days before Will, paving the way for him. Predictably, she adjusted beautifully. The fact that not a single classmate spoke English seemed virtually irrelevant to her. More a bit of trivia than a barrier to creating friends.

Getting Will adjusted to HIS school would be more difficult. The warm and fuzzy feeling of American schools was void. Chinese primary school students were tasked with hour after hour of homework each night. Extracurricular activities. Outside tutors and weekends of extra classes. Parents were welcome in Eden's school, but strictly forbidden to enter the school grounds at Will's. In addition to the institutional restrictions, his personality provided a litany of challenges. He wasn't game for new experiences. Totally unwilling to try anything that might cause embarrassment. His days consisted of trying to remain under the radar screen. Will's likeability factor was high and he had many friends in Denver. But he didn't want to do anything that might appear outside the norm. That was true in Denver, and it doubled in importance here.

To counter his nerves, we visited the school and his class-room just before he was scheduled to start. The school principal and his classroom teacher urged me to enroll Will in full days, though I'd worked tirelessly in my conversations with them to allow him to start with half days. We sat in the principal's office as I explained my desire to start slowly, transitioning to full days later in the year. His teacher was called Teacher Che. She had the look of a woman who could be both compassionate and strict. Wise eyes were hidden behind dark frames. Dressed in comfortable clothes that would allow her to wrangle a class of 40-plus eight-year-olds. I addressed Will using his Chinese name, the one he'd use in school.

"We feel it will be better for Zhi Yong to take time to get to know the Chinese way. Improve his language skills." I spoke in Mandarin with the rest of the family sitting behind me as usual. My language was formal as I tried to match the respect I wanted to convey for their willingness to school our son.

"Mom, you're just really not making a lot of sense. Your Chinese needs help, Mom." Will grumbled under his breath, but I could tell that my point was getting across.

"But Zhi Yong will not make friends if he's here only half days. He must behave like other Chinese students."

The principal was insistent. I glanced at Ernie for reassurance, and he nodded. Our expectation that we'd continue to face resistance on this issue was being met. Our tactic was to kill them with kindness.

"Thank you so much for understanding our hopes for Zhi Yong. We're so very grateful that you are able to educate our son. We hope he'll be a good student."

The principal pursed her lips a bit, but then smiled and showed us to his classroom.

The students, all 44 of them, were enthusiastic about having a little American boy in their class. At the end of our class visit, they jumped to their feet and clapped to welcome Will. It was a touching scene I could never imagine in an American school. The energy was infectious and it eased our nervousness. And the number, though staggering, seemed as though it could work in his favor. Cautious optimism settled over us in the days before the first day of school. Our goal now was to keep Will's spirits high and his anxiety low.

Will's nerves began to kick in the night before his first day.

Unable to sleep, he panicked about everything from the food to the lack of friends. His stomach was constantly in knots, he said. He peppered questions to us that we both could and could not answer.

"But how will I know when to go where?"

"What if I don't like the food?"

"What if I get sick?"

"What if I don't understand anything?"

I got online and researched school anxiety. I contacted a school psychologist friend of mine in America. Posted on my mom listserve from 10,000 miles away. Trying to find any way to ease his fears in what was undoubtedly one of the most stressful situations a child could go through. A new school. In a different country. In a different language. His Mandarin was decent, but not at the level of his classmates. It would be difficult to follow the flow of the day. I knew that. I tried bribes, encouragement, meditation tricks, breaking down his day into small and achievable goals. I offered to stay at school with him for as long as it took. Sitting next to him or sitting in the back of the room until he was ready for me to leave. I even, gulp, compared him to Eden. My string of endless attempts spilled out as I tried to find one that might fit:

1. "Honey, what you're doing here in China is more challenging than anything that I ever did when I was your age. You are awesome. So proud of you."

2. "Look at your sister. She doesn't speak ANY Mandarin and her school days are longer than yours."

Crap. I had just compared him to his six-year-old sister. Bad mom. Bad, bad mom.

3. "After you get through this, you'll be able to conquer anything you want. There's nothing that you won't be able to overcome after this. You'll always have this experience and it will

help you control your anxiety."

4. "What if, after every day of school, we plan to get a treat at the store across the street? That might be fun? Something junky, even?"

5. "How about if we watch a little funny cartoon on the iPad each morning before school?"

6. "Let's try some breathing exercises. Let's breathe in the scared and breathe out the brave."

7. "Why don't we break down your day and talk about how you can get through each piece?"

In the end, it was clear that we would all just need to walk over the hot coals together. There was no escaping it.

I woke before the alarm. Lying there, I felt panicked for my son to begin his day. With a deep breath, I rolled out of bed and got myself ready for whatever might await. The room the children shared had a bunk bed and giant windows on two sides looking out onto the road below. I slid open the curtains and chirped the same thing I always did.

"Rise and shine! Rise and shine, peanuts."

"Mom. My stomach hurts." Will looked down at me from the top bunk.

There it was. I felt an equal mix of sympathy and anxiety. We'd tried so many approaches to overcoming Will's fears that I had no idea which one would work best in this moment. Ernie had less sympathy than I did with Will's plight. He'd overcome anxiety as a child and though I thought it would make him MORE sympathetic, the opposite happened. Ever the sensitive child, Ernie viewed this moment as the one in which Will should buck up. For me, it looked like the hardest moment Will had faced in his young life, and I carried the burden of being the one who'd brought him to this. Hell, I was terrified myself!

I decided to go with the team approach.

"We're gonna do it together, buddy. I know we can do it. I'm going with you and we'll march into those school gates and show them what we're made of."

"Mom, I'm serious. I'm really sick."

Here we go. I don't want to come across as the mom who doesn't believe him, but I KNOW that this is just anxiety. Please, someone help me. Help me figure out what to do.

"Come on, Will. Time to get up. Your sister's already at the breakfast table," Ernie commanded.

Oh, crap. Ernie's taking a hardline approach. That's different than mine. Why didn't we consult on this before we got out of bed? Rookie mistake. We're both unequipped to deal with this. We suck.

We plodded through breakfast, Will eating nothing. Scared beyond scared. He got dressed, but as time came to leave the apartment, he stood his ground.

"No. Mom, I'm not going. I feel sick and I can't do it. I can't do it. I can't do it." Again and again he repeated his new mantra, while I countered it.

"Buddy, I KNOW you can do it. I'll do it with you. We'll do it together. I'm not going to leave you. You can do it."

"Mom, I can't. I can't!"

"Will, it's time to leave. Get your coat on and put your backpack on please." Ernie was losing patience.

Will didn't budge from his stance in the front hall. Ernie lost it.

"Will, get your jacket on this instant. Your mother is walking you to school and that's the end of it." Ernie's voice was raised, a sound unfamiliar in our home, though heard recently on a Beijing street corner. I couldn't take it. I left the room and sat on our bed. Breathing in the scared and breathing out the brave. *Give me strength, give me strength, give me strength!*

I heard voices from the other room and could tell that Will had done what Ernie had asked. His jacket was on, but the bickering continued.

I winced as I heard Eden say, "But Daddy, Will's tummy hurts. You shouldn't make him go to school if he's sick."

I stood from the bed, forcing myself into the front hall. We walked out the door together, Ernie strapping Eden in the bike seat on the back of our bike for the ride to her school. Will and I began walking. I took his hand.

"Just take one step at a time, buddy. All we need to do is make it to the gate. Then the corner. Just think one bit at a time like we taught you."

"I can't do it. I can't do it. I can't do it."

I could feel my heart aching for my son. Helpless, but with no other option but to move forward, we walked. The school was across a major street that was just outside our apartment gates. We approached the street. Cars flowed past us, their drivers going about their days as if all was well.

"No. Mom, I can't do it. I don't wanna go. Don't make me go, Mom."

I felt like I might throw up. Time slowed. The cars on the street sped past. Chinese people stopped to stare at us as I knelt down in front of Will and looked up at him.

"You CAN do this, Will. I know you, and I know you're scared. And so am I. But once we do this, it'll get easier. Every day will be easier. Let this moment wash over you, buddy. I'm right here."

"No. No, Mom. I'm not going."

"Will. You must. I want you to at least try. I'll pick you up and carry you if I need to. All I'm asking is that you try. For me. Do this for me, for your father, for your sister. But mostly for yourself.

You're strong, Will."

He didn't move. I took a breath and picked him up. At nine years old, he weighed less than fifty pounds and was no match for me and my strength. I put him on my hip and we crossed the street as he began to cry.

"MOM! Mom! Don't make me go! I can't do it. Mom, why are you doing this?!" His tears came without hesitation now, and he didn't care that we'd become a spectacle. I moved slowly as he continued to lash out at me, kicking and screaming.

"I hate you, Mom! I hate you! I hate that you're making me do this! I want to go home! To America. I hate this place! I wanna go home now!" There they were. The words I'd hoped to never hear. My ears burned as his thin legs squirmed in an attempt to get free from my grasp.

I replied, calm and steady. "I know it's hard, Will. Let it go. Let it go. It's okay. If you're mad at me, let it out. Let it all out."

I wanted him to let out his anger at me, though his words were the worst I'd ever heard. No amount of bad breakups or job rejections had prepared me for this. *Give me strength, give me strength, give me strength.*

"I hate you, Mom! I hate you! I hate you!"

I began to cry as I walked up the slightly inclined sidewalk towards the school gate. We were both crying now, Will still in my arms twisting to release himself from my grip. I was sure he'd run home if I let him go.

"I want my China mom! She'd never do this to me! I hate you, Mom! I want my China mom! I want my real mom!" The words were all he had left and felt like poison dripping into my heart. I inhaled with shock, but not loudly enough for him to detect.

"I know, buddy. I know. Let it out. It's awful. It's just awful. I hate this, too. It's okay. It's okay. We're gonna do this together. I'm never leaving you. Nothing you will ever say or do will make me stop loving you. I'm never leaving you."

Oh God help me! There aren't words for this. Brutal. Awful. Staggering. Heartbreaking. It's more than that. What have I done? I hate myself, too. I'm a terrible mother. I'm a terrible, selfish mother.

Time froze as I forced myself to walk the final few steps up to the school. Tears rolled down my cheeks. We got to the school gates and Will said, "Let me down! I can walk on my own."

I put him down but held tightly to his hand. We strode into the gates and then to his classroom where we were met by Teacher Che. My Mandarin was filled with bad tones and sniffles as I tried unsuccessfully to hide my emotions.

"I'd like to stay today and sit next to Zhi Yong."

"Mom... this is embarrassing."

Teacher Che led us upstairs, leaving the classroom of 44 students completely unsupervised. I made a mental note to be grateful for our class size of 25 back home in America.

Teacher Che calmly explained to me that it wouldn't be possible for me to stay with Will. I'd expected this answer, but wanted to follow through on my promise to him. She spoke to Will in Mandarin and asked if he was cold or hungry. He'd calmed down once we'd entered the school grounds and said that indeed he was both cold and hungry. The impression I was giving of American mothers was falling flat. She tracked down an old jacket for him while I dug out a granola bar from my backpack. One of the last from our stash brought from home. They were like gold.

We sat in the teachers' lounge for a long time. Breathing. Will eating the granola bar. And listening to Teacher Che tell him that it would be okay. She would take care of him, and the other students were excited to have him here this year. *This woman radiates kindness,* I thought.

Finally, she stood, taking Will's hand and heading for the classroom. He followed. We got to the classroom door and I said as cheerily as I could, "I'll pick you up at 11:30, Will." It was nine o'clock and he'd come home at lunch. He could do anything for 2.5 hours. And all I had to do was breathe. He didn't bother to look at me as he stepped into the room and was swarmed by his giddy classmates. Each asking him questions in rapid succession. The sight buoyed me as I stepped away and began to walk towards home. I took deep breaths, hoping to make it all the way inside before I collapsed. As our metal door swung open, I let my backpack fall from my hand, closed the door and took a final three steps to the couch. Where I lay for the next hour sobbing.

chapter twenty five

As we'd hoped, the pain of the first day of school passed. Our decision to have Will stay at home and study with Helen in the afternoons saved us. The mornings were still tough, but knowing Helen would be by his side to wade through Chinese homework slowly eased his anxiety. Her patience and sense of humor lifted him into a sense of normalcy. He had a friend. His first real friend in China at a time when he was aching to escape from his sister and parents. Despite the fact that she was 23 years old, Helen's demeanor was closer to 14. I spent time talking with her about childcare and reminding her not to hit Will if he did something wrong. Her hits were playful, but took me by surprise. Given her lack of siblings, she had no real experience with children, and only mirrored how she herself had been treated in school. Teachers hit children over the heads or on the hands. With books and rulers. It happened regularly, though I'd made it clear to Teacher Che that their sole American student was "unfamiliar with being hit."

We swept our scene from the first day of school under the rug. We concentrated instead on the little accomplishments we each continued to have, and on Thailand – our next vacation was approaching, complete with the authentic phad thai and beaches that I'd been dreaming about. We counted the days.

Our plane touched down in Bangkok. We'd left China to deal

with my visa drama. Needing to simply leave the country as part of the runaround, we'd picked Bangkok, but then had been instructed by my university to go to Hong Kong. Too late to change our plans, we decided to do both. Thailand first for some relaxation, then Hong Kong for the paperwork.

After a short layover, we boarded a smaller plane and made it to the small island of Koh Samui. The children were beside themselves with the warm, clean air. Fruit trees and lizards at every turn. Our hotel was about as far away from our stark apartment in Kunming as it could possibly be – lush gardens spilling out into a pool lined with fountains, a bathroom the size of our apartment, a menu that included chicken nuggets and corn dogs for the kids, and an enormous breakfast buffet that nearly brought tears to our eyes. Settling in took no time at all.

This was our second big trip since arriving in China. It was obvious to me that traveling outside of China would need to be part of the pattern to get us through the year. The lack of Western amenities in Kunming meant that escaping every now and then would help us keep our sanity. It wasn't lost on me that the reason we could do this was because of Ernie's job. His work would make it possible for us to enjoy a periodic dip into luxurious Asian resorts. It seemed yet another in a long line of contradictions in my life. We'd come to Asia to live a simple life, yet here I was in Thailand, full of angst over whether I should have fresh squeezed papaya juice or a lychee smoothie with breakfast. I hated myself for the moment of silly stress. And then I took the smoothie.

After a couple of days in Thailand, our tough China exteriors were shed. Our moods were lighter, laughter more present. We hugged more. Dug in the sand. Breathed. We had gratitude. We wrestled with the children on the floor of our room, an activity that had been present daily in the States, but all together absent since we'd arrived in Asia.

One afternoon, Ernie and I sat poolside with books. Eden was at my feet playing with shells she'd collected on our morning walk. Will dove in and out of the pool and the adjoining hot tub. A few other boys splashed, trying to engage him in their horseplay. My eyes fell shut, but were opened with a start as I heard a commotion. My gaze drew to a figure lying on the side of the pool deck. A boy. The same size as Will. Chinese. And there was a figure above him – an adult, performing CPR. Time stopped.

The book I was reading fell to the ground as I looked at Eden and jumped to my feet, shouting, "Where's Will?!"

My eyes raced to the hot tub where he'd been just seconds before. *Oh my God! How long had I been sleeping?* Ernie scanned the pool and I called to Eden as I ran, "Stay with Daddy!"

The distance from where we sat to the hot tub was no more than 25 meters, but required going through a small path around the pool. As I ran, I began to hear shrieks. Hotel staff poured out of every nook to help, walkie-talkies buzzing. I reached the hot tub and looked down to see my son in the water, swimming at the bottom. I recognized his navy swim shirt, but my panic remained. I knelt down, my fingers breaking the surface of the water. *I'm not going to lose him. I won't lose him.* The water felt like honey as my fingers strained to reach my boy, going deeper and deeper. My arm was just long enough to reach his shirt. I grabbed it hard, pulling him up, up into the air and back to me.

"Oh my God, Will. I'm here. I'm here. It's okay." I shook as I squeezed him into me and sat on the side of the hot tub, his wet body warm from the water. I began to rock back and forth. I held him so hard that I began to frighten him.

"MOM! Mom! Why did you DO that? MOM! What's wrong? You're hugging me too tight, Mom. Stop!"

He'd missed the entire affair. All he knew was one moment he was diving for rocks in the hot tub and the next moment he was being pulled up and out of the water by a terrified mother. We heard the screams continuing just a few meters away. The little boy's chest was being compressed over and over by a burly man in a swimsuit. The pool had cleared of swimmers.

"Buddy, a little boy was under the water too long. He got pulled out and I thought it was you. I ran over here and saw you were still playing and I pulled you out because I just needed you out of the water."

"Is that him over there? Did he die, Mom?"

"Buddy, I don't know. We need to leave now."

I looked across the pool and saw Ernie holding Eden. I motioned for them to join us and we walked quickly back to our bungalow, passing more hotel staff running toward the pool. I carried Will, a nine-year-old perfectly capable of walking on his own. The patio door slid open and Ernie and I stepped inside, each holding a child in our arms. I moved towards the king-sized bed and crawled in with Will in my arms, both of us soaking wet.

"Come here. Come here." I reached out to Ernie, who brought me Eden. She slid into bed next to me and I wrapped her up in my other arm. I began to shake, both from the cold and from the fear of losing my children. We sat in bed and I rocked both of them, wrapping them up in the comforter.

"Mom, did he die? Did that boy die?" Will asked.

"Momma, why are we in bed? Is it time to sleep? I want to go swimming," Eden said.

I stared at Ernie, whose eyes, buried in a novel just a few minutes ago, were now full of horror. The past two months had been hard. We'd left our home, our country, our friends, and our family. We weren't going to lose each other. The screams of the parents at the side of the pool seeped into our bungalow, causing me to cover the children's ears. I stayed in bed, clutching Will and Eden for a long time, the sheets soaking through to the mattress.

chapter twenty six

The rest of our days in Koh Samui were subdued. Because we never found out whether he lived or died, visions of the little boy lying on the side of the pool haunted me. I saw his lifeless body and the image of his spirit lifting slowly upwards. He rose above the pool and hovered, looking down peacefully at his distraught parents. Then drifted out over the Gulf of Thailand.

Thankfully, the children had a different reaction. By the end of the week, they'd forgotten about the boy and had stopped asking about his fate. Long walks on the beach captured their attention, though my mind remained fixated on the contrasts of our life here in Asia. Serene and full of joy on the surface, but messy underneath.

We packed our bags with a carton of stowaway seashells. The week had added much-needed weight to our frames and a glow to our skin. We looked ahead to our trip to Hong Kong and the paperwork that needed finalizing for us to be able to remain in China. It made me nervous. My experiences with Chinese bu-reaucracy had taught me to never trust what looked like the final step in any simple process.

Hong Kong. My visits to the city with Ruby had been frequent because of our shady Taiwanese visa fiasco in our 20's. We'd flown back and forth between Hong Kong and Taiwan sever-al times, each visit stocking up on Western snacks and trashy

American magazines. As adoptive parents, we'd stopped here with brand new babies on our hips. I adored Hong Kong for its ability to bridge the gap between East and West, just as we were striving to do this year.

Despite my concerns about my visa being approved, things sailed smoothly in Hong Kong. It took several days for the paperwork to be processed at the Chinese consulate, and while waiting, we ate sushi twice a day, spoke English, and toured the islands on a double decker bus. Hong Kong Harbor was about as far away from Koh Samui as possible, but its bustle was welcome nonetheless. The visa paperwork was processed with ease and soon we were on our way back to Kunming. Going home once again to our real life.

As the final step in our process, we needed to register with the local immigration authorities. We were reminded that they needed to know exactly who we were and where we were. I had no doubt that these were well known facts already. Nevertheless, we played by the rules and made preparations to appear at the local immigration office. Invisible for months in helping us get established, my university sent me a list of paperwork.

"What the hell? It says here that we need to bring the children's original citizenship certificates with us." I grumbled to Ernie as I read through the email from the department chair.

"Did we bring those?"

"Negative, Ern. I brought almost every conceivable document, but the idea of traveling with original ANYTHING was unnerving. They're in the fireproof safe at home in the basement."

"Why do they need those anyway? The kids are U.S. citizens and we carry their passports."

"Good question. I'm sure they just want proof that we got the babies through legal channels. Who knows? It's China. Well, they're gonna have to deal with the copies. That's all we've got."

A little voice screamed at me as I collected the documents we needed and picked up the phone to call Mr. Zhang. *You ridiculous woman! Just watch as China bites you in the ass again, girlfriend. You're totally whacked if you think photocopies are going to fly. I'm gonna just go with the naïve, Wisconsin, sweet-girl route and see how far we get. Here we go.*

"Nǐhǎo, Mr. Zhang. It's Johanna. Just want to check with you on the paperwork you said we need for this last immigration check in. It says here that we need the children's original citizenship certificates, but we only have the copies. I'm sure that's fine."

Silence.

"Johanna, don't be so naïve. When China says we want the original, we mean the ORIGINAL."

"I got that, but here's the thing. Americans don't carry around original *anythings*. That's why we have banks and storage systems. So hopefully the copy will be fine."

"I don't think so."

I felt my blood begin to boil. It was not, of course, Mr. Zhang's call. He was only the messenger. But the message was so futile. Unnecessary.

"Why does China need anything more than the children's passports? And what does this have to do with getting ME a visa? I'm the one they should be concerned with."

"I don't know, Johanna."

Of course not.

"Well, our temporary visas are expiring in, like, three days. We don't have the documents they want. Why didn't anyone tell us to pack them when we came to China?"

"We didn't know."

"Oh my gosh. So, now what?"

"If China wants the documents, you need to get the docu-ments." Mr. Zhang's voice was flat, showing no signs of sympa-thy. If anything, he seemed irritated at this *má fan*. It had been his responsibility to get the information to me, but he'd failed. And was now passing the buck.

"But you don't understand. They are locked up in a safe in the U.S. I can't get them in time."

"Then you must leave. You'll be deported."

"What?! Leave China? No way. We're not going anywhere."

I began to have an out-of-body experience. The struggles we'd overcome to get here were now crashing into the real-ity that we might not be able to stay. Was this not a welcome opportunity? Life had been so hard since we'd arrived. Was this a chance to escape?

"Let me see what I can do, Johanna. I'll call you back."

Ernie had overheard the conversation and rolled his eyes.

"Jo, we need to think about packing our bags."

Like 20 years prior in Taiwan, I calculated the likeli-hood of our phones being tapped as high. I assumed history was repeating itself, and we began to take care with our phone conversations. The next day, I heard back from Mr. Zhang, who wanted to meet with me that afternoon. His voice radiated hope-lessness, and we prepared for the worst. I pulled up a map on my laptop and began to look at countries in Southeast Asia we could get to via nonstop flights out of Kunming.

Ernie came in, peeking over my shoulder as my mouse moved over the tiny images of Indonesia, Malaysia, and Singapore.

"So, you won't even consider going home, will you?" Ernie asked.

"Are you seriously asking me that? No way. How long have we been married? Oh my God, Ern, do you even know me?" *Wait. Maybe he already answered this question last month in Beijing. Damn.*

"You know as well as I do that this is an uphill battle."

"I realize that. But going home? That's whackadoodle, Ern. We've come this far; we're not going home. This is home. We're gonna find a way to stay. I refuse to leave the continent. I'll look at going elsewhere within Asia, but I'm not going back across the Pacific. No way. I'm not failing at this," I said.

Failure. I'd had plenty of it in my forty-two years. Bar exams, poor performances in track meets, men who were terrible boyfriends, men I wanted who didn't want me, rejections from jobs I'd ached for. Failure had shaped me in the best ways, and it wasn't something I was scared of. Leaving China felt different. If we played this game well, there wasn't any reason we should have to leave. Should China decide otherwise, I'd do whatever I could to salvage the year for us. Failure seemed fruitless to discuss. We'd find a way to stay and live out our wanderlust.

"What about India?" I asked Ernie. There was potential work there for him. His company was contracting with businesses in New Delhi and Bangalore.

"No, too intense," he replied. "The kids would lose it, and if we have to leave, don't we want to be somewhere relaxing? India? Give me a break, Johanna."

"What about Cambodia? I love Cambodia, and there are expats and beaches and lots of non-governmental organizations. Maybe I could pick up some work with the United Nations."

"Maybe," he said. "What if I call Julia in Beijing and ask if she can arrange for you and the kids to get transferred onto my visa?"

"I suppose that would be the most logical option. But if the Chinese really don't want us here, there's nothing we can do about it. I'd hate for her to use her *guānxi* when it's a lost cause."

"It can't hurt to try, though," Ernie said.

"Okay, but I still think we should have a backup plan if we need to get out of here fast," I answered. "What about the Maldives? It's gorgeous there. On our list of places to visit in the next few months. Or Thailand? The kids loved it, it's easy to get to, and maybe I could teach English there."

"The Maldives, Jo? It's full of expensive resorts. And even if you DID get a job, what would the kids and I do for the rest of the year?" Ernie wondered.

"Fish, surf, swim, eat fruit. Learn Thai. Ride elephants. I think it sounds great," I said, sounding like I was 22 and not 42 with two small children in tow.

"I think it would be great for awhile, but what about my work? They'd figure out sooner or later that I wasn't in China," Ernie said.

"But would they care? Why would they care? Your China project is bumping along so far. Will they even notice where you are?" I asked.

"What about Alice? She's coming next week. Here. To Kunming. She could get the documents and hand carry them."

"Ludicrous. This whole thing is just ludicrous. Look at us. How is it even possible that we're here? Again. Being screwed by China. What is wrong with us?" I started laughing. Frustrated at my own idiocy.

My laughter was interrupted by Mr. Zhang calling. He asked me to step outside, where he was waiting in his car. Pulling on a coat, I ran outside, approaching his car as he waved for me to get in. *Damn, he could at least open the door for me*, I thought. There was none of that here. Men didn't open doors for women or let them get off buses first.

I had barely sat down in the passenger seat when he said, "Johanna, there's nothing to be done." *Whoa, he got straight to the point,* I thought.

In reality, this shouldn't have surprised me. We'd been educated by example in the brevity of Chinese conversation styles. Whereas Westerners would consider it rude to speak so quickly, getting to the point so directly, the Chinese thought it honorable. In a country of one billion people, time wasn't to be wasted. Drawing out conversations in long narratives was seen as disrespectful. The manner in which I used please and thank you relentlessly was laughed at. Even more so, my tendency to use a particular Chinese phrase that meant roughly, "I am so sorry to trouble you with this inconvenience" frequently brought giggles. I couldn't stop. I needed to remain polite. At least in the way that I had been taught. But in this situation, I appreciated Mr. Zhang's ability to cut to the chase.

Nice. I like this. Now we can work through it. I'd prepared a rebuttal worthy of something I'd pulled together in law school. Mr. Zhang started driving away from the apartment. I had no idea where he was taking me, but I didn't care. I just needed to present my case.

"Okay, I heard you yesterday. But surely there must be SOME way that they can accept what I have to offer... the photocopy, that is?"

"No. Not possible."

"But even if you explain it to them, and tell them that I have children who are now in school here, and students who are depending on me to teach?"

"I cannot get involved."

Oh, crap. I had a sinking feeling that we were quickly descending into the complicated realm of guānxi. The university's main campus was just a few blocks from our apartment. Mr. Zhang navigated his car into a small university parking lot and turned the key, killing the engine.

"You mean you won't come with me to the immigration po-lice?"

"That's right."

Well, there it is. I felt the reality hit me in the face. It was pay-back time. I had refused the housing arrangement set up for us. And though I'd been a great teacher so far, the slap in the face from my initial rejection stung. We were alone. We were alone in China. The children and I had only two days left on our visas. They were in school. Had started to make friends. We had paid in full for the entire year's worth of rent for our apartment. I was teaching. We were finally making a go of it. This couldn't happen to us. Mangoes on the beach in Thailand for the rest of the year sounded fun, but what I really wanted for us was a regular life. Here. In Kunming.

"But there must be some way. I mean, what am I supposed to do tomorrow? I have classes to teach."

"You shouldn't go to your classes. You will need to leave, Johanna. You need to go home now."

Tears began to well in my eyes. I knew unquestionably that this would make Mr. Zhang uncomfortable. But I couldn't help it.

"I don't believe it. There must be something we can do. That YOU can do. You have a responsibility to help my family." I reached up and quickly brushed a tear away. Mr. Zhang looked at me and then quickly away. He looked irritated.

"Don't be so stupid, Johanna. You know how this works."

"But I don't have any guānxi and you do."

"You just don't understand. I can't help you anymore."

Anymore? Did you EVER help, I wondered?

"Alice is coming to Kunming next week. It's after our visas ex-pire, but if she can get the papers we need, and bring them here, maybe that will help?"

"Perhaps, Johanna. You could write a letter to the immigration police explaining your situation and telling them the documents are on the way. You could try that."

"And I would go there alone? To the immigration office?" I sniffled a bit and pulled out a tissue.

"I could have a student go with you."

A student. Wonderful. The university wouldn't put their name on the line, but they'd throw a student into the mix. It was like feeding a large bucket of chum to the sharks. The poor student wouldn't have a chance to refuse the university request. And I knew the fear young people had of the Chinese police. Still, I had to accept the offer. I pulled myself together at this last chance.

"Okay. Find a student for me and have her call me. I'll write a letter and arrange a time to meet her and go to the immigration police."

There were no apologies as Mr. Zhang drove me back to the apartment. No explanation as to why we just couldn't have had this conversation in a coffee house. There was silence. *Did he want me to give him a bribe*, I thought? *Is that why he took me in his car? I'm so confused.* The wooden massage beads laying over the passenger seat dug into my thighs. I got out of the car and waved good-bye. A sliver of hope remained with two days left on our visas.

The clock reached midnight as Ernie and I stayed up late that night. We counted the minutes until the time in Denver was an acceptable hour. Then we picked up our red telephone and made a call to Melissa and Dan who were living in our home. Sleeping in our bed. Using our fancy espresso maker. Sitting on our cozy porch swing. Walking to our local bakery. The cold marble floor of Ernie's office was no match for our couch in Denver. That Melissa and Dan were likely sitting on. Right this instant.

"Hello?"

"Melissa, it's Johanna."

"Who? Johanna? Where are you? Is everything okay? What time is it there?"

I quickly explained the situation. The two-minute version felt like pure fiction, but Melissa, having had experience in China, had an immunity to the preposterous nature of the whole affair. I told her in detail where to find the key for the fireproof safe in our basement which contained the documents China need-ed. How to contact Alice and arrange a time for her to collect the documents. I then called Alice and filled her in on the plan. Moving forward, despite the fact that we had not gotten the thumbs up yet from the immigration authorities. It was a Hail Mary pass. But it was all we had.

Will's tutor, Helen, looked at me with concern.

"It's gonna be fine, Helen. I'm sure it's no big deal."

It was a lie. I had no idea if it would be fine, and it certainly WAS a big deal. The biggest deal. If we didn't get good news when we walked into the immigration office, it was game over. We'd be on a flight to Thailand. Tomorrow. Leaving Ernie, legally secure in Kunming, to figure out what to do next.

There were six of us standing outside the offices of the re-gional immigration police. The look on the faces of Helen and the college sophomore who'd been sent to "help" us was nothing short of pure terror. They knew nothing other than what we'd told them. Which was a version of "We don't have the paperwork we need and our visas expire tomorrow. Could you give us a better option?" This sounded bad to the two young women. It was bad.

The fear of the communist police was serious business, and the two of them knew that they could easily be asked to provide their names, their stories, and their connections to this messy, messy American family. The six of us padded up the stairs to the correct room. We waited, watching other helpless foreigners with similar visas problems try to navigate the system as we were about to.

"Ernie, pick up Will. Cuddle him a little. Let's look sympathetic."

We each picked up a child as our number was called. I approached the desk with Edie in my arms. The appearance of the woman behind the desk screamed All Business. We handed over our passports and I explained our situation in Mandarin. We have the photocopies of the certificates of citizenship. The originals are in America. We hadn't been told to bring the originals when we moved here. We can get them, but this will require more time. All Business looked dubious. She was about to say no. I took a breath and pictured myself on a beach in Thailand.

Looking at Ernie, his face set in a bland grin, I thought about what a selfish, blind woman I'd become. *I can't believe I've brought my family into this mess and now these two, poor Chinese undergrads –what's wrong with you, Johanna?*

"Where are you from?" I turned to see that a young Chinese man had joined All Business behind the desk. With a strong American accent, he was somehow different than All Business.

"We're from America."

"I know. I guessed that. I meant, which part?"

"Colorado."

"I went to university in Ohio."

Yes! I knew an opening when I saw one. "I'm from Wisconsin originally. We're practically neighbors!" I flashed a grin and showed him my dimples, though I wasn't sure that Chinese men went for that sort of flirting.

The young immigration officer smiled at me. He'd been passing by All Business, and now she turned to him and asked a series of questions, none of which I understood. I looked at Helen and the terrified college student for an indication of what was being said, but got nothing. They stared at the officers, but I could tell they were trying to look as invisible as possible. I rubbed my finger along the charm on my necklace. It was the one my friend, Jill, had given me before we'd left the States. With the word "Believe" on it.

"Your visas expire tomorrow?" He looked over our passports.

"That's right. We can get the documents you need, but it'll take a couple weeks."

He spoke a few more words to his colleague, who nodded. As he handed our passports back he said, "One week. Get us the documents in one week."

I felt a mix of relief and terror take hold of me. How the heck were we supposed to do this in one week? Alice wasn't scheduled to leave for three days, and wouldn't be in Kunming for 10 days. I thanked him, and looked at the rest of our pack. Ernie looked stunned. Helen and her sidekick took baby steps backwards, as if they couldn't get out of there fast enough. The children bolted for the stairs, leaving us to whisper our debrief as we followed.

"One week? That's like handing us half a solution! This is so – this is so Chinese!"

Ernie chuckled at me. "Jo, we've been given a lifeline. Let's work with it. I know Alice won't be here for ten days but maybe I can fly to Shanghai to get the documents from her. I'd normally suggest that the documents just travel all the way from Colorado to Kunming via FedEx, but these are too important. We want them hand-carried, don't we?"

"Yes. Yes, we do. Okay. We'll figure it out."

And we did. Melissa found the key to our safe. Opened the

safe. Retrieved the documents. Alice and Melissa connected. And with the documents in hand, Alice flew across the Pacific Ocean, landing in Shanghai. She promptly put them in the hands of a high-end Chinese courier who delivered them to me on the eve of our visas expiring. I could practically smell our basement on the edges of the certificates as I brought them back to the young immigration officer on the final day of our seven-day reprieve. As I watched, he glanced at each certificate for roughly five seconds before handing them back to me. China scores again. Johanna still only hitting the rim.

chapter twenty seven

A few days later, Alice arrived. She'd worked tirelessly to get me the job in Kunming, and now she was the first American we'd laid eyes on since O'Hare. She'd traveled with her adorable husband, Jon, and brought boxes of my favorite energy drink and copies of Runners' World magazine. Alice had an infectious laugh, which we reveled in for the duration of her stay. We shared our already-full suitcase of stories about the bizarre. The unbelievable. The depressing. The full-on insanity that was life in China. It was contagious and we both hated it and loved it. Alice understood. She'd been coming here for twenty years to cultivate relationships with Chinese universities. Every year for the past five I'd heard her complain about the bureaucracy. The red tape. The bribes.

"Oh yeah, the university officials used to take cash, but now they just prefer cigarettes," she said with a chuckle at dinner one night. We'd taken them to our favorite restaurant overlooking Green Lake Park.

"Did I tell you about the time I was sitting in an airport in Kunming and pieces of the ceiling started falling on my head?"

"Yes, but Ernie and the kids haven't heard it yet, so tell it again."

"Incredible. So I'm just sitting there, and chunks of ceiling tile just start raining down on top of me. And nobody thinks there's anything odd about it. Nobody even really notices! And then a cat fell out of the ceiling! A CAT! What is THAT?"

We laughed uproariously, raising our glasses to toast China.

Our visas were finalized the day before Ernie's 40th birthday. He was deathly sick with food poisoning, the sort that's rare in the United States. So far, we'd all had at least one brutal bout. The previous week I'd been out to lunch with my new gang of girlfriends and all nine of us came down with it in the hours after we got home from our lunch date. Nine. I had laid on the floor of the bathroom, the chill of the tile amplifying my discomfort.

"Take me home, Ernie. I just wanna go home," I moaned. "Look at me. I'm not running, I feel out of shape, I'm ingesting too much MSG every day and I can't find proper snacks for the kids."

"Johanna, I know you feel like crap, but this is kind of part of the deal. You like to be in control of your life, but you moved your family to a communist country where we have zero control over practically everything. You're crazy, Jo. And now you're down for the count with food poisoning. You'll be fine, but next time let's move to Italy. You can run there. And they have gelato."

But now, roles reversed, I was full of energy and tried to sound excited as he lay in bed looking green. Certainty ruled. The knowledge that we wouldn't be kicked out of our apartment and sent to the airport boosted my spirits. All we had to do now was concentrate on having meaningful experiences. My head exploded as I went through the laundry list of things that I wanted the children to see. The places we needed to take them, as fast as possible. The year was already well underway and all of Southeast Asia was waiting.

"Isn't it great, honey? We're all set. We can stay. Let's *really* do it now. Let's *really* do this Asia thing!"

Ernie looked at me with disgust. And irony. I handed him the trash can just in time.

chapter twenty eight

Our desire to stay in China tugged at us a little deeper now because of something else. Friends. In the days after our arrival, a university colleague of mine introduced us to Nina and Alex, a young couple with three children who lived close to us. Nina was Finnish, and Alex was Australian. Alex worked for a multinational company, and their two boys, Miro and Mishka, sandwiched Will in age, while their daughter Sofia was the same age as Eden. Simply put, they saved us from ourselves. Having lived in China for years, Alex and Nina spoke the language fluently and knew the tricks to surviving in a place that felt nothing like the lands we'd grown up in.

A series of panicked phone conversations marked my early interactions with Nina. A typical call sounded like a juxtaposition between comedy and terror. Sitting perched on my window seat, iPhone pressed to my ear, I'd call Nina after our kids were at school.

"So wait a second, if I go to the market, how do I ask for the chicken that's not blue? And also, I want them to cut the head off. Will they do that?" I laughed as I asked the question, but seriously, the chickens were blue and they creeped me out. Our housekeeper Xiaocui bought nothing but.

"Can't Xiaocui go to the market for you?" Nina asked.

"Well, yes, but she always goes for the blue chickens and also she won't buy mangoes for us, even though I've told her I love them," I responded.

"Let me guess. She says they're a 'hot food' right?" I heard the smile in Nina's voice.

"Totally, Nina. I just want a little mango but she says it's going to give me a rash and a fever."

Nina laughed and I continued with the inquisition.

"What about bug repellant? Where can I buy that? Or should I just bite the bullet and put us on malaria meds for the Laos trip?"

"Don't bother. Just cover yourselves up. Those medicines are toxic."

"Yeah, agreed. Speaking of medical stuff... a pap smear... holy crow... one of the doctors at the international clinic wants me to get my annual pap smear here. I'd rather have hot pokers stuck in my eyes, right?"

"Yes! Don't let anyone put anything near you like forceps! I'm getting some dental work here and it's a total nightmare. Wait until you go home."

"Yeah, the idea of unsanitized forceps going into my crotch makes me queasy. One more question. A sandwich. Ernie's starving. He just needs a sandwich. Where can he get one?"

"French Café. Near the university. Or Lost Garden. Wanna meet there on Sunday? No. That's not a question. You NEED Lost Garden."

Nina brought me back to life after our first few weeks in Kunming. She loved yoga just as I did. Had a wicked sense of humor. In no time, she was my new bestie. Providing advice – and more critical than even advice – laughter. We began to meet regularly at Lost Garden on Sunday mornings. The sunny rooftop café near our home served Western-style breakfasts and Bloody Marys, which we sipped while telling the stories that made up our week. These stories buoyed us, each one being more ridiculously unbelievable than the one told before it. Living in China was both heartbreaking and unbelievable. Akin to an unhealthy relationship that you just cannot escape because it's so addictive that each sip draws you in further. All we could do was give voice to the hilarity that was all of our daily lives here, pushing each other forward.

"Did I tell you about the guy who paid for an entire pile of Chinese movie stars to come entertain at Jake's company party last week?" Alex chuckled as he began to elaborate.

"No wait – let me be clear. Prostitutes. They were totally prostitutes."

The boys were playing in the alley while Eden and Sofia drew pictures and listened to their parents joke about the week's events.

Ernie waited patiently for the story to end before adding, "So listen to THIS one! Yesterday there was a man laying spread-eagle in the middle of our street. And cars were just going around him? I mean, really?"

"Nobody noticed?" asked Nina.

"Sure people noticed, but nobody seemed too concerned," Ernie responded.

"What about the oil spill we saw at the apartment entrance last week that the scooters kept going through," I added, the image still stuck in my brain like slapstick comedy.

"One after another they kept slipping. Like a bad movie. Until one of the guards spent a few minutes and just cleaned it up."

Our brunch was served and the children descended on the tables, ravenous after skateboarding in the alley. Will knew we were likely venting about our week and I nearly spoke the next line before I deferred to him.

"I saw an entire skinned cow hanging out of our neighbor's window yesterday!" His eyes glowed as he recalled the sight. Ooohs and ahhhs fill the tables as the kids carried on where the adults had left off.

"There was a man fixing our pipe last week and he made our bathroom wet," said Eden. I'd forgotten that story, but she was right. A plumber had come to fix a leaky faucet and drilled directly into the wall, causing a pipe to burst. Water flew out of our walls at a ninety-degree angle as Ernie and I had rushed to get towels.

As stories flowed and coffee was consumed, I smiled to myself. *Here we are,* I pondered. *Totally immersed in Chinese life. We live in an exclusively Chinese apartment building. I work for a Chinese university. The kids are in Chinese public schools. We eat mostly like the Chinese. Live in a city with very few Westerners. And it's hard. This is harder than I thought it would be. Positively exhausting, in fact. But we did this willingly. As did our small group of expat friends who have become our lifeline. And when we see them, we don't exactly day dream about our home countries, but almost all our time is spent kvetching about China and her drama. Her remarkable ability to leave all of us speechless every day.*

We left America to get away from endless school functions and drama. Carpools and traffic. Exactly the types of things that people loathe but cannot break away from. But now here we are, complaining about how silly life here is. At the end of the day, it's all about community, isn't it? There's no way we'd be surviving without our friends here. We're short-term visitors in their world, but they've taken us in and pushed us forward. They've been strong when we've been weak.

Still at the restaurant, I picked at my eggs and took another sip of coffee, smiling at Nina, who was helping the girls fold origami. My thoughts of gratitude were overrun by the story Ernie was now telling from just that morning, when an elderly Chinese woman had rung our doorbell.

"So she rings the doorbell and I open the door and she just totally bursts in! She shoved past me and started ransacking the house!"

"What?! Oh Lord, what was she looking for?" Alex shouted.

"It was crazy. She was opening dresser drawers and kitchen cabinets and talking so fast that Jo couldn't understand her."

I chimed in, adding the outlandish conclusion. "Turns out she had been given a package that was for us, and she opened it before she realized it. It was full of socks and English books. She gave it back to the security guard and we got it, but she was just coming over to make sure we had everything. Basically, she was just a form of delivery confirmation. Looking for the socks and books."

"Inexplicable," said Nina.

"Outrageous," added Alex.

"China. Oh my God, we're living in China," sighed Ernie.

chapter twenty nine

We'd begun to integrate a family blessing into our dinners. Giving thanks for the day. Thanks for the meal. And thanks for each other. It provided daily gratitude, but also levity. We ended the blessing with "I love you" repeated three times to each other member of our family while we looked at each one. But because each of us was doing the same, the chances that we would each make eye contact at the "I love you" with everyone else was, well, small. When it happened we let out delighted shrieks, then dove into dinner conversation.

"Xi'an. Seriously, let's try to do this before Christmas."

My tone was urgent, but the plan unclear to Ernie. He had no idea where Xi'an was, or why I needed to get there. I'd failed to connect the dots for him. The Terra Cotta Warriors were waiting for us and Xi'an, their home, was on the itinerary this year. The fact was, I'd scribbled down a list of places that were on my radar screen. The list had begun small and manageable, as if just writing it down would will each trip into existence. Once the travels began, of course, the list grew. I was convinced I couldn't miss Xishuangbanna in southern China, with its jungles and wildlife. The Maldives called to me through in-flight magazines. We found ourselves spoiled, planning one vacation while on an entirely different one. The small piece of paper was now covered with names and places of destinations that stretched beyond the walls of our one-year stay in Southeast Asia. But Xi'an – nonnegotiable.

"Dad, really? The Terra Cotta Warriors."

Will had been in awe of the Warriors for years. Where Ernie was showing his weakness at Chinese geography, Will knew exactly where Xi'an was. I also knew that while the stress of school had lessened, the children needed breaks to look forward to. A visit to Xi'an brought with it the promise of a cozy hotel room and maybe even a swimming pool. Once the picture became clear to Ernie, there was no debate. We booked a trip three weeks out and started the countdown.

In early December, we walked into a Hyatt in Xi'an and exhaled. Just as we'd done in Beijing. And Thailand. And Hong Kong. Surrounded by creature comforts that we'd grown used to living without. Orange juice. A Western-style bathroom. And heat. Our apartment in Kunming was without it because the outside temperature never dropped much below 50 degrees. But when it did, life was brutal. We had one small electric heater, which we often huddled around. Sleeping in layers had become the norm. But here in very chilly Xi'an, there was heat. And more. Much more.

We'd booked a room on the executive level, after learning in Beijing that this often provided an additional level of comfort at a low cost. Often times, it meant a little extra attention. Sometimes it meant a plush lounge on a special wing of the hotel. The staff in the lounges were used to seeing only business people, so they frequently fawned over the children. In our time so far, we'd had box lunches packed for us and dinners ordered up from the restaurants downstairs. Ernie and I had even used the staff as babysitters on a few occasions so we could take a tour of whatever city we were in. Xi'an's lounge delivered at just the right time.

"May we help you, madam?"

Two hotel staff members jumped from their seats at the entrance to the lounge as we stumbled in, tired after a day of travel. Startled by the formality, I asked for a cup of tea.

"And for the children?"

Eden and Will heard the question and weren't sure how to respond.

"What do you have?" Will asked. I could see his wheels turning. The list of foods he'd been denied since August was long.

"What would you like, young man?"

Holy crap, I thought. I could see where this was going, and I wasn't sure how I felt about it. Though we'd been in Asia for four months, I still hadn't let go of all my American food foibles. Children overdosing on sugar was at the top of the list. Eden and Will looked at each other. Wide-eyed. Salivating.

"Hot chocolate!" Eden blurted out before Will had a chance to unload his epic list of wants.

"Me, too!"

"That's two hot chocolates. Anything else?" The children were now surrounded by additional wait staff who'd come to inspect them. I knew that the fact that Eden and Will were Chinese was causing additional curiosity, as it usually did.

"Cookies! I want cookies!" Eden realized her bargaining power as she noticed the growing number of people she could wrap around her little finger. Ernie looked at me, his eyes pleading for me to release the children into a happy, sugar-induced coma. I smiled and remained silent.

"Of course, Miss. Right over there." The staff member pointed to a large, glass bowl filled with more cookies than we'd seen in the past several months. Eden and Will broke into a sprint, racing across the lounge to get to the bowl.

"And for you, sir?" Ernie was last to be served, but his request was no less important than the rest.

"A beer. I'll definitely take a beer."

I smiled at my husband, knowing what was beneath the surface. He was no different than many other men in his love of a good microbrew and a night watching football. His guy friends had slowly gone their separate ways once they'd started getting married, and he'd been one of the first. His life in Denver provided fulfillment, but no longer included the long mountain bike rides, nor the late nights out playing pool with his friends. Not because I'd banished those pieces, but just... because. It happened. He stood here in China as the one who was now responsible for most household management and shepherding the kids to and from school. His engineering work provided comfort, but he worked alone. His life was, in no small matter, radically different than what it had been a few years prior. My husband had been cast into the unlikely role of being my sidekick on this so-far-not-totally-easy undertaking of ours. And he needed a beer.

chapter thirty

The cold of Xi'an wrapped around us the morning of our visit to the Terra Cotta Warriors. The children had been pumped up on sugar, then spent hours in the pool the night before. Sleep deprived, we hauled them out of bed early for a packed day. Our guide took us to several local sights before the drive out of town to the excavation site, which held the Warriors. The massive pits were still considered a working archeological dig site. I couldn't believe we were about to set foot in this place I'd only known through National Geographic articles. But as we approached the sight of one of the wonders of the world, the children both began to lose it. Will's earlier enthusiasm about the Terra Cotta Warriors had faded as he'd been dragged all over Xi'an for hours already.

"Mom, I wanna go back to the hotel."

"Dad, I'm hungry."

We responded as calmly as we could, but the complaints continued to escalate. Our guide gave me a sympathetic look. The kids began playing a game in the van, which Ernie and I hated. Whenever we were out of earshot, we called it by the only appropriate description we could think of: High Stakes Grab Ass. Poking one another out of sheer boredom. Followed by whining.

"Hey guys, let's get a little perspective here. I know it's hard to hang in the car for so long, but isn't this amazing? Right now all your friends back home are probably sitting in math class. And here YOU are, about to experience one of the most remarkable things ever discovered. Holy cow, you guys are so cool!"

"Uh, Mom, it's the middle of the night at home. All our friends are sleeping."

"Buddy, you get my point. Take a moment and just think about your life for a second."

I glanced at Ernie. Today his look said *nice try, but it's not even remotely working, honey.*

He was right. We exited the van and started walking towards the first dig site. Complaints with every step.

"I'm tired."

"I don't like the snacks you brought."

"My feet hurt."

"Eden pushed me."

"I just wanna go swimming."

I honestly think I might lose it. They're tired and their feet hurt but they want to go swimming? What the hell? I'm definitely going to lose it. And then, I did. A final complaint sent me over the edge.

"Mom, can we go back to the hotel and swim? How long is this gonna take?"

"Enough!" I screamed loud enough to get the attention of both children, the tour guide, and Ernie, who promptly took me by the arm and led me a few steps away and out of earshot.

"Pull yourself together, Jo. They're just exhausted from the day."

"I get that, Ernie. But we're at the freaking Terra Cotta Warriors! We only have a couple hours here. I want it to be perfect. I want this to be something they remember. I want this entire YEAR to be something they remember. Fondly. Not like this. This sucks."

"I know, Jo. I want that, too. But they're kids. You've just gotta let go of your expectations."

It's not pretty, I thought. *This entire experience so far. It's been messy and glorious and depressing and exhilarating. All at the same time. Today is no different. My expectations are misplaced. Damn.*

"Okay, okay. Let's just do our best to separate them."

I walked back to the children and lifted Eden onto my shoulders as we entered the first dig site. Her 30-pound frame was no easy weight to carry on my shoulders for long periods, but it got her up and away from her brother.

We moved forward, leaning over the railing to look down into the pits, which held the Warriors. They took our breath away. They sat in peaceful, even lines. Their goal upon being buried had been to protect the king in his death. Each Warrior was life-sized and individually carved, with specific characteristics unlike the one next to him. Our two hours at the pits passed quickly, the children quieting as they marveled in their own, child-like ways. As we left and began to walk back to the van, I asked the guide if he could wait. I wanted one more look. I ran back to one of the excavation sites alone and peered up and over the guardrail. Releasing gratitude for being there, however contentious the day had been.

chapter thirty one

Christmas was approaching, and we had an enormous present in store. Visitors. When we'd first announced our intent to live in China, we'd been overwhelmed with offers of potential visits. So much that it seemed like the time we were alone as a family might actually be in short supply. As life caught up with people, the number of potential visits dwindled until it stood at only one. My cousin, Liz, and her family carried through on their promise to use our time in China as an excuse to visit Asia for a month. They would arrive just before the holidays. Our family traditions would be carried across the sea. We spent every other Christmas at Elkhart with Liz and the rest of my extended family. As in the summers, the merriment continued, though in a wintery form. Family parties every night of the week. Piles of children. When did there get to be so many children in our family? Ice hockey on the frozen lake. And food. So much food. My cousin, Nelli, liked to joke that when you arrived at the lake you just "strap on the feed bag."

The timing of the visit worked well. The children had finally adjusted to school as best they could. Eden reported daily interactions with friends that sounded typical for a preschooler. We could only imagine her Mandarin was progressing bit by bit as none of her friends, nor the teacher, knew a word of English. Will's days still involved angst, but we saw improvement. He and his tutor Helen had developed a sweet relationship. The hours they spent together solidified his Mandarin skills and gave him a buddy.

We had fallen into nice routines, as well. Ernie had taken over the role of house husband seamlessly. He sandwiched his work hours in between taking the kids to school and interacting with Xiaocui with his ever-improving Mandarin. Meanwhile, I had become close to the students I taught at the university. A few in particular had befriended me outside class and I was spending my lunch hour chatting with them instead of eating alone as I'd done in the early months. Slowly, life was coming together.

We walked the streets of Kunming on the weekends, exploring new places and calling out to each other when we spotted particularly adorable old Chinese men and women. Typically this meant someone over the age of 80 with lots of wrinkles who was wearing some traditionally Chinese outfit – a Mao suit for the men or a silk dress with slippers for the women.

"Mom! Adorable old Chinese man alert!"

"Totally! He's about a 9.5 on the cuteness scale, Will. Nice spot!"

Before we welcomed our cousins into this unusual life, there was the matter of a tree. A Christmas tree. This holiday in China was purely about kitsch. Shops became decorated in over-the-top displays of tinsel. Restaurants played screechy Chinese versions of holiday songs. Entire families donned Santa hats, not having any idea what they represented. It was, frankly, pretty hilarious. Christianity and the birth of Jesus were completely meaningless. The time of year meant only an opportunity to pick the most garish of American traditions and embrace them. Our family wasn't terribly religious, but we made a point of explaining the significance of Christmas, and it didn't include the Chinese version.

We bought the hats, the tinsel. But I wanted a tree. In a place where trees of that sort were unavailable. We needed a tree worthy of the ones Liz and I had grown up with. We needed something. Were we in Colorado, we'd be out with Ruby and Philip, cutting down a Charlie Brown tree and making its home in the corner of our living room.

I'd looked in the local paper for things like this before, but inevitably all I'd find were ads for an odd assortment of mish mash. My favorite classified ad so far was posted by someone looking for three things: A dozen earthworms, coconut oil, and an electric saw.

"Mom, when are we getting a tree?"

Eden looked concerned as we fell within a week of Christmas. My heart raced at her next question.

"If we don't have a tree, where will Santa put the presents?"

We'd carted two believers across the ocean. We needed a tree. In times like this, I determined there was only one place to turn. Pinterest. And it delivered. Amidst the pages of elaborate holiday crafts that I'd never be competent enough to make, I saw a tree that looked like a ladder. Each rung was decorated with homemade ornaments. I reasoned we could make the ladder out of bamboo or sugar cane, both of which were overflowing here. I called to the children on a Sunday afternoon just before Liz and her family were due to arrive.

"Guys! Get your coats on. We're going to the market to get our Christmas tree."

Ernie looked at me and asked what I had up my sleeve.

"Not totally sure of this idea, but we're gonna need twine. Can you manage a bit of twine?"

"Twine? For what? Jo, I can't WAIT to see this."

The kids and I hauled to the market, past the corner where children squatted, urinating on the sidewalk through pants that were purposely split. Past the woman who sold the only real French bread in town. Past the school supply store with the endless choices of fancy, colorful ink pens that sucked me in every time.

We landed on a corner with a vendor selling sugar cane. The tall stalks were at least 9 feet. Perfect, I thought. People were lined up to buy smaller chunks of it, which he chopped down with a rusty old machete. The man saw us coming, as did some of the people in the market. Before long, we drew a small crowd. This had become normal for us, and we expected the steps that followed. The people approached, stood within a few feet of us, looked directly at us, and started discussing what they saw. Assuming that we didn't speak Mandarin. Usually I'd just chuckle inside as I listened to their dialogue, but on this day, I shocked all of them when our conversation went down roughly like this, my bumpy Mandarin skills paving the path:

Me: Hello, Sir. I would like to buy that sugar cane from you.
Vendor: Hello, foreign woman. How much would you like?
Me: The whole thing.
Vendor: But this is a large branch. How will you eat it?
Me: We would like to use it as a Christmas tree.
Vendor: A what?
Me: A Christmas tree. It's an American thing.
Will: Mom! This is totally embarrassing. Can we figure out something else?
Eden: Momma, I want the bigger one!
Vendor: Why are those Chinese children speaking English?
Me: They are my children.
Vendor: What?? But they are Chinese. Hey, everybody! Look at this foreign woman with these Chinese children! She says they speak English!

The crowd closed in on us.

Will: Mom, we don't need a tree. Santa can put the presents on the table.

Me: Zip it, buddy. We're getting a darn tree.

Eden: Can we make the biggest tree EVER, Momma?

Vendor: Okay, I will sell you this sugar cane, foreign woman, but it will be expensive.

Me: How much?

Vendor: Thirty yuan (This was the equivalent of about $5).

Me: What! Too much! How about twenty-five yuan?

Vendor: Okay. Deal.

Me: Can you cut a few pieces off so we can make branches?

Vendor: I don't understand, but okay, foreign woman.

Passerby: Hey you, Chinese boy! Do you speak English?

Will: Yes, I'm from China and was adopted as a baby. This is my mother. I speak English and Chinese.

Will rattled off the answers that he could say in his sleep because they'd been asked so much of him.

Passerby: Is that your sister? She is fat.

Will: Yes. She eats a lot.

Vendor: Here you go, foreign woman. How will you carry this home?

Me: I am strong. I can carry it

Vendor: Where is your husband? He should carry it.

Me: He's at home cooking dinner.

Vendor: Hey everybody! The foreign woman says her husband is home cooking dinner!

The crowd burst into laughter.

Will: Mom... I'm soooo embarrassed. Let's get out of here.

Eden: Momma, that is the best tree EVER!

We walked back home and the guards at our apartment building gave us a puzzled side-glance. We now knew them only as the Happy One and the Older One. The Happy One laughed and waved, no doubt cooking up a story about us to tell his family over dinner. The Older One grimaced. I suspected his family was getting slightly less enthusiastic stories around their dinner table.

We entered the apartment as Ernie emerged from the kitchen wearing an apron and holding a handful of twine. He looked at the branches and laughed as he reached out for them, lightening my load.

"They asked you where your husband was, didn't they?"

"Yes, and I replied he was home cooking a lovely chicken dish."

"Ha! I see you two got the tree you were after! Just as nice as any we'd find in Colorado, right?"

The kids grinned as they walked to the living room and began to assemble our makeshift tree. Paper chains were glued together. The outrageously expensive imported candy canes I'd bought from the grocery store tied to each rung.

Christmas could now arrive for our family.

chapter thirty two

The Kunming Changshui International Airport. We'd been in and out of this airport what felt like a hundred times already. This and other Chinese airports seemed predictably futuristic. Lots of glass, soaring ceilings. Loud travelers with all manner of plants, food, and oddities to carry on board. And all of them, it seemed, staring at us. This time we were here to pick up my cousin Liz and her family. Free of their usual travel gear, the children were bouncing off the walls with excitement.

A series of reality checks had marked big events in our year. Standing in the Kunming airport, I had another. The distance between the time Liz and I were teenagers and this moment. How could it be that we were *just* sitting on the pier at Elkhart dangling our feet into the water and talking about boys with the rest of our cousins? How could it be that I'd blinked my eyes and now we'd found ourselves married with four children between us?

Liz had been the first of my cousins to get married, and her husband, Kirk, set the bar for the rest of the incoming husbands. A tall, soft-spoken man, he had intelligence in droves. From Kirk, Ernie had learned the best approach when dealing with Garton women, which was a version of "just step back and enjoy the show."

Liz had a mess of dark, curly hair that hadn't seen a brush in years. Like the rest of the Garton women, she spoke with emotion, her articulation overlaying all conversation. Their two girls, Finlay, 14, and Willa, 12, had picked up similar mannerisms. Both girls were tall and lanky like their father, creative like their mother. Full of spunk and ready for anything, Finlay had studied Mandarin since she was a little girl. Liz liked to joke that she seemed so enthralled with China that perhaps she was Chinese in a former life. This was her first trip to the mainland and we heard her excitement resonating in the pre-departure emails. Eden and Will knew they were in for a treat.

"Which door, Momma? Which door will they come out of?"

Eden was antsy. The promise of our time with the cousins had lifted us out of nearly every down moment since we'd arrived. Our family was abnormally close. The time at the lake in the summers solidified the relationships they had with their second and third cousins, among them Finlay and Willa. In this moment, the relationships were amplified, with the word "cousin" equating to the same in the children's small minds as "a pile of gold." Every second of sadness for the past four months had been laced with the reprise...

Wait till our cousins arrive.

We just have to make it until our cousins arrive.

Our cousins will make everything better.

In fact, Ernie and I had talked offline about the emergency plan as it related to this visit. We reasoned that if we just couldn't cope with life in Asia, we could await this visit, and then join Liz and family on the journey home.

But no REAL emergency had arisen. A visa kerfuffle that had seemed to be an emergency, but was really just a game of chicken with the Chinese authorities. Or the fact that Ernie and I were recycling the same jokes over and over, not even needing to say the punch lines anymore. We weren't thriving, but we were surviving. Laughing more at the absurd things that unfolded each day. Finding small wins. And so here we stood, in the Kunming airport with handmade signs and ready to pounce.

Piles of travelers streamed out the sliding glass doors and into the waiting area. Each one into the arms of waiting friends and family.

Finally, "Mom! There they are! I saw them first!"

Will raced forward and jumped into the arms of Liz, his whole body wrapped around her, feet around waist, arms around neck. I nearly lost it as I watched him in the arms of another trusted adult. People stared unabashedly at us. A bunch of white people and two Chinese children having a love fest in the Kunming airport.

I took in the sight of each one of them, whispering to Liz, "Holy crow, we are soooo glad you guys are here. We've been *dying* for your visit."

We gathered luggage and made our way to the waiting van, which was sufficient for 4 adults and 2 pieces of hand luggage. We were 4 adults, 4 children and 6 suitcases. There was momentary confusion as we all looked at the situation. And then I realized, *Oh yeah, we're in China. This driver TOTALLY has it covered. Just watch.*

And sure enough, we crammed our way into the van, leaving just enough space for the oxygen we'd need to sustain us on the 35-minute drive home.

"So, how's it been?" Liz asked as we raced towards the apartment.

"You have no idea. It's been – intense."

"I've been reading your blog. Is there more?"

"Way more. I couldn't possibly put the REAL story on the blog without one of two things happening: My mother having heart failure. Or being deported."

"Oh my God, let's chat."

"Sounds good. And welcome to China, by the way. It's crazytown, here!"

chapter thirty three

The visit shook us each back into ourselves. An infusion of laughter and love that we'd been craving more than we realized. Our days were filled with family stories and silly kid jokes. Updates on all things Americana. I wanted to know about as much about the health care legislation as what whacky drama was happening with the Kardashians. My true personality resurfaced and I felt reassured that I wasn't the total lunatic that I appeared to be so many days on the streets of Kunming.

We led our pack of eight around vegetable markets, back alley restaurants, and our favorite school supply stores. Wrapping them into the comedy that made up our every day life was the entertainment. Even such simple things as a pile of bed sheets became an adventure.

We needed a dryer. We hung all our clothes and linens on a laundry line to dry, but with a house full of guests needing clean sheets fast, I stared at the washing machine one afternoon – perplexed. Dryers didn't exist here, or if they did, I'd never seen one.

"Hmmmm... " I thought out loud about this prospect.

Finlay tipped her head into the laundry room.

"What about a laundromat? Can they wash and dry the sheets?"

"That's not really how things work here, laundry-wise. But we can try. We can go to the cleaner down the street and maybe they'll have a dryer in the back. Who knows. It'll be fun to see."

For Finlay, an outing of any sort was a chance to practice her

Mandarin. "I'll go! Let's go now!"

We set off, my wheels turning as I tried to remember all the vocabulary I'd need to undertake this request. I was fully aware of my bad grammar, weak accent, and questionable sentence structure. But the dry cleaner was close to home. They knew me and surely they'd understand what I was asking for. We strode up the steps and the woman behind the counter recognized me. Obviously. After general hellos, I spoke.

"Excuse me to bother you, but do you have a machine that will make clothes dry?"

"No."

There it was again. The very distinct, very Chinese way of answering what was, after all, a very simple question.

"But surely you must have one in one of your other stores in Kunming? Maybe?"

"No."

The shopkeeper wasn't getting irritated. Rather, as we'd discovered, the majority of Chinese thoroughly enjoyed their interactions with us. Mostly for comic relief, it seemed.

I turned to Finlay. A goofy smile on my face. I'd learned how to play this game. To make it enjoyable for everyone.

"Fin, this is a lost cause. There's probably not a dryer within fifteen miles of this place. That said, it'll be fun to just sort of chat her up, don'tcha think?"

Finlay's eyes got wide. An interaction in a Chinese dry cleaner was right out of a high school Mandarin textbook. I continued, smiling. The shopkeeper smiling back at me.

"Hold the phone. Is it possible that there's a dryer in a building nearby to where we stand now?"

"No. Not possible." The shopkeeper giggled. Whether at my questions or the way we looked, I wasn't sure.

I could tell Finlay was following the conversation perfectly.

I hoped she'd jump in.

"What about another store somewhere else?" Finlay asked. My heart swelled with pride as she stepped forward to create more conversation. Her Mandarin tones were superior to mine, her sentence structure perfect.

"No. Not at any other store," the shopkeeper replied. One of her co-workers had joined her, delighting in the silly scene.

"What about at a friend's house? Do you have a friend who has a dryer?" The shopkeeper chortled at the presumption. I laughed back. It was becoming a game, and we were all having fun with it.

"Absolutely not!"

"Really?" Finlay acted shocked and I was thrilled. She laughed now, along with the rest of us.

"Not at a friend's house. Hmmmm... tell me this... do you HAVE any friends?" I asked.

It was all in jest, of course. Simply to continue to shine a bright light on the cultural divide between us. No offense meant. Or taken. I had hit the jackpot. The shopkeeper could barely breathe due to her cackling. Finlay, likewise, could barely breathe. This was good.

Laughter came easily in this moment. As it washed over me, I realized that I'd missed it. I missed laughing and smiling and boy, did I need it.

You've just gotta go with it. Someone told us this early on – don't try to understand China or you'll drive yourself crazy. I decided to just go with it, laughter being more valuable than angst.

❦

The day before Christmas. Our two families had walked all over town and were now buried in last-minute preparations for our China Christmas.

"Mom, what's the deal with Santa?" Will was helping to put the final touches on our sugar cane Christmas tree. The question came out of nowhere.

Oh crap, I thought. *I wasn't ready for the Santa conversation. Here. Ever, actually. How old was I when I caught Dad putting the presents under the tree? OMG, I was 10. Will's almost 10! Didn't I learn something about this in our adoption training? That we should never tell lies to our children. It goes against attachment parenting or something like that? What WAS that lesson?*

I tried to act casual in my response. "What do you mean, honey?"

"Well, you know the whole chimney thing. We have a fireplace and chimney at home. How will he get in here? No chimneys."

"I guess he just has his ways, " I responded.

I held my breath and hoped it was enough. When I looked up, Will was staring at me. I looked at him. *Let's please move on.* Two seconds passed. *Crap. Where's Ernie right now? Why is it always ME who gets stuck with these moments?* Then three seconds. He changed the subject. I made a mental note to myself to revisit this topic with Will in a few months. To let him have Santa for one more year.

I had mentioned to Will's teacher that we had family coming into town for Christmas, asking if we could come visit his classroom. The entire request was based on the fact that I, too, wanted to see the classroom. It hadn't been allowed up to this point, but I was dying to get in there and see how one of Will's days really unfolded.

Knowing the visit coincided with Christmas, Teacher Che sprang into action. Christmas continued to look downright silly here in China. I'd heard something about people spraying fake snow from cans in big masses in the city center. What? I didn't get it, but I imagined we'd get a taste of it when the time came. I wasn't sure how the kooky Christmas the Chinese celebrated would translate into our classroom visit, but Teacher Che had a plan.

The eight of us were told we should visit Will's classroom on Christmas Eve. Liz, a children's book author, would read one of her books. Helen and Will had translated it into Mandarin and Will and Finlay would read the Chinese translation. Aside from that, we were clueless. Frankly, as we'd received less than zero communication from the school since Will had started, I expected little to nothing.

On noon of Christmas Eve, the eight of us climbed the hill to the school gates.

"Brace yourself," I commented as we entered.

"From the one visit we had early on, I remember that the decibel level of Will's classroom is unreal," Ernie added.

"Hello! I hope you and your family are well and Merry Christmas!" I piped in Mandarin to the guard sitting at the metal gates.

"How many kids are in the class?" Liz asked.

"Forty-four." Will answered.

"Oh my gosh!" Liz responded.

We turned the corner and approached Will's classroom. I saw flashes of something red and white. What the heck? We entered the cramped classroom and were welcomed with 44 cheering third graders. Each wearing a fuzzy, red and white Santa hat, smiling and clapping their hands. They sucked us into their energy, treating us as if we were movie stars. *Abso-*

lutely freaking adorable, I thought.

Teacher Che led us through the throngs of children to seats in the front row. The room had been arranged with a circle of chairs to create a stage atmosphere. Once Will, Finlay, and Liz had read the book, I assumed we'd depart. But there was more in store. So much more. After their reading, each student was offered the chance to perform a talent. And what a scene it was. Flute-playing. English-poem reading. Dancing. Each talent no doubt practiced for hours at home under the watchful eye of a strict Chinese mother. Performances were followed by a buffet of treats brought in by parents. Preserved eggs. Chocolate. Small cakes. And chicken feet. Will and Willa toughed it out and nibbled while the rest of us sat in awe.

When we left, it took a herculean effort to get us out. Goodbyes and Merry Christmases were repeated ten times over. The students wanted to know what we were doing for Christmas, how long our cousins were staying and where they were from. The kids had grown accustomed to seeing me and Ernie at the school gates, but these new Westerners were exciting. I loved feeling like an old shoe. Answering their questions as best I could, I told them we were going to Lijiang near the Tibetan border, then Cambodia, then India, and then Nepal for the holiday. Christmas would stretch into Chinese New Year, giving us almost six weeks of vacation to play with.

"But those places are so far away. You should stay here!"

Their protests wrapped me in warmth. Never mind that the distance from Kunming to Cambodia was relatively the same as from Chicago to St. Louis. They just wanted to know that Will was returning. According to his reports, he rarely spoke in class, but it was clear that Will was beloved by his classmates.

"Zhi Yong will be back," I reported, using his Chinese name.

"Will you fly on airplanes?" asked Chu Guo, Will's best friend.

"We will."

"Ahhh... " The children seemed stupefied.

We departed. Overloaded with boxes of pastries and chicken feet to take home. The screams of Will's classmates followed us as we made our way back to the school gates. Finlay, Willa, Will, and Eden chattered with amusement about the entire scene. Liz and Kirk smiled as they listened to the recounting. I looked at Ernie.

"Wow."

"Yeah," he replied. "That was awesome."

Maybe this made up for the trip to Xi'an, I thought. Where I expected so much and got less. Maybe there's something inherently positive in expecting nothing. Can I do that? I'm a Type A fruitcake. Oh my lord, I don't think I have a choice. I may be Type A, but I'm living in a communist country. I hereby resolve to empty my cluttered mind of expectations. I'm a black hole. I'm an empty vessel. This feels silly, but more manageable.

"That was more than awesome, honey. THAT is what we came here for."

chapter thirty four

Christmas Day exploded in a mix of Chinese and Western traditions. We sang our favorite family tunes, Skyping with our parents in the States. The sugar cane tree served as a humble reminder of the simplicity of this holiday. Our gifts to each other were small and meaningful. Late on Christmas afternoon, we walked to a meal of hot pot. Traditionally Chinese, it involved each person at the table getting an individual bowl of broth placed over a burner. Into the broth went vegetables, meat, fish... whatever you desired. But the best part of all was the sauce room. An entire room dedicated to every paste, dressing and oil one could dream of. All there to be combined into the perfect dips. Kirk's sauces were the spiciest. Eden's leaned peanut butter-y. Ernie's laden with garlic.

Our tummies full, we walked home through the city center. As we'd heard, it was packed with people of all ages spraying each other with white, canned string. It was designed to resemble snow, I suppose. The result was more like a carnival on crack.

"What the heck is THAT?" Finlay pointed towards a corner of the square where there was a crowd gathered.

It was, as best we could tell, a man on stilts. Stilts that bounced. He wore a clown outfit. And sprayed the white, stringy stuff from cans onto the cheering crowd. We stopped. We stared. Our minds trying to comprehend what we were seeing on Christmas afternoon. There was nothing to do but laugh. Which we did. The hold-your-stomach-doubled-over kind. Right there in the middle of the square.

The day after Christmas we ventured to our favorite Japanese spa in the mountains outside Kunming. Built in a forest on the side of a hill, it was a glorious retreat from the city. Pool after pool of warm, colored water. Each pool had a delicious fragrance. One of roses, one of lavender. Another bright green and minty. Yet another filled with tiny fish, which nibbled on the dead skin lining our feet as they swayed under water.

We then flew north to Lijiang, close to the Tibetan border, for a week of hiking in the Himalayan foothills, exploring small villages and enjoying a visit with an old Chinese medicine man. At every opportunity, I cornered Liz to soak in every bit of parenting wisdom I'd ached for since arriving in Asia. We talked about Will's struggles prior to departure, which were now absent. Or so it seemed. I suspected they lurked below the surface, and we talked about our upcoming visit to his orphanage and how we'd handle its impact on all of us.

Eden had grown more sassy than I remembered her at home in the States. I suspected it was the only way to release her four-year-old stress. Liz and I sat sipping our cocktails in the lobby of our guesthouse one evening, my floodgate of motherhood angst flowing like mad.

"I think the Eden behavior is pretty standard. But I just don't know about Will. It's so hard to tell what's identity stuff and what's just holy-crap-I'm-nine-years-old-and-I'm-living-in-a-foreign-country stuff," I stressed.

"Johanna, I think you're doing great given the circumstances. I'd say trust your gut with both kids. And really, you'll be home before you know it and you'll have all your usual parenting resources again."

We were interrupted by Will, who wandered over to confirm our location.

"Mom, we're up near Tibet, right?"

"Roger that. We are indeed."

"Okay, well I wanna know a lot more about the Dalai Lama. Eden wants to know, too."

Oh, this is going to be good, I thought. I left Liz to nurse her beer and headed back to our room, running through the shaky political innuendos that would color the conversation. I'd already had an awkward discussion with my university students about this exact topic. Alice had told me not to mention "The Three T's" which were Tibet, Taiwan, and Tiananmen Square.

So I chose to discuss just one. One "T" at a time seemed logical.

Tibet was a part of China, they insisted.

Not so much, I'd countered. The Chinese invaded Tibet in the 50's, forcing the Dalai Lama to flee. Tibet had its own culture and language. It was – separate.

The students had glared at me. Some of them were members of the Communist Youth League. I pulled back and returned to verb conjugation.

Back in Lijiang, I flopped on the bed, asking the kids what they'd like to know.

"Basically, Mom, I told Eden what I know. About how the next Dalai Lama is chosen and all that. And she thinks it's her." Will smirked.

"Huh? She thinks what's her?"

"She thinks she's the next Dalai Lama, Mom. So we just kinda want to talk about how this works."

I was nearly bursting inside, hoping that I could bottle this conversation. Eden was now sitting on the bed with a giant grin on her face. This was too good to be true.

"So Momma, how's the next one picked?" she asked.

"Well you know he's chosen by a group of wise people. When he's little. About three to four years old, I think."

"That's how old I am! I'm four."

"Indeed you are, Edie."

"And he has to be Chinese?" she asked.

"Well, I think he needs to live in Tibet, but usually that means he's Tibetan. Not Chinese. Though the next one chosen will probably be Chinese."

"I thought he lived in India. Why does he live in India if he's Tibetan? Why doesn't he live in Tibet? Does he miss his mom?" Eden wondered.

We were getting into shaky political territory. Far above where her four-year-old mind could stretch. I hated to slam China in front of them, but the truth was, I felt strongly that Tibet was a separate country and had been wronged by forcing the Dalai Lama into exile. Thankfully, Eden crashed my need to respond with yet another question.

"And it has to be a boy?"

This was a question I didn't have the answer to. I punted.

"I'm not sure, honey. I suppose it could be a girl."

"Momma... maybe I'M the next Dalai Lama!"

Mamma Mia! My son wants to know why Santa doesn't need chimneys in China, and my daughter thinks she's the next Dalai Lama. What next?

Over the years, I'd so far successfully skirted the fact that neither of our children could ever become President of the United States. Though they were American citizens, they'd been born on Chinese soil and thus, ineligible. If Will gets to keep Santa, I will let Eden keep her dream, too. Just a little longer can't hurt. I sighed, buying a lottery ticket for Eden's dream of becoming the next reincarnation of the Dalai Lama.

The sun rose on January 1. It was a new year. 2013. Departure Day for Liz and family who were on to Laos and Thailand. And us, onward to other travels. Their visit had been healing. The kids had played themselves silly; Willa and Will becoming buddies with a shared sense of humor and a love for sports that played out as they kicked a soccer ball through the cobbled streets of Lijiang. Finlay and Eden had sat together for hours reading.

Liz had given me plenty of girl chat and family gossip. The husbands had talked music and sipped bad beer together. Perfection. We weren't even halfway through our year, but felt on the upswing. They left as they'd arrived. Crammed into a car far too small for the four of them and all their luggage, yet smiling. We lingered over hugs and kisses and told them we'd see them at the lake in a few months.

Will found me later, crying as I made dinner.

"Why are you crying, Mom?"

"Oh, honey, I'm just so happy that we had such a nice visit with them. But it's hard to say goodbye, isn't it?"

"Yes. And it makes me want to go back to America. Sorta."

"I get that, honey. But believe me, we have a lot more adventure ahead of us here. It's not nearly time for us to go home."

chapter thirty five

Our cousins progressed to Laos and we began to pack our bags for six weeks of travel. We'd planned two trips on opposite sides of our home base of Kunming, leaving just enough time to return home to do laundry in between the two. Destination number one was a circuit around Nepal and India. Early in the year, I'd pressed Ernie to offer himself up for a site visit at the New Delhi offices of a company sub-contractor. As our location in Kunming was significantly easier and cheaper to manage than sending someone over from the States, the offer was accepted. As for Nepal, it was just plain amazing as a 24-year-old, and I presumed the magic would remain.

The destinations we'd planned for the next six weeks were not easy to manage with children in tow. Many of our friends thought we were downright crazy for even considering such an itinerary. I patiently listened to the criticism, did my research on the current state of things and carried forward with our plans.

Will joined me in the bedroom as I packed our rolling duffel bags, a task I could practically do in my sleep now. Word searches, Chinese antibiotics, travel guide, US dollars, extra passport photos, a Frisbee.

"It's a lot of traveling in the next month, Mom."

"It is, Will. Think you can handle it?"

"I can, but I'm thinking we should bring something that makes us feel like we're at home."

I wondered what that might be. Flashes of People magazine and frozen yogurt shops ran through my vision. Kentucky Fried

Chicken or McDonald's? Where was he going with this? What did we have here in China that would feel like home as we traveled?

"I'm thinking some chopsticks. Or some calligraphy paper. Or we could just relax. We do that a lot at home."

Smiling, I nodded. Relaxing was definitely not in the cards back in Denver. Nor were regular calligraphy sessions. Or chopsticks. Home was now China.

In preparation for visits to both Nepal and India, Ernie and I introduced crash courses in the week before our departure. We provided the children with the basics. We looked at a map so they'd understand where we were going. Taught them how to say please and thank you in the local language. Discussed what the people might be like, what they'd look like, the language they would speak. How we'd chosen traditionally Nepalese hotels instead of the fancy Western options. The kids beamed as we talked over details each night, the wheels on their tiny rolling suitcases ready to gather more miles.

When we landed in Nepal, I realized immediately that it hadn't been enough. I had focused so much on the cultural aspect of the countries, that I'd overlooked the necessary discussion of poverty. We'd seen a bit of it in rural China, but the Nepalese version ached in its contrast. It was nothing the children had seen before. Or Ernie, for that matter. Our first morning in Kathmandu hit us hard. We sat in a taxi. The street scenes almost too much to bear. Dirt. Noise. Beggars at every corner. Ungroomed children running in packs on what should have been a school day.

"What are those silver things on the side of the road,

Momma?"

"Honey, those are homes. Made of tin. People live inside."

Silence. A group of children raced down a dirt road with tires and sticks, pushing as fast as their skinny legs would take them.

"And what about their toys? Why are those kids playing with tires?"

The kids on the side of the road wore clothes that hung off their thin frames. Sandals many sizes too big were wrapped around their feet. Some of the girls had babies strapped to their backs, and it was unclear if those babies were younger siblings or children of their own. Our taxi slowed and my eyes locked on the kids, immersed in playtime that looked unfamiliar to my own children. It was minus the fancy balls, the walkie-talkies and the large fields of thick, green grass to tumble upon. Yet, the Nepalese children were still happy. They'd never known anything different, and would likely be just as awe-struck if they caught a glimpse of our world.

"Here's the thing, guys. Most people in the world don't have what we have. You know how I always say that there are kids all over the world who go to bed hungry and don't have toys?"

"Yeah."

"Here. This is it, guys. It's here. We're here."

We backtracked the first night in the hotel. We'd be swarmed with beggars, we told them. We agreed that each child could carry a small amount of money to give out as each pleased. Preferable was giving tangible things, food being primary. The children stuffed their pockets with coins and gum, ready for what the days might hold.

Amidst the massive poverty, we found pleasure. Sitting on

a rooftop café overlooking the Boudhanath Stupa, the largest stupa in Nepal. Watching pilgrims circle with prayer wheels while we sipped tea and mango smoothies. The children receiving lessons from us in Hinduism. We talked about compassion, gratitude and how to give to those unable to feed themselves. The lessons were received well, but I noticed as our days in Kathmandu passed, that the children would need to rest on our laps in the back of taxis. It was too much to bear to look outside at the real world. I understood and sympathized, thinking that this time, I may have erred in bringing them here.

One afternoon my desire to teach compassion caught up with me in a big way. We walked the back alleys of Kathmandu. Gorgeous, handmade souvenirs met us at each corner. As usual, we stood out. Not just for the fact that we had children, but because of our racial makeup. As often happened, we were approached by a beggar. But this time, there was a hitch. It was me who was being approached and the beggar was a woman with a baby in her arms. *Oh God*, I thought. *She's playing on my motherly instinct.* I ran through the mental checklist of things we would not provide. Money, alcohol, dollar bills. But then...

"Milk, ma'am. Milk for my baby."

Her voice was weak. But she spoke English and her request was clear. The baby in her arms looked dirty and unkempt. I melted. Looking at Ernie and the children, I felt full with the promise of a real time lesson in all that we'd been lecturing. In Denver, we rode around town with a box of granola bars. I refused to give money to people on the street, but if we saw homeless people with signs, I'd hand a bar to the children and they would roll their windows down and deliver the goods.

"What do you think, guys? She wants milk for her baby."

"Mom! We have to do it. She's not asking for money."

Ernie nodded. "Seems legit."

The woman could tell we were willing and led us to the nearest grocery store. Inside, I paid for a can of milk powder, which the woman took and graciously thanked us. We left, feeling warm with the glow of having given something tangible and needed. Eden and Will talked about the baby and how pleased they were that we had now fed him his next meal.

The shine wore off several hours later, when we were being led through town by a local tour guide. He asked us flat out, "Have you gotten the milk powder scam yet?"

My heart sank. "What do you mean?" I cried.

"Yeah, the women carry these babies and they partner with the grocery store owners. Split the money after the foreigners buy the milk and walk away."

Ernie and I looked at each other and groaned. The children, several steps ahead of us, were safely out of earshot. Their giving glow remained.

chapter thirty six

Coming from Colorado we were accustomed to mountains. But I knew that the Rockies paled in comparison to what we could see just outside of Kathmandu. When Ruby and I had been here, we'd trekked for three weeks, reaching the summit at Annapurna, which touched nearly 18,000 feet. I knew that wasn't in the cards for us this time. Eden's struggles with altitude sickness were enough for us to avoid such heights. Still, I wanted to at least see the Himalayas from a better vantage point than the city. We traveled to the hill town of Nagarkot, hoping to catch a glimpse of Mt. Everest. It would be only a dot on the horizon, but we ventured anyway.

Sheets of rain greeted us as we arrived in the village. Though only at 7,200 feet, Eden began to vomit within hours, signaling our need to consider returning to a lower altitude. We stayed a night, hoping for improvement in her condition, but there was none. The speck of Mount Everest remained hidden by thick rain clouds. As we made plans to leave early, the skies cleared enough for us to see a bit of the mountains and a spectacular, full rainbow gracing the valley below. I took Eden in my arms and we reached out to touch it.

The yin and the yang of our year began to hit me in Nepal. Our daily life in Kunming was simple. A struggle, at times. We were still grasping with the basics, such as what to feed ourselves for dinner each night. How to avoid getting sick at restaurants. Living with a single bicycle as our only means of transportation. But this, I felt, was what we had come for. Simplicity. I wanted to escape the trappings of American life, but also help us all understand how privileged we were to be living in the United States.

Yet now, here in Nepal, the struggle was continuing. We had stayed in typical, concrete Nepalese hotels and walked the poverty-ridden streets. Our meals cost us next to nothing. The poverty stared us in the eyes all day, creating a stress that I hadn't planned on. We were experiencing Nepal. There was no doubt about that. But enjoying it? That was a stretch. Every day provided an intense experience for which I was grateful, but maybe I just wanted us to have a little relief. Ernie and I considered our dilemma as we made plans to return to Kathmandu.

"This is stupid, Ern." I sat with Edie on the bed as Ernie packed our bags. A hot water bottle lay softly on her tummy. Her face still pale from the nausea of being at altitude.

"We're going back to Kathmandu. I get that. There's no reason to suffer up here."

"Agreed. But I don't want to stay at the same place we stayed at a few days ago. I've had it."

"What are you thinking, Jo?"

"We're drawing your American salary and it's costing us, like... $5 a day to live in China. We have the resources. And we need to refuel. The nicest place in Kathmandu, honey. *That's what I'm thinking.* The kids need this. We need this."

My voice conveyed irritation and desperation in equal parts. Ernie could sense it, and he'd done his research behind my back. He told me a driver had been called to take us back down to Kathmandu. And then to my surprise, the hotel name slipped off his tongue in less than two seconds.

"It's the Hyatt Regency, Jo. We're going to the Hyatt. I've already booked it."

Two hours later, the gates of the Hyatt greeted us. The contrast with the world outside those gates couldn't have been more stark. Our room cost us the same as what an average hotel in the U.S. would have cost. But that price got us the nicest room in the hotel, complete with an unlimited breakfast buffet overflowing with made-to-order eggs, trays of sushi and every kind of fruit imaginable.

I felt guilt once again at having caved in to my need to be pampered. And yet pure relief at being able to feed the children, sleep in a comfortable bed and enjoy our vacation. The mix of these two emotions was now a familiar feeling. Walking with me through Asia and our year.

Our last stop in Nepal was Chitwan National Park. Chitwan was south of Kathmandu and populated by wild rhinos, elephants, crocodiles, Asian tigers and birds of every conceivable size and color. We woke in the mornings to elephants trumpeting. Took long rides by canoe and in jeep safaris to spot animals. Will and Eden played in the river that lined the edge of the forest, being careful to avoid the crocodiles. Our lodge was comfortable. Not the Hyatt, but comfortable. A balance, for the moment.

One afternoon our guide took us to the edge of the jungle. We were scheduled to go on a jungle walk, but as we got our gear together, our guide threw in a twist.

"I've heard from another guide that there's a wild elephant in the jungle. A mother. With a baby."

Having been on the receiving end of a charging elephant in Tanzania years prior, I had no intention of repeating the experience, especially with our children. I stopped putting water bottles in my backpack and chuckled, "That's too bad. Another day, then."

"We can still go. We just need to stay at the perimeter of the park."

"I want to go! I want to go! Let's go see the baby elephant!" Will was adamant. Clueless, but adamant.

I looked at Ernie. No words needed. I had no intention of taking a step closer to the jungle than we already were. But he looked me in the eyes, looked at the guide. Then at Will.

"Will you carry a weapon?" Apparently Ernie wanted to appear at least a little bit aware of the danger ahead.

"Of course – this!" The guide held up a stick the size of a golf club. I choked back a laugh. *An elephant could use that thing as a toothpick*, I thought.

"You've gotta be kidding?" I said.

"No. We will be fine, ma'am. I know this jungle and we'll give the mother elephant a lot of space."

Yes, I thought. *And the head of my husband and son. Holy crow! Ernie's totally going to do it!*

"We're doing it, Jo. We'll be fine."

"You're not taking Eden. No way. I'm keeping her here." I clutched her tiny body and pressed it into mine.

The boys walked off into the jungle as I began to count the minutes. When they emerged an hour later, my heartbeat returned to normal.

"No biggie, Mommy," Will laughed.

Ernie shrugged. "We were totally fine."

"Totes. We were fine, Mom."

"Happy to hear that, boys. I guess it's my turn for a little excitement."

"Johanna!" I could hear Ernie yelling something to me as I sat atop an elephant.

Our last afternoon had brought us to the river spot where elephants bathed. And tourists climbed aboard for rides. My elephant ran her trunk through the river and splashed herself. The sprays hit me in the face. Water ran down my body, soaking my clothes. Overwhelmed, I released shouts of glee and laughter. I was having the time of my life, but Ernie looked concerned. Finally, I heard him.

"Johanna, for the love of God, close your mouth!" Ernie's pleas caught up with me on the final minutes of my ride.

What an over reactor, I thought.

"You're nuts, Ern. What's the big deal?" I inquired as I dismounted, feeding my elephant a handful of mini bananas.

"Jo... this river is filled with all sorts of stuff. I don't want you getting sick."

My sweet husband, rarely wrong in such matters, proved himself again. He had hiked with our son in a jungle occupied by a wild elephant mother and her baby. And been fine. Me? I was a hot mess of diarrhea. His words of warning, and a wicked case of giardia, followed us to India the next day.

chapter thirty seven

Slowly, I was learning my lessons. Third world countries deserved my respect. Stay at the Hyatt and safely enjoy the banana smoothies. Opt for the elephant ride in a dirty river and pay the price. If you want to go to native, be prepared to not really feel like you're on "vacation." If you want to go plush, be prepared to feel guilty for not being more native.

We landed in New Delhi.

"Cows! Dad! Look at all the cows just hanging out on the side of the road!" Will couldn't believe what he was seeing as we drove from the airport to the hotel.

As we drove through the city, the poverty was less apparent than the cows. At least to the children. Shack after shack lined the roads, but it was the cows roaming free which appealed the most. Sacred to Hindus, they sat in the middle of roads. Walked through construction sites. Led their calves to the middle of roundabouts where they lay in the hot sun.

Oblivious to it all, my stomach preoccupied me. It was making noises I'd never heard. Ernie had been right about the Nepalese river water and now gave a sympathetic look in my direction. My misfortune was both poorly timed and perfectly timed. We were here in Delhi so that Ernie could attend a series of meetings with his company's offshore subcontractor. The kids and I tagged along and we all planned to enjoy the bliss of another five-star hotel.

We checked into the hotel, a fancy suite awaiting us. As soon as the hotel staff heard about my illness, they sent a doctor to our room. He took blood work and prescribed me antibiotics based on my description of the past 24 hours. The river water, the elephant, the open mouth, the noises from my stomach, and the emptying of its contents ever since.

"Yes, well, those people in Nepal are dirty," he commented. I noted the irony, as we had just come through slum after slum on our way to this over-the-top hotel.

"I'll have the hotel staff bring you a lime tonic." The doctor seemed eager to please, but all of it seemed unneeded. I could take care of myself. I began to tell him so, but stopped myself and simply thanked him. *You're so ungrateful. And furthermore, you'd probably offend him by refusing an offer to help. Stop fighting and just enjoy the simple pleasures, Johanna,* I told myself.

My illness prevented me from going to the Taj Mahal with the boys the next day. Eden and I stayed back, resting, brushing each other's hair, and swimming at the pool while the boys took in the sights of yet another wonder of the world.

Recovery came quickly once the drugs hit my system. Within 24 hours, I was gorging myself on fresh naan, curry, and chocolate cake. The children and I had been assigned a private driver to stay with us while Ernie worked. He took us to Akshardam, an unbelievable Hindu temple made entirely of white marble. We walked, shoeless, out of a sign of respect, touching the statues of elephants that lined the grounds.

By the time we left two days later, we'd become addicted to naan and infatuated with cows. India had left her mark.

chapter thirty eight

Cambodia. More than any other destination we'd planned to visit during our time in Asia, this one called to me. I'd been there in the early 90's with Ruby. Magical. I remembered the flight to Siem Reap in the north of the country. Looking out the airplane window, we'd seen pockmarked countryside. *What in the hell are those little, dry lakes?* I'd mused. Until it hit me. Land mines. Bomb craters left from shelling campaigns waged during the Vietnam War, which at that time was still recent history. I walked in the Killing Fields. Looking down at one point to realize that Ruby and I were walking on still-exposed bones, teeth and bits of clothing. I wept. Felt sick. Wept some more.

Ruby and I had clung to the backs of our guides and entered the fabled ruins at Angkor on motorcycles. Stopping to wait until the United Nations minesweepers had done their morning rounds. Once inside, the beauty of the temples transfixed me.

The main temple at Angkor Wat had been constructed in the 12th century as a dedication to Vishnu. Built primarily of sandstone, the walls were covered with intricate carvings depicting stories from Hindu mythology. Aside from this main temple, the ruins, buried in jungles, covered 75 square miles. For better or worse, the ruins were mostly free for us to touch, crawl on and experience to the fullest. Once we knew we'd be spitting distance from Cambodia, I vowed to take my family.

We returned to Kunming for a few days to prepare for this second trip. As with India and Nepal, I launched our pre-departure shtick. I talked about the Vietnam War. About what it would be like to see amputees, their numbers plentiful here because of the number of landmines that continued to dot the landscape. I talked about genocide in terms that were barely understandable to our four-year-old and nine-year-old. Ernie hung on the sidelines for most of these conversations. A little digging revealed a side of him that I'd always wondered about. And didn't necessarily like.

"What's the dealio with you, honey? Why aren't you more, I don't know, participatory in these discussions?"

"I know it's important to you to fill the kids in a bit, but it just feels too heavy."

"Too heavy? We're not exactly taking them to Key West here."

"I get that. But genocide? Johanna, honestly, they're too young for that."

"I disagree. I think if we frame these things in the right way, they can handle more than we think they can."

I could have left it there, but he'd cracked the door on a long-standing issue, and I pounced on it.

"Personally, I think YOU'RE the one who can't handle it, Ern. You've never liked to hear me talk about my human rights work."

"Jo, that's totally unfair."

"It's not unfair. It's the truth. Every time I talk about something really tough, you can't handle it. You change the subject. All the work I did with torture survivors. The asylum cases I've worked on. You've always seemed detached from that part of my life and I don't get it."

"I don't know what to tell you, Jo. You might be right that I can't deal with hard stuff, but I never intended to seem so detached. You know I feel the same way about going to visit Eden's foster mother. It seems too upsetting."

"I know you feel that way, and I think it's selfish. There. I said it. It's selfish. I know you can't stomach the idea that Eden and Will had lives before us, but get over it. It's tough, but buck up, buddy."

"You realize it's only because I love them so much, right? I don't want them getting hurt all over. Will at the orphanage or Eden with our visit to her foster mother."

"I get that, Ern. I do. And I can tone down the talk about genocide and death a little bit. But I want you to put aside some of your hangups and see if you can just show up a little more for some of these hard things."

"And I want you to treat our trips as vacations and not lessons out of a social studies book. Believe me, the kids are getting plenty of that by just being here. By just living."

Ernie displayed a look of exasperation. I quickly searched my mind seeking a solution, but the areas of potential compromise felt remote. Our marriage, one which had always been relatively smooth, felt as if it was falling into unknown territory. I knew from experience that sometimes the best course of action was to let these moments pass without trying to fix them. As difficult as it seemed in that instant, the alternative would have been both uncomfortable and unwelcome. We tabled the discussion. Never to be revisited.

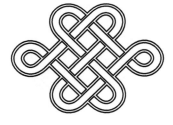

chapter thirty nine

The grin on my face stretched my cheeks as we landed in Phnom Pehn, Cambodia. I wanted my family to be as captivated by Cambodia as I had been. So it was with relief that my hopes were realized. Our first days in the country were spent in the capital, devouring delicious meals of fresh fish and French-infused cuisine, swimming in the small pool at our quaint, European hotel, the children befriending other expat kids and speaking English, glorious English.

We moved onward to Siem Reap, arriving late in the day. In time to catch sunset at the temples of Angkor Wat. We were met at our hotel by a tour guide, a man in his 40's who held many of the same characteristics that drew me to the other Cambodians I had met over the years. A spirit of steel. A brilliant sense of humor. And a mountain of stories he seemed open to telling.

Without expecting the brutality of his stories, I inquired about the impact of the United States bombing campaigns of the late 60's. Though I meant it as a general inquiry, he launched into a personal tale of his own family, many members who had been killed by the Khmer Rouge. As we drove, he told us about how he and his sisters had been spared because his father had talent as a cook.

"The Khmer Rouge planned to take us away, but my father told them he would prepare their meals."

The children knew from our pre-departure conversation that the Khmer Rouge were... the bad guys. Will looked over as our guide spoke, recounting how his father would cook all day for the enemy and then return at night to their family. Exhausted and morally challenged.

"Finally one day he couldn't do it anymore. He escaped from the Khmer Rouge by running into the jungle. He hid there for a long, long time. Until it was safe and he could find us."

I had about a billion follow up questions begging to be asked, as did Will, whose expression showed confusion at taking in the story. Looking at Ernie, I hesitated, recalling our conversation from the previous week. A discussion of the architectural significance of Angkor Wat seemed more appropriate right now. I took a breath and told myself I could always seek out the end of the story away from little ears. Another time.

Our driver let us out at the main gates. My heart raced as I looked at the spires of Angkor, set back from the road by a long bridge. Surrounded by smaller temples, each still able to be walked upon, touched, and explored. Throngs of tourists now speckled the acres stretching around the maze of temples. It was a sharp contrast to twenty years prior, when Ruby and I had traveled practically alone in these same footsteps.

We crossed the road and the children stared at the sight in front of them, but didn't move. The vision of something built so long ago and not in a museum sinking in slowly.

"Guys, this is Angkor. This is the place Mom has been talking about for so many years. Do you see it? Do you see how beautiful it is?" I nudged them forward, one hand on each back.

The children were silent for a moment, looking at the temples as if they were just postcard pictures. I looked at

Ernie and he smiled,

"Spectacular, Jo. It's spectacular."

Will and Eden shifted and took a few steps forward.

"It's okay, guys. This is a place where you can run. Explore. Go ahead."

They began to walk towards one of the outlying temples. The only children for miles, they could tell this was different than the museums we had hauled them to in other Asian cities. Or the pagodas in China where we had instructed them to be silent. Here was a place outside. A play park. Built for exploration. Freedom. Their walk towards the temples turned faster. Ernie and I lengthened our strides. The children began to run. They skipped, their feet barely touching the ground. I hadn't seen them run like that in months. Far ahead of us, I heard them squealing as they reached the first temple, climbing upwards on the stone steps surrounding the structure. In and out of the porticos. Peeking around corners and playing hide and seek. Laughing.

"Ernie! Look at them. Look how happy they are." My voice cracked as we walked towards the children and their cries of joy.

"Mommy! Mommy! This is the best place we've ever been! This is the best place you've ever taken us!" Eden was on her hands and knees, her face smashed against a 3,000-year-old seated Buddha.

"Can we stay? How long can we stay?" Will had found a small pond and was looking for frogs.

We stayed. A long time. Watched the sun set. Ernie falling just as hard for the place as I had so long ago. I felt waves of gratitude wash over me. The children had never been to Disney World and may never be. But, we had given them Cambodia. Which, over the next few days, turned out to be an elixir for all of us. Pushing us forward into the light.

chapter forty

Returning from our Chinese New Year travels felt freeing. We'd reached the halfway mark of our year and had our footing. The steady decline in weight we all saw in China had been put back on through our travels, and we had new plans to prevent ourselves from losing again. The eight-dollar bag of imported tortilla chips from the fancy grocery store that had seemed so unnecessary became... necessary. We hired my friend from the Slice of Heaven cafe to teach our housekeeper Xiaocui how to cook a few Western meals. I relented on the constant requests to go to McDonald's.

The children grumbled a bit about their return to classes. But nothing like the tornado we'd faced in the early months. They had both made friends and came home daily with stories about the antics in the classroom. Will's best friend Chu Guo played an important role in his days. The two of them played basketball while chatting about regular boy stuff.

I loved taking Will to school and picking him up. I bounced alongside him and waved to his classmates, speaking to them in my imperfect Mandarin and embarrassing my son to no end.

"*Nǐhǎo! Zǎo shàng hǎo?*" (Good morning, how are you?) I asked.

The cultural divide between the Chinese moms and me was glaring. I smiled, wrapping Will in a hug at the school gates. Stealing a kiss if I could. They wore scowls, straightened their children's neckties and provided only a gentle push into the school grounds.

Eden's school drops and pickups bore no resemblance to those of her brother. For Eden, the school day was full of hugs in the beginning, middle, and end. She received plenty of play-time and a two-hour nap. Her friends didn't seem to notice that she lacked the language skills to grasp what they were saying. They carried on speaking to her in rapid Mandarin months after it was obvious she wasn't understanding much. Their eyes locked on her, they'd relay the details of a game or joke. I would look at Eden, whisper a translation and let her shake or nod her head in response. Slowly my role disappeared and Eden began more independent play with her friends.

Both children astounded us. Doing things that we weren't even remotely asked to do at their age. We told them so often. The refrain in our home slowly became a version of, "If you can do THIS, you can do anything. Anything you want."

I'd taken on the task of homeschooling them in English. The outcome taught me swiftly that I wasn't cut out for the job on a long-term basis. My time was better spent on my college students. Teaching was providing both highs and lows every week. The bus that I rode from the center of Kunming out to campus was packed with other professors. They'd chosen an honored profession, which was evident in the salutes from the university military police that greeted our bus at the main gates of campus. My students were motivated, attentive, diligent and full of energy. In short, they had many of the qualities that were lacking in their American counterparts. For years, I had dealt with excuses ranging from computer problems to I-just-found-out-my-roommate-is-a-meth-dealer to my-dog-has-fleas to general overwhelm. Directions were routinely ignored and it wasn't uncommon for students to plagiarize entire papers. I frequently had students protesting their grades. While I was a strict grader, I considered myself fair. Over many years of teaching American graduate students, I'd become increasingly frustrated with the quality of student that I was teaching.

"Why do these students think it is okay to complete master's level work without knowing how to properly cite sources?" I roared many evenings from my home office in Denver. But here in China, the motivation to learn English was high, and I would often enter the classroom to a room full of students seated, 30 minutes early and practicing their English. In hushed voices, they'd repeat poetry or paragraphs from novels. Whispering in an almost monk-like chant I would never be able to understand, this practice was clearly something that they were comfortable with. Memorization was the center of China education. It didn't encourage creativity. Yet it leveled the playing field, some thought. All Chinese students, from primary school age, worked from a standard, national curriculum. The goal was to provide the same education to all children, churn out the best of those students at the end of the line, their senior year in high school, and send them to the top universities in the country. What constituted "best" in China was not nearly the same as what our Western standards would judge it to be.

Among my students, I had expected many to approach me and want to spend outside time learning from me. Yet, this didn't happen at first. Even more bizarre, none of the other Chinese professors were approaching me since my arrival. In fact, they seemed to avoid me all together.

Finally one day I asked a colleague I was close to, "What's the reason that none of the other professors speak to me?"

"Well, it's most likely that they're worried about their English accents," she replied.

I couldn't believe it. "But isn't this even more reason to chat with me? For practice, you know?"

"No, it doesn't work like that. They are more concerned

about losing face if they pronounce something wrong or do not know the correct word."

"Well that is so... so... " I struggled to find the right way to describe my sadness, my frustration. "That's just so Chinese," I finally blurted.

My colleague laughed the same laugh that I was now familiar with. After many months I had come to accept the way that the Chinese viewed us. Our family was an oddity, not conforming to anything that made sense to the Chinese mind. And when we tried to push a point or get further explanation, I was often greeted with just such a chuckle. I'd learned that unless I wanted to drive myself batty, it was best to laugh in turn, and move forward. There was no point in becoming frustrated about such matters, as it would only lead to days of running a hamster wheel. Trying to understand the rationale behind so many things we saw each day was fruitless, and my time was better spent appreciating my surroundings for what they were.

After several months of lonely lunches, a brave student approached one day asking if he could have lunch with me. His English was excellent, and he said his English name was "Dang."

"Dang?" I asked.

"Yes, you know... like dammit. Someone tells me it's a bad word?"

"Yeah, kinda, but we can work on a new name if you'd like," I replied.

What was it with the odd names? In my classes so far I had three students named Cherry, two named Christmas and one Train. I also had a Sunshine, a Mint, and an Echo.

Dang and I began to have lunch together a couple days each

week when I was on campus. Laughing about the differences between American and Chinese culture. I told him things I loved and things I found perplexing about China. His enthusiasm for learning about Western culture differed from anything I'd experienced. He had a sense of humor similar to mine. I spoke Mandarin to him, and he spoke English to me. Slowly, this 19-year-old boy from Inner Mongolia worked his way into my heart.

"But Dang, ping-pong, isn't a REAL sport, is it?"

"Of course it is. The Chinese are very good at it."

"I got that part, but you don't even, you know, break a sweat!"

"Break a sweat?"

"That means get hot. You don't even get hot. It's not real exercise, is it?"

"It's in the Olympics, isn't it?"

"That's true, but so are other funny things like race walking and trampoline."

"The Chinese are also very good at trampoline, Johanna."

Though I loved the uniqueness of his English name, Dang had plans to spend a semester in Hong Kong. Suspecting that his name would eventually cause problems, we began brainstorming on new ones.

"How about Walt?" I suggested.

"Like Walt Disney?" he inquired.

"Right. Exactly. It's short. Strong."

"I'll try it!"

Weeks passed before I got the report on the name.

"It's going okay, but when I pronounce it, it sort of sounds like I'm saying the word 'what' to other people."

"I can see that happening. Does it become clear pretty quickly?"

"Not really. I say Walt and then they repeat the question. 'What's your name?' and then I repeat my name but they think

I've got bad hearing." I pictured the old Abbott and Costello routine, "Who's on First?"

Walt kept his name as well as our lunch dates. Our conversations covered ground from the One Child Policy, same sex marriage, China's relationship with Japan to the National College Entrance Exam. This became a framework for the contrasts we were experiencing in Western and Eastern culture. Contrasts that spanned from what we ate to how we perceived politics. We disagreed on whether Taiwan was part of China. I told him that childhood was for playing, while he thought it was for studying. Laughing, he explained to me that he thought it amusing that Americans had different hair and eye colors. I'd use this outlandish concept as a running joke whenever he'd try to describe particular students in my classes.

"Which one do you think will be most successful?" I asked.

"Cherry. Definitely Cherry."

"I don't think I know her. How tall is she?" I inquired.

"Hmmmm... your height," he said.

"Hmmm, what color hair does she have?" I asked.

Walt stopped for a second, started to answer and then giggled. The answer being perfectly clear. And perfectly black.

chapter forty one

The list of Asian travel destinations on our refrigerator began to shrink. With each successive trip, I'd strike out one of the expeditions we'd planned for and conquered. As if each were a simple carton of eggs or gallon of orange juice, the items typically contained on the list that hung on our fridge in Denver.

Even though we were on the back end of our year, I'd added Myanmar to the list after seeing that President Obama was visiting. The images of the president's trip flickered on the iPad which streamed CNN in the kitchen as we cleaned up from dinner one night.

"Check it out, Ern! Obama is in Myanmar! I didn't even know that it was open to tourists. At least not easily. We should go. It's supposed to be spectacular... undeveloped, beautiful, peaceful."

Ernie rinsed a plate, handing it to me to dry and put away.

"Jo, you're crazy. We've already got multiple trips planned... to Will's orphanage, Thailand, Vietnam, Laos and Eden's foster family, in like, the next two months. You're whacked if you think the kids could handle another."

"I know, but it's only a two-hour flight. That's like going from Denver to Chicago. How can we pass it up?"

"If you're dying to go, feel free. Just don't expect the kids and me to tag along on this one. We're totally tapped out on airports and travel."

Here we were. The point at which our need for family routine collided with my desire to see as much of Asia as could be seen in our remaining months. Could I go alone? That felt selfish and extravagant. And also not totally safe. Myanmar was still in the midst of civil unrest in parts of the country. It had recently undergone a series of political reforms, and seemed to be on the path to democracy, but the atmosphere in much of the country was still shaky. I'd have to at least enlist a travel partner.

I finished the dishes, wandered into the living room and crashed on the couch. I picked up my phone, dialed Nina's number and sprang my plan on her.

"Burma? You're such a gypsy! What does Ernie say?"

Nina's reaction convinced me that her answer would be "no," but I wanted her to hear me out. I sank into the couch, a tattered, oversized monster. Its pillows were looking worn from the number of times the children had built "couch caves" so far this year.

"Well, it's technically 'Myanmar' again now. And as far as what Ernie thinks, are you kidding? He thinks I'm batshit crazy!"

"So do I. You want to go to Burma for, what did you say, a long WEEKEND!?"

"Well you know... I've gotta teach and all that jazz."

"Right. That regular life stuff. I love the way you operate, Johanna. Count me out for this one, but what about Helen?"

Will's tutor Helen was the perfect suggestion. Very few Chinese young people were as willing to travel as she was. We'd gotten to know Helen well, as she'd continued to tutor Will five afternoons a week. I soldiered on, successfully recruiting Helen to come with me. Her sense of adventure would be ideal for Burma. I guessed she'd be an easy-going travel partner and game for the overloaded agenda I'd already crafted.

Ernie and the kids were more than happy to take a pass on the Burma trip. They planned a weekend full of the sorts of things that I would veto. Multiple trips to McDonald's, a visit to a local arcade, late night movies. As the weekend approached, they seemed as excited about their days minus Mom as I was about having a few days of space to travel on my own.

Myanmar was unlike any place I'd been in Asia. The city of Yangon was clean and orderly, with heat that caused people to move slowly and dress in long, flowing skirts, including the men, who wore traditional sheets of fabric called longyi. As we drove into town, we passed a flat, monstrous new building that had a sign out front: Embassy of the United States of America. I'd heard about the embassy, a multi-million dollar complex that had been moved from one part of town to these outskirts, a safer location. It was located across the road from the University of Yangon where President Obama had spoken with human rights activist Aung San Suu Kyi.

As with so many other places we'd visited in Southeast Asia this year, the rate of change in Myanmar was breathtaking. Our taxi driver on the ride from the airport commented that we'd landed the same day as Eric Schmidt, the chairman of Google. He was in town to talk technology, tapping into a country still in its infancy in this department. The driver told us that Google would itself be introduced to the country that day, another step towards democracy.

We settled into our hotel, changing clothes as we prepared for a visit to Shwedagon Pagoda, the country's most sacred Buddhist pagoda. I pulled out my phone and got on the hotel Wi-Fi.

"An error message, Helen," I said.

"What do you mean?" she asked.

"I just searched for Google and all I'm getting are error messages."

"Give it a few hours. Perhaps it hasn't launched yet."

The afternoon sun was setting as we arrived at Shwedagon. It was covered in 60 tons of gold leaf, making it stunningly visible from all parts of the city. The monument was said to contain eight hairs of Buddha and attracted hundreds of pilgrims and monks daily because of this. Many of the monks in and around the pagoda were of the kid version. Young boys in training to become monks at local monasteries. I dubbed them "mini monks" and fell in love with their adorable shaved heads and saffron robes. Though only children, the mini monks seemed mature, their emotions in check as I smiled at them and tried to make them laugh with my silly waves.

Helen and I wandered the grounds of the pagoda slowly, keeping pace with the monks who were doing the same. We fell across a small corner with a shrine dedicated to the Burmese zodiac animals. Statues of animals dedicated to each day of the week lined a wall. We'd been told to bring flowers to place at our own symbolic animal, determined by the day on which we'd been born. A quick look at a reference book at the shrine helped us identify that Helen had been born on a Monday and that she was a tiger. I was born on a Friday.

"So what am I, Helen?" I asked as she flipped through the pages of the book to find the answer.

"Oh dear," she said.

"Lay it on me. What am I? A dragon? A lion?"

"I don't think you're going to like it, Johanna. It says you're a guinea pig."

"My spirit animal is a guinea pig? I love it. That's perfect."

We shared a chuckle and finished our tour of the pagoda,

climbing back into a taxi as the sun set. My desire to be tied to some animal other than a caged rodent overtook me, and as we clicked back onto Wi-Fi at the hotel, I tried again to pull up Google to do a bit more research on the subject.

In the six hours since I'd last checked, technology had invaded yet another small Asian country. The website loaded, the familiar flashy logo and search bar filling the screen of my iPhone. Google had officially been launched in Burma.

An early morning flight greeted us the next day. Though we'd just landed in Yangon 24 hours prior, our desire to see Inle Lake in the north of the country required a short, additional flight. The departure lounge at the domestic airport showed its age. Hundreds of people crammed into an area with one bathroom and not enough seating. No actual signs were provided to give travelers any indication whether their flight was on time, or even which gate it was leaving from. Given that neither Helen nor I spoke Burmese, we were left on edge for several hours, patiently waiting until a man with a cardboard sign bearing our flight number began screaming for passengers to board. He collected our hand written tickets, giving barely a glance, and off we went.

Our flight to Inle was short, though as our plane descended, it seemed a little too short. We landed, and I gazed out the window, the terminal laying just ahead. As we drew closer, I gasped. The words on the terminal wall read "Mandalay Airport."

"Helen! Oh my God! I think we got on the wrong plane! We're in Mandalay!"

I looked around and saw passengers getting off the plane.

"But, but... that cardboard sign had our flight number on it!"

Helen said.

"God, Why did we trust a cardboard sign? We're a bunch of dummies. For God's sake, I'm a guinea pig, Helen! I'm such guinea pig material."

Rows of passengers began to unload while Helen and I tried to get the attention of a flight attendant. I managed to communicate my question, with a version of, "What the hell are we doing in Mandalay when we thought we were going to Heho?"

The flight attendant answered in broken English, with a version of, "You silly American. You ARE going to Heho, but we stopped in Mandalay to drop off other passengers."

Oh, I see, duh...it wasn't a nonstop flight. Relief blanketed us, and we settled back into our seats. The plane was nearly emptied, the only passengers remaining being me, Helen, and five monks. In no time we were back in the air for the short flight to Inle Lake in Northern Myanmar.

The part of Myanmar that Helen and I had entered was in civil conflict. Free elections had taken place in the country in 2012, but there continued to be small clashes with government troops. Riots had killed 30 people in the days before we arrived, rendering a state of emergency in a town three hours away. A quick check with our guide and the State Department website revealed nothing for us to worry about, but we were on high alert, and made sure to check with our guide about the latest developments. I crossed my fingers that my mother hadn't read the New York Times that day – an unlikely wish. Sure enough, the news about the unrest had topped NPR for a few cycles and made its way to her, requiring a few quick emails back and forth to serve as reassurance that Helen and I were far from danger.

Inle Lake spanned miles and miles. An enormous, freshwater lake, it was covered with small villages on stilts, floating gardens and men rowing fishing boats while standing with one leg attached to a paddle. The sight took time to adjust to, the mechanics of paddling this way incomprehensible. We traveled by motorized longboats complete with cozy chairs and blankets. The boats were made of wood, twenty feet long, and low to the water, almost like stretched-out canoes. The ride on our first day was over an hour, our destination being a trailhead leading into a bamboo forest. We hiked to a field with over 500 small pagodas, each in a different state of collapse. Accompanied by our guide, Helen and I were the only ones wandering in this place that was as historically worthy as any I'd been to in the world. The structures had been built in the 16th century and were covered with intricate Buddhist etchings.

The people of Myanmar were genuinely excited to see tourists, a refreshing change from some of the other places we'd visited in Asia. In addition, the people had a collective sense of humor that I hadn't seen in other parts of the world. In a way, the place reminded me of Cambodia, another country where the sense of humor seemed relative to the magnitude of tragedy the country had survived. Our guide for the time in Inle was a man in his 40's who talked passionately about the survival of his country and about "The Lady." Aung San Suu Kyi held that term of endearment, as well as a special place in the hearts of the Burmese. Her many years of house arrest cemented her status as the country's leader, despite her simple position now as a member of parliament.

The longboat rides over two days soothed me. This was the first time in months that I'd been away from the children for more than a few hours. Without the call of little voices, I fell into a natural pattern of awareness and reflection. Beauty surrounded us in way that was more simplistic than anything I'd seen all year long. It was March, and I'd spent the past eight months since our arrival trying to force us into a place of gratitude. The truth was, we were all finding our own ways there this year.

Each relationship within our family had grown. Each had gone through stages that were messy. Our marriage, once the most unquestionably solid fixture in our home, had been tested. Will struggled, as he continued to describe China as a place that felt both comforting and foreign. In a few weeks, we were scheduled to visit his orphanage, an event that would mark a pivotal moment in his life. In May, Eden would meet her 75-year-old foster mother for the first time since she'd been adopted. The uncertainty and excitement of both visits kept me up many nights.

I hoped to tie everything beautifully together with a prover-bial red ribbon, but it sat in my mind, out of reach. I'd brought us here to Asia to grow closer. To learn about the world. To develop a deeper passion for life. I'd chosen this unlikely and very diffi-cult path on purpose, but the reality was, those goals could just as easily be achieved in undertaking a different path – through studying music, practicing a life of spirituality, caring for a loved one. Our journeys would continue wherever we ended up back in America. We'd find our own ways to be fulfilled, without the need for struggle to accompany us at every moment as it had this year.

We'd make it, I told myself. The lessons learned wouldn't be apparent right away, and they wouldn't be packaged with a red ribbon. It was an awakening. Slow yet steady.

chapter forty two

"We're here," chirped Susan.

The van pulled around a corner and I gasped. "I remember the street, Ernie! This is it. I see the building." I grabbed for Will's hand. His eyes were cast upon the large white structure that was once home. And he was smiling.

The gates of the Kunming Social Welfare Institute lay before us. Its tall, white walls crumbled as its base met the sidewalk. Our van rolled inside. My heart was pounding as I scanned the grounds, looking for anything familiar. I'd been here before, alone, a couple days after we'd received Will. We'd been told not to bring him back just after we received him because it might cause undue trauma if he thought he was being returned. I joined several other parents in a visit without our new babies. Nine years later, that visit felt as if it were just a few days prior.

Will was wide-eyed, looking around at the series of buildings that crowded into one another. Usually full of questions, today he was utterly silent. Once parked, we got out of the van, were led into an office and introduced to the Director of Foreign Adoptions, Miss Zhao. I spoke Chinese, hoping that efforts to communicate that way might soften my approaching inquiries. Miss Zhao didn't appear to recognize Will, but that was understandable as nine years had passed.

Susan sat us down on a couch and I slipped my iPhone onto the table, hitting the record button in the audio app while nobody was looking. I knew full well that if discovered, our visit would end immediately. But I took my chances, hoping the risk would be worth the value in having our visit documented for Will.

Another member of the orphanage staff came in with cups of warm water and a bowl of hard candy. She placed it in front of Will who took one, unwrapped it and popped it into his mouth.

I looked at Susan, who indicated that I should start in with my list of questions. But I turned to Will.

"Sweetie, do you want to ask any questions? I have a list of the ones we've talked about, but I want to give you the chance to start first. This is your time now."

"No, Mom. You go."

I looked at Ernie. He nodded. *I don't know what I'm doing,* I thought. I felt my preparations slip away as I looked down at my list of questions. *These are shitty questions. All of them are going to be answered in a typically Chinese, non-confrontational way. All we want today is something new. Something more than the façade. They're never going to tell me what they think about the One Child Policy. Who am I kidding?*

We'd been exposed to the One Child Policy all year long. We'd met very few families who had two children. Those who did had a backstory – an exemption that allowed two children. They were from a minority tribe. From a rural area. Had been successful in influencing officials to look the other way. Or perhaps, they had flown to the States for the birth of the second child, rendering that child an American citizen, and thus exempt.

The piece of paper in my hand was all I had. Realizing that once again our fate today was unknown, I began. Our expectations were to fill in bits and pieces of Will's story. Allow him to have more to hang onto than our version of events starting when we got him at twelve months of age. I started with the softballs. And got the expected dry and formal answers in return.

No, Will was not in foster care.

Yes, Will was one week old when he was found.

Yes, the report of his finding place was accurate.

Yes, aside from jaundice, his health was good when he was found.

Yes, he had several nannies care for him.

Hoping that Miss Zhao might not notice my quiet slide into the questions that were more pressing, I continued.

"Is it possible for us to see the original police report from his finding?"

No.

"Is there any way for you to tell us which police station he was brought to?"

No.

"Could we see any part of his actual file?"

No.

Miss Zhao was polite but firm in her responses. I was cheery but getting nowhere. I tried the last question. The one that had nagged at me for nine years.

"Is there any way for you tell us if he was found with a note?"

No. If he'd been found with a note, the police report would have stated this, we were told.

Ugh. I felt Ernie shift in his seat as the last question was answered. He had gone over the questions with me, but I was firmly in the driver's seat today. Meanwhile, Will was unwrapping his fourth piece of candy. And seemed only mildly interested in the dialogue we were having. Was he angry? Mad at us or at his birth parents? Did he miss them in this moment? We tried to talk about them as often as we could, but this silent treatment was killing me. I tried again.

"Will, is there anything you want to ask? You had all sorts of questions before we got here. Have they all been answered?"

"Yeah. Guess so."

Holy crap. I don't need any of this pre-adolescence I'm-too-cool behavior today. We'd spent time devising hand signals for him to use if he was getting uncomfortable, wanted more questions asked or needed escape. He wasn't using them, but I began to wonder if I was just missing them.

Damn. Was it a tap on his nose? Or a scratch on his knee? Which signal was which? Oh God, I'm such a goon. I began a silent conversation with my uncle Joe and my grandmother, long deceased, but two of the wisest people I'd known and both, adoptive parents.

What am I supposed to do here? Press on or back off, I asked? I pressed.

"Buddy, we don't know when we'll be back here again. If you have any questions, now's the time."

He hesitated and then I looked at him and knew the question that he wanted answered. We'd discussed it before. It lingered, unasked. At last, I spoke for him.

"Will wants to know about boys. He was a healthy boy when he was found. And abandoning boys is not common. He wonders why he was left."

Susan translated the answer quickly, which was something about boys not having been left much before the year 2000, but more in following years.

It wasn't good enough. I heard Ernie next to me whisper, "Again." He wanted me to ask again.

I asked the question again, partially in Mandarin this time, desperate for additional information for my son. The journalist in me wanted every possible detail, and this outweighed the mother in me and the fact that the answers might be painful.

Susan spoke quickly as she gave us the expected answer.

"Miss Zhao says that it is hard to know. And yes, it was rare for a boy to be left. But perhaps if the mommy was not married, didn't have enough money or had too many children already, it could happen. Just a guess."

I knew Will had heard, but I turned to him and repeated the answer. I looked in his eyes.

"It sounds like they cannot tell you for sure, buddy. But that it might be because your mom was a single mom, or because she was poor or because she had too many children already."

Will paused. I had no idea what he was thinking. Whether it was sadness at the answer or disappointment in the lack of certainty in that answer.

"I'm guessing poor." His voice radiated strength.

"What, honey?"

"I'm guessing it's that she was poor. I'm pretty sure it's poor. She was too poor to keep me. Yup. That was it."

The certainty in his words took my breath away. He had what he needed for the moment. His story. His birth mother had been too poor to care for him. That was that. A look of melancholy covered his face. We waited for him to add more, though nothing tumbled out.

Ernie spoke up at last, asking if we could tour the grounds. Happily, the answer was yes. We gave Miss Zhao several bags of baby clothes and supplies that we had purchased as a donation, then stepped outside into the sunlight. The courtyard held the shadows of several buildings. Miss Zhao pointed to one of them, telling us that it was to be torn down next month. It had been damaged in the earthquake that had hit Sichuan Province to the north a few years ago.

"She says this was the building where Will lived." Susan

passed on the news matter-of-factly, but I was taking in each detail, categorizing each one as it entered my brain.

"We'd like to go see it," I said.

"That should be fine," Susan replied.

We began walking toward the building, but stopped when an older woman approached us. She appeared to be from the orphanage staff. Her short, black hair looked professional and she wore a crisp, white uniform. She and Miss Zhao exchanged a few words, no doubt an explanation of who we were – foreigners coming back to visit our son's orphanage. She sized up Will and smiled at him. We were told that her name was Dr. Liang and that she was the orphanage medical director. At her age, was it possible she remembered Will? It had been so many years... nine years, to be exact.

My hand reached into my backpack and I pulled out the match photos of Will with the little basketball that the orphanage had sent us so long ago. I continued to speak in Chinese, burning with anticipation.

"This is Wu Zhi Yong as a baby. His English name is Will." I handed the photos to Dr. Liang. She gasped. Then laughed.

'Wu Zhi Yong! You were such a good baby!"

Oh my God! She remembers him. The weight of the past year lifted further off my shoulders as I looked over at Will. He smiled a half smile, continuing to try to act nonchalant. But I could see through it. I slipped my finger back into my backpack, hit the record button on my phone and started in with more questions. I needed to have all of this. For him.

"Buddy! They remember you!"

"Oh yes, he was a good baby. He didn't cry very much. He was very healthy," Dr. Liang chirped. She looked at the photos and up at Will. Again and again. Continuing to make the connection. She reached out and stroked his hair.

Thousands of babies had passed through these doors. How many actually return, I asked? The answer was not many. And certainly none who went to American families and now lived in Kunming, spoke Mandarin and went to school just a few miles away. Dr. Liang warmed at our story as I filled her in, and I could see Miss Zhao brighten. *Now we're getting somewhere.*

I took a series of photos of Will with Dr. Liang and we then moved on to the building where he'd lived. Empty now, it still had the look of a place that had once been clean and full of life. The room where he'd slept had held 10-15 cribs. Lined up end to end in long rows.

"I'm so glad we made it here. What do you think, Will? We made it before they tore it down." Ernie sensed Will's mood just as I had. Knowing our son well, we knew Will's lack of chatter didn't indicate disinterest. Rather he was taking in the scene in his own way. He'd been the same as a baby, not speaking until 2.5 years, at which point he began with complete sentences. Silent observation worked for him.

Susan helped us step out of Will's old home and into another building. Walking up a flight of stairs we heard the coo of babies and turned the corner. We'd hit the mother lode. A room full of 15-20 rosy-cheeked, round-faced babies under the age of one year. Each propped in a baby bouncer. Not one crying. Not one looking underfed.

A middle-aged nanny approached us, a baby in her arms. Miss Zhao explained again who we were, why we were here. She held the baby photos of Will in her hand, giving them to the nanny.

"Yes! Zhi Yong! I remember you! You were a little bit lazy."

A second flame of recognition! The nanny was named Miss Tong, and she handed the baby in her arms to another nanny so she could get a better look at Will.

"Oh yes, I remember you, Zhi Yong. Miss Zhao, don't you remember him?" Miss Tong was addressing the Director informally, and I was momentarily confused.

"Miss Zhao used to be a nanny before she was promoted to the Director of Foreign Adoptions position," Susan clarified.

"He was the baby who didn't like to be on his tummy. We had to call his name again and again, remember? We used to call 'Zhi Yong, Zhi Yong!' Trying to get him to work on his crawl! You just started to cry. All you wanted to do was relax and sleep. You were a good sleeper." So many babies had passed through these doors but in this moment, Miss Tong was desperate for Miss Zhao to remember only Will.

After a few back and forths between Miss Zhao and Miss Tong, I could see the light bulb moment. Miss Zhao remembered Will, too. She grinned. Nodded. They both looked directly at Will and spoke to him.

"Yes, Zhi Yong, you used to get so frustrated. We wanted you to get stronger, but you just wanted to go back to sleep." Miss Tong took Will in her arms in a proud, unashamed way. American culture had taught us caution when embracing children we didn't know. Not so in China. Miss Tong held Will close, then pulled him back for a better view.

"And now look at you. You're so handsome. How old are you?"

"Almost ten," Will responded in Mandarin.

"You understand Mandarin!" Miss Zhao was animated now, having finally remembered her former charge. She turned to me and Ernie.

"You are such wonderful parents. You teach your child Mandarin and now you have brought him back to China," Miss Zhao said.

Her gratitude in our presence filled the hollow inside me. Uncertainty lived there. Uncertainty as to whether we'd made the right decision to uproot ourselves from the only place we'd known to be home. It was a void I wasn't sure would ever be filled before this moment.

"And look at him! He is so well-behaved!" A small group of orphanage workers gathered around us, Miss Tong and Miss Zhao filling them in on our story.

Will glowed. He didn't need answers about his birth parents. About a note. Nor what condition he had been in when he'd been found. Apparently he just needed to know that he had been loved his first year.

We lingered for a long time, the same questions and observations coming up over and over from various orphanage workers. Slowly then, we made our way back to the courtyard to say our good byes.

"He is such a lucky boy," Miss Zhao stood with us as the van pulled up to take us away.

"No, no, it is US, his father and I who are lucky," I responded.

"He is so handsome and you have given him such a great home. You are wonderful parents."

I could feel my emotions rising with each additional kind comment. The persistent praise we'd been hearing for the past hour was wearing me down, bringing me to that weepy place I preferred to avoid in front of other people.

Ernie and Will stood silently as I took Miss Zhao's hands in mine. I could feel my husband stiffen as he sometimes did when I was about to cry. *Oh my gosh! I was totally about to cry.*

"Mom, you're totally going to cry now, aren't you?" Will knew me. And also knew that it was hopeless to try to bring me back from the brink. I turned to Susan. Because I had one more thing to say.

"Susan... I can't say this part in Chinese. Can you translate for me?"

She nodded and I continued, looking at Miss Zhao.

"I want to say thank you. For taking care of our son. He was in good health and very happy when he came to us. And I can tell now that there were many people who loved him."

"I promise we will give him a good home forever." I tried to keep from completely losing it, but I could see that Miss Zhao, too, was struggling. I clung to her hands as the boys stood behind me shifting and ready to escape the emotional scene playing out before them. Instead, Miss Zhao and I embraced. Sniffles filled the space as we both repeated over and over, to each other, "Thank you. Thank you. Thank you."

The van pulled away as I continued to sniffle in the backseat sitting next to Will.

"Mom, what's up with that? Why are you crying?"

"Honey, I'm just so happy that we had a chance to visit. To see where you lived. To meet those wonderful nannies. I'm so grateful for them. They loved you when we weren't there."

"But why was Miss Zhao crying?"

"I'm sure she's just really happy to see one of her babies in a good home. You know they never really get to see the babies after they leave. It was special for us to come back and visit."

The next spot was the Civil Affairs Office, where we'd received Will. The area had been full of trees nine years ago, but now the neighborhood was almost entirely concrete. We stepped out of the van and walked to the area where we had sat with other families on the grass. The wall of ivy remained.

We led Will there, showing him how he'd reached out and grabbed for the leaves. We lingered only briefly, as our third destination loomed.

Outside of a one-line description, we had nothing on the place where Will had been found. We knew he'd been left at the age of one week. I thought often of how agonizing it must have been for his birth mother, father, or both to decide not to keep him. How they likely wrapped him in a blanket, gave him one final suck from a bottle or breast and then left him alone. Was he crying? Was he cold or scared? How long was he alone until he was found and who found him? These were all questions we would never get the answers to, of course. Yet, the one line description we'd been provided could lead us to the place where his life forever changed. The place that ultimately brought him to us. Will wanted to visit as much as we did, and his little Lego creation made the trip with us.

As we got into the van one more time, I handed Susan the name of what we called the "finding spot." It was an apartment complex in the city. That much we knew. But we had no idea where it was located. The driver began to navigate in a direction that seemed familiar. Each turn brought us closer to our apartment. Then past it, and along a busy road we'd walked countless times.

"Mom, it looks like we're going to Slice of Heaven."

Indeed, that's where it appeared we were headed. The café run by my teacher friend. We had gone there many times this year, and now it appeared we were heading back. The van slowed, Susan looked out the window and called out, "We're here!" A tall series of buildings created the apartment complex where Will had been found. And it was right across the street from the café we knew so well.

"I can't believe it," said Ernie, incredulous.

"My spot is right across the street from Slice of Heaven!"

I shook my head in amazement. The café had been our oasis all year. We'd dined here for Thanksgiving dinner, saying our Thanksgiving blessing just steps away from where Will had been abandoned.

"Yes, it sure is, Will. Unbelievable. Let's check it out."

People strolled by as we took up our spots in the entryway to the apartment complex. A large sign towered above the main gate, the Chinese characters none that I recognized. On either side, gray concrete boxes rose upward, divided into small apartments. In typical Chinese style, there were laundry lines hung outside each window. Each hung with laundry, some also with the carcasses of animals drying in the spring sun.

Were Will's parents residents here? Was he placed in a box, or wrapped in a baby blanket?

"Mom! Look at this bush. This might be a good place."

"A good place for what, honey?"

"My spaceship. The one I'm going to leave."

Right. We had stopped to buy a helium balloon to release at the finding spot, but I had forgotten about the Lego spaceship Will had built. The bush he was pointing to was sparse. Set upon a tall planter, it was surrounded by bits of garbage and dirt.

"I think I'll put ten yuan in it and then some little kid will find it and be happy. Is that a good idea?"

"It's a perfect idea, Will."

He took a ten yuan bill out of his pocket and wrapped it into a square, placing it in a small opening in the spaceship. He parted the branches of the bush and set the spaceship deep within its folds. He had an air of satisfaction. The three of us walked inside the gates of the complex. There was very little to say as we took in the scene. In my hand, I held the balloon we'd purchased. Our plan was to say a prayer of gratitude and release it into the air. But as I surveyed the sky above, I saw nothing but a tangle of wires strung from building to building. China's furious race to develop had apparently not included a plan to bury wires, and this fact was staring us in the face. *Damn. There is no possible way this sucker is going to clear those things, I thought.*

"Mom, I'm ready for the balloon!"

"Do you want to say a few words before you release it, bud?" Neither of my boys had noticed what I had. *Best not to say anything. Let fate carry the balloon where it may.*

I stood next to Will as Ernie took a video.

"I want to thank my birth parents for giving me an awesome family."

A second round of tears filled my eyes as Will let the balloon slip from his hand. It sailed upward as I held my breath. Clearing the power lines by inches on either side, it made a path towards the clouds. The three of us watched it float away.

Smiling, we headed out of the apartment complex. Slice of Heaven seemed the perfect place for a celebratory lunch, and it was just steps away. I glanced up at the sign looming over us and called over to Susan. She had let us enjoy these moments here alone, but I was curious about something. Of all the places in Kunming, why had Will's birth parents decided to leave him here? What was so special about this place?

"Susan, could you tell me what those Chinese characters say? I mean, what's the English translation of this place?"

Her answer stopped me. Shocked me. Humbled me. Soothed me.

"It means 'safe.' The name of the complex is the 'Safe Place Apartments,' Johanna."

Smiling, my eyes lifted to the skies to see where the balloon had gone. It was only a red dot now, moving further and further on its journey. Destination unknown.

chapter forty three

The most dramatic scene of the movie approached. Leonardo di Caprio was hanging onto a piece of lumber while trying to keep Kate Winslet afloat. The students in my film class had requested *Titanic* and I was happy to deliver. Nothing like a good cry in the middle of the day. As class started, I passed around a box of tissues. They giggled at me, but as the ship sank deeper into the ocean, I heard the proof that my judgment call was a wise one. Sniffles. Full on nose blowing.

The subtitles flashed relentlessly as I glanced at my laptop screen. Sitting in the back of the room, I'd made the mistake of thinking I could get some work done while the movie played.

A text popped up on my laptop and I hit the mute button, looking to see who it was. My cousin Chris.

Chris: Hey there! You up?

Johanna: I am! It's 10 a.m. here. I'm in class. You?

Chris: It's 7 p.m. here. OMG! Lana and I are watching a movie. We need tissues for this one.

Johanna: OMG! Here, too! I'm in my film class and we're watching *Titanic.*

Chris: No WAY!!! That's what WE'RE watching!

Johanna: You're joking!

Chris: I'm totally not joking. Leonardo and Kate just took deep breaths and went under.

Johanna: Unbelievable! We're nearly at the same part! They're floating on the log and he's about to let go and bite it.

Chris: OMG! It's too much to handle. Lana's already crying.

Johanna: Here, too. A room full of weepy 19-year-olds.

Chris: It's so damned tragic.

Johanna: That's true. And it gets me every time. Can you imagine having a love like that when you were 19 and keeping it a secret your whole life?

Chris: No. Pure hell.

Johanna: Oh God! He's about to go under. I'm a total puddle, Chrissy.

Chris: Me, too. I cannot believe this really happened. I spent a semester on a boat and never once thought about it sinking.

Johanna: I always thought I could go for a cruise with the right person but after watching this, uh, not so sure.

Chris: OMG! I gotta fly. Lana's starting to hyperventilate.

Johanna: Go! I love you!

Chris: I love you, too!!!

The last scene of the movie played out, the sounds of weeping filling my classroom. I flicked on the lights as the students tried to compose themselves. With only a few minutes left in class, I prepared to engage them in a short discussion about what they liked and didn't like about the film.

"What did you like most about the movie?" I inquired.

Twenty-five pair of bleary, red eyes gazed back at me.

"I liked the love story," one of them responded.

"And Rose, she was so beautiful. Such white skin." I didn't really understand that comment, but filed it away to chat about with Walt, who I was meeting for lunch.

"The people who were in the lower classes didn't get on the lifeboats. That part was sad," said another student.

"Well yes, that IS sad. And unjust. Do you know that word? Unjust?" I asked.

Silence gripped the room. The definition of unjust, in my mind, included all three of Alice's banned topics. So, I moved on, choosing another illustration before finishing class.

I met Walt outside my classroom for the walk to the student cafeteria. Spring had brought warmer temperatures and the doors of the cafeteria opened onto a large patio. Inside, the lunch lines exploded with upwards of 250 students congregated to find their meals. Every student started the same way. Grab a tray and proceed to the rice station. Behind the counter sat giant rice cookers, with multiple cooks scooping out piles of rice into bowls and handing them to students. Next it was the decision of what to pile onto the rice. Counters lined the rim of the cafeteria. One for meats. One for vegetables. One for eggs of all sorts. One with some food that looked fermented. And a station with drinks. Freshly squeezed watermelon juice. Lemonade. And my favorite, fresh made sweet soybean milk, also known as dou jiang. The final stop was the station that held chopsticks. This stop always made me grimace, as I looked around every day and saw 250 students using a disposable version. For just one of three meals. Consequently, I'd recently made a mental note to bring my own, reusable version.

Walt and I sat in a corner, far from the chaos and noise. When speaking to each other, we needed relative calm so that we could fully understand one another. His English was far superior to my Chinese, but I tried valiantly to carry on my portion of the discussion in his native tongue. Walt was the only student who knew I spoke Chinese. I'd kept this fact a secret in order that my students wouldn't fall back on Chinese if they needed to discuss something with me. There had been many an instance during which students had approached me in groups and fumbled through an English explanation of something. The piecing-together usually consisted of the group consulting with each other in Chinese to try to determine how to phrase something in English. I'd remain quiet, fully understanding what they were saying to each other, but unwavering in my desire for them to work it out minus assistance from me in Chinese.

Tofu hung between the ends of my chopsticks as I launched into my questions for Walt. Most every opportunity we had together was like this. Me digging deeper to try to really understand the meaning behind Chinese customs. Him grilling me about life in America. His desire to leave China was palpable, and the two of us talked regularly about when he might leave the mainland to study abroad.

"What's the big deal with the white skin?" I asked.

"It's more beautiful," he replied, matter-of-factly.

The tofu dropped into my bowl as I leaned forward, certain I'd misheard him.

"Say again?"

"It's more beautiful. The white skin. Yours. Though you have all those... what are they called? Those spots you have."

"Freckles?"

"Yes. Freckles. You have so many freckles, Johanna. You should carry an umbrella to shield your face from the sun."

"Well, I wear sunscreen. But back to what you said before. You don't really think white skin is more beautiful, do you?"

"I do. And I think most Chinese people feel that way. If you have dark skin, people associate that with being a laborer. Working in the fields."

"Really? So it's not about race? It's about social status?"

"I suppose so. Rich people get to stay inside. Away from the sun."

"Huh. Okay. That's fascinating and kind of creepy."

"Creepy?" Walt repeated the word in question form, not knowing what it meant.

"That means 'weird.' But I shouldn't say that. I guess I'm just intrigued. And happy that it's not about race. You already know how I feel about adoption, and that my kids are Chinese." Walt and my other students had met the children at the start of the year.

"Yes. I understand how you feel about it. And you had to tell the children they were adopted, of course. Because they look different from you."

I chuckled at the comment, given the conversation I'd had with Nina just a few days prior. She'd called to tell me that she'd made an offhand comment to her son Miro about our visit to the orphanage. Miro flew into a state of disbelief, totally unaware that Will and Eden were adopted. In his eight-year-old mind, our children looked just like us. Nina laughed as she recounted the story, telling me that the rest of the day, Miro had walked around the house mumbling,

"I can't believe Will's adopted. Why didn't anyone tell me?"

Somewhere between an eight-year-old such as Miro and a 20-year-old such as Walt, a shift in thinking was bound to happen. I tried to clarify.

"We didn't HAVE to tell them, but it wasn't a secret, if that's what you mean."

"Right. In China, it's a secret."

"You mean there are adopted children who don't know they're adopted."

"Right. I have a cousin who's 20 and has no idea he was adopted."

"What? Why not?"

"His parents think he would be sad if he knew. Or angry. Or that he'd try to find his real parents."

I cringed at the term "real parents" as the words used to describe "biological parents."

"But doesn't your cousin have the right to know this information?" I countered.

"He would be so upset. His parents don't want to hurt him."

Walt and I played ping-pong on the issue, neither of us understanding the perspective of the other. I continued to try to explain my point of view, thinking that if perhaps I used different words, he might agree with me. Walt didn't budge. Telling your children they were adopted was not common practice in China, and he understood why.

"It's not as if Chinese parents don't love their children. They do. They just value their children's feelings and want to protect them."

I nodded, convinced we were at the end of our friendly banter. Then thought about our own situation. And what WE must look like here among locals. Not only had we adopted, but we were parading that fact in the faces of our children by virtue of coming back and creating a life here. While we saw this as a progressive and beneficial step in the long run, I shuddered to think that the Chinese might think it cruel.

chapter forty four

I began to feel myself try to slow time. There had been plenty about our year that grated on my nerves, but much about China that I now treasured and wanted to enjoy in our remaining months. I'd become a regular at the traditional Chinese medicine clinic around the corner. For everything from running injuries to digestive problems, I wandered in. The front of the clinic stood out from the boring concrete buildings around it. Festooned with an ornate Chinese arch, its glass doors constantly open, emitting the scents of medicinal concoctions of all kinds.

My visits to the clinic were as much for comic relief as anything else. Every interaction with one of the doctors left me swimming in the cultural divide between these visits and one I might have at home. Most recently I'd gone in for plantar fasciitis, an injury of the lower leg and heel. The doctor, sitting behind a desk, reached over and started by looking at my tongue. Then moved to taking my pulse. The room in which we sat was large and housed desks for other doctors. Patients streamed in and out, medical conditions openly being discussed without closed doors.

"Should I slip off my shoes?" I asked, my Mandarin now solid enough to communicate freely.

The doctor laughed, reaching down to scribble notes onto a prescription pad. He'd examined me for less than one minute.

"No. No need. It's your kidneys."

"My kidneys? No, it's my heel. It hurts when I run."

"I understand that, but it's a problem with your kidneys. You need some tea and bath herbs."

I'd been here before with similar, outlandish suggestions. The last time I was given acupuncture to treat a digestive problem. The needles had been boosted with electric currents, and the treatment sent me squirming all over the table. I walked out cursing, but the next day, my digestion was singing.

In the doctor's office, I began to laugh at this familiar scene. Not rudely. More in disbelief. As I laughed, the doctor laughed with me. He handed me a prescription, which I should have filled at the pharmacy attached to the clinic.

"Mix the herbs with white wine and soak in it for 20 minutes each night. Warm bath water. Not hot. You Americans like your baths too hot."

The pharmacy he directed me to wasn't so much a pharmacy as a kitchen. A dozen cooks in aprons and chef hats. They scurried behind glass windows pulling out herbs from a giant chest of drawers. Each mixture was tossed in a mortar, ground with a pestle, and scooped into little bags. Each bag contained the magic potion, which was to be boiled and consumed as warm tea. And, in my case, used as a bath tonic.

I walked the three-blocks home clutching my bags and giggling to myself. I loved this little juxtaposition of life. The life outside our apartment contained absurdity and wonder. All those things that had both driven us crazy and also drawn us to China in the first place. After many months, the absurdity had become...routine. Our life inside the apartment provided comfort. Both had their place now. Both were welcome.

The things I missed about the States were real but sometimes random. I missed avocados. I missed the smell of fresh cut grass. I'd recently been transfixed by the sight of a lawn mower on the university campus. There was barely any grass in the entirety of Kunming, yet the lawnmower had found a tiny patch and was doing its work, powered by a maintenance man. I'd waited for it to stop, looked around to make sure nobody was watching and then grabbed a handful of grass shavings and stuck them in my jeans pocket. The thought of sharing this scent with my family made me smile all the way home.

As I entered our apartment, I heard Ernie on our landline speaking English. It had to be someone in America. Our phone was wired to receive international calls through the Internet. Free of charge, free of static, and free of the weird phone delays of international calls in years past. Friends and family called our same old number as if we were still living on Newton Street.

"It's the sprinkler head in the front yard or the back yard?" Ernie questioned. He saw me, looked up and grinned.

I could tell from his end of the conversation that it was the tenants in our rental property in Denver. Not our primary home, but a secondary property we'd bought as a source of income. The same family had lived there for years, and we'd always communicated almost entirely by email and text. Their rent was deposited electronically each month, and any problems could be handled through a few phone calls or email messages. As we'd prepared to leave the States, I'd proposed a game of sorts. There was no NEED to tell them, I argued, that we were moving to Asia. Let's see how long we can hold out and not tell them.

"Right. Why don't you call that lawn company we used last year? They ought to be able to fix it pretty quickly. Have them send me the bill."

I covered my mouth so I wouldn't laugh. All our mail had been diverted to Ernie's father, who had access to our bank account and promptly paid all our bills. I looked out the window, past Ernie, and saw a dead pig hanging out of a window in the complex next to ours.

"The rent – yes, it's due today. No – actually, if you can deposit it electronically this month, too, that would be great. We're not home right now."

Ernie covered the mouthpiece and whispered, "She wants to come over to drop off the rent!"

The two of us were bubbling, and I couldn't wait anymore. We'd made it all year and I knew we could easily get home with the secret in tact. But our tenant had a wicked sense of humor and I knew she'd love the news.

"Tell her!" I said in a loud whisper.

"To be honest, Naomi, you should know that we won't be home for a few months. We've been away for awhile." He paused, listening to her response.

"Everything's fine. It's just that, we're not in Denver right now. We've been living in China this year."

The yelp from the other end caused Ernie to pull the phone from his ear. All three of us laughed generously.

"That's right. We're not exactly 15 minutes away from you. We're 15 TIME zones from you."

The woman in the apartment across the way pulled the pig in the window. It had been nicely cleaned, though small bits of hair remained on its chinny chin chin.

"What time is it? It's morning here. It's still Tuesday night for you, but we're already at lunch on Wednesday here."

Ernie finished his conversation and joined me in the kitchen.

"Hilarious, Ern. Did she love it?"

"She totally loved it."

"The sprinkler heads in the front yard are broken. Can you imagine if there was enough grass here to NEED a sprinkler system? That grass you brought home the other day was the most I've seen all year." I laughed and held up the packages of herbs.

"Another successful trip to the witch doctor?"

"Stop! You're missing out. You should go. For your knee problem or that pain in your lower back."

"Maybe. The price is certainly right, isn't it?"

"It is, and as crazy as it sounds, the treatments have worked without fail. I'm gonna miss this part, Ern."

I glanced at the receipt. The value of herbs relative to the time with the doctor was the opposite of what it would be in the U.S. The bath herbs equated to a $10 bath every night for a week. The consult with the physician = $1.75.

Weekends on our calendar had filled just as they had in the States. When we weren't scooting in and out of the country, we were home in Kunming. Trips to the park mixed with trips to the market. The routine of four hour Sunday breakfasts at Lost Garden with our friends became something we couldn't imagine living without. Ernie and I began to talk about how we'd convert our friends at home by hosting brunches every weekend complete with Bloody Marys and room for the children to play all morning.

Our credit card statement showed evidence of our constant traveling, but suddenly there was only one set of tickets left to buy. The one-way tickets that would get us home.

I bought them quietly one afternoon and then filed away the confirmation email. We'd decided to make our journey home one last escapade. We'd stop in Shanghai for several days, then fly to Hawaii for a week to recover from jet lag and finally proceed to Wisconsin and the lake.

chapter forty five

As we marched on with our adventures, we tried our best to keep up with those of our friends and family. Our attention was captured by that of our friends, Kristy and Dave. Their family had helped launch the school that Will attended in Denver. Kristy and I had known each other for years, having met on the playground when Will and her daughter, Emma, were toddlers. She'd struck up a conversation with me about Chinese adoption, telling me that they were considering adopting from China as well.

Many years had passed since then, and they had indeed decided to adopt not just one, but two. They'd switched from the traditional adoption program to the special needs program and were anticipating a trip to pick up their toddlers soon. After years of waiting, they'd be in China shortly, just two hours away by plane.

I poured over their blog as their trip to China started. First the actual travel overseas, with its usual ups and downs. Then the arrival of their toddlers, Gia and Jude. At first joyful, but then a quick turn to the difficult. Gia was severely underweight and not eating. Jude had the spunk of a typical toddler. Together the two of them were mixed with new parents and two new siblings. Dave and Kristy had brought two of their daughters with them on the trip.

The blog entries grew more downcast. Each member of the family was falling victim to the flu. The hotel was unreasonably hot without air conditioning. Nobody was sleeping and the crying of the little ones seemed difficult to contain. With just one adopted child, this would have been a handful, but they were dealing with two.

I knew that I didn't have all the answers and that time would be the elixir for many of their present experiences. Yet we were only a few hours away and I knew we had the resources to help them in some small part.

I curled my legs under me on our tattered couch after dinner. My laptop was open, the page showing their blog. I scanned it once, then again. Their words seemed more exhausted than the day before.

"Ern, I can't read this much longer without feeling like we should do something more."

Ernie pulled up next to me, taking the computer onto his lap and reading the entry.

"Wow, yeah, that sounds pretty grim. What are you thinking, though?"

"Well we're only a couple hours away. Maybe I could just offer to go help. I don't want to intrude on their trip, but they sound desperate."

"You could always offer and just see, right? They would probably say NO if it didn't feel right."

"That's true. Maybe I'll offer to come and bring Will. I bet their girls could use a playmate."

I sent a quick email message to them, having no idea if they were even able to receive their mail. When the response came within hours, they jumped at the chance to have us join them for a few days.

Twenty-four hours later, Will and I were on an airplane headed to meet them in Guangzhou.

We arrived at the hotel several hours ahead of them, as they were traveling from another city within China. We parked ourselves in the lobby and waited for them. The bus arrived, an exploding mass of adoptive families clutching overtired babies and toddlers. We saw Dave and Kristy and their two girls, giving them hugs. Kristy had the look of a mother of six who hasn't slept in days, but is concurrently overjoyed with parenthood. Gia's eyes were huge and alert, though her tiny waist reminded me of photos I'd seen of children starving in third world countries.

I spent the next several days dividing my attention in halves. One half entertaining the three bigger kids with ice cream, pizza, swimming, boat rides, and movies. The other half having long brainstorming sessions with Dave and Kristy. The topic never changed: how to survive the next 24 hours. Jude seemed well, but he'd taken to running off with strangers, unsure of who his parents were. Gia was barely eating, and as we sat in the hotel hallway with the toddlers running up and down, we pondered the list of possible causes. A parasite? Ringworm? Food allergies? Or just simply the shock of being ripped from one life and placed in another?

On our final afternoon in Guangzhou, I took Dave and Kristy's older daughters to get pedicures. I pretended to read a magazine while I waited for them to finish, my thoughts elsewhere. On a conversation Dave and I had just shared.

"Johanna, can you talk to Kristy? I think she's just overwhelmed. I know we can do this, but it's more than we anticipated."

"I know she can get through this, Dave. The actual adoption trip is not – how do I say this? It's not real life."

"Could you just tell her that? It'll be better coming from you than from me. Trust me."

"The two of you have an incredible family. Six children. It's so much love, Dave. I know you've put your faith in God to help you get here and get through it and it's remarkable to watch."

The reference to God was welcome, and I could see Dave relax. I knew that they'd been called to adopt in ways that were different than ours. Spirituality held a presence in our lives, but not in the same way it did for them. As with any parenting journey, the adoption journey was unique for every family.

The girls marveled at their finished pedicures as I lined up a few talking points in my head for a discussion with Kristy.

"Mom! Look at our toes!" The girls bounded into the hotel room they all shared, being careful not to smudge their fresh paint.

"Thank you, Johanna... SUCH a big help. They'll never forget it. You and Will were so sweet to come all the way here to help us."

I nodded and pulled Kristy into the hallway, which had become our de facto living room. Gia and Jude crawled on us and wandered back and forth from the elevator to where we sat. I shared the stories of our adoption trips, being careful to not make comparisons. Focusing instead on the humor. Eating my daughter's poop. Getting her head extracted from crib slats in the middle of the night. I told her about my own mind racing in those days at the hotel. Worried about everything from giardia to developmental delays. I gave her advice on how to heat Gia's bottles to a practically scalding temperature to see if that might help her take them easier, as it had with Will. My advice felt trivial, though I knew our presence alone must have been comforting. Will and I returned to our room down the hall, settling into pajamas. As we curled up in bed, the phone rang. I answered it.

"It's Kristy. And my gosh, Gia just drank an entire bottle. I made it hot, just like you told me to. It was so hot I was sure she'd burn her lips." I laughed, reminding her that I'd felt the same way making Will's bottles this way so many years ago.

"Thanks again, Johanna. There just aren't words."

"None needed, Kristy. I understand."

The next morning Will and I had an early flight. The sky over Guangzhou choked with pollution. One new piece of our daily routine in China was now "checking the AQI" also known as the Air Quality Index. The number usually proved acceptable in Kunming, but in Guangzhou even when the sun appeared to be out, it was covered by haze and grime. My worries turned from Gia and Jude to the state of our planet. *How in God's name can people live in a place where it's this hard to breathe?* Will noticed the dejected look on my face.

"What's up, Mom?" he asked.

"I think it's just been a very overwhelming few weeks, buddy. I'm tired."

"Are you ready for our vacation?"

"So ready. For elephants and fresh fruit and the beach."

We'd planned a week in Thailand once again, having loved it so much on the front end of our year. Our experience had been intense from start to finish. There were days that I came home from work and simply lay on the couch, unable to speak. The kids were unaccustomed to seeing me on the couch in Denver. Their mother was a constant ball of energy, rarely sitting down. But Mom's "couch mode" had been well interpreted by now. It meant I'd encountered something funny-ridiculous or confusing-ridiculous or I-just-wanna-cry ridiculous.

Our flight to Kunming appeared to be on time. The two of us checked our bags and headed to the gate, passing a fruit and vegetable vendor.

Will scanned the produce and then screamed, "MOM! Look! It's an avocado!"

Hot damn. It WAS an avocado! I held it in my hands like a glass egg, rolling it around and staring at the sticker, which said,

"Imported from Mexico."

"I'm buying it for you, Mom. You NEED this avocado."

Twenty yuan poorer and one avocado richer, Will and I smiled as we walked to our gate.

chapter forty six

Spring in Kunming was in full swing, the cherry blossoms exploding on trees all over town. The temperatures had only dipped to the low 50's during the winter, but the addition of another 20 degrees was welcome. With only a few months left, a trip to Eden's foster mother approached. We'd saved the visit until the end of our year in order to maximize the chances that Edie, now five years old, would remember it.

Eden's foster mother was a woman named Yu Li. She lived in central China, requiring us to fly inland, spend a night in the city of Nanchang, then drive several hours the next day to her remote village. Yu Li pushed age 75 and from what we understood, Eden had been one of many babies she'd fostered over the years. The photos we had showed an elderly Chinese woman holding our daughter, a baby who looked rashy, but well fed and smiley. We hadn't met her when we'd picked Eden up, but knew immediately that she'd been taken care of properly. Her pudgy legs and cheeks remained, as did a cheerful disposition amidst the trauma of being taken from her foster mom and given to us.

As the time approached for our trip, Eden grew more and more animated about meeting Yu Li. She asked to see photos of her foster mom regularly, and we talked about what it would be like to meet her. The thought of seeing where Eden had lived and being able to ask questions about her first few months made me as giddy as it had with Will's orphanage trip.

"Mom, can I see the pictures again? The pictures of me and my foster mom?"

I clicked into the file containing a dozen photos of Eden and Yu Li. Eden's smile brightened as she looked at herself in Yu Li's arms. Bundled in several layers of clothes, she grasped Yu Li's shirtsleeve in several shots.

"Why do I have those red marks on my cheeks and where are all my toys?"

The photos had arrived while we'd waited to pick Eden up and we hadn't been given an explanation of where they'd been taken. It looked like an outdoor market, but for all I knew, it could have been her home. I hoped that perhaps any toys she'd had were just in another room, but the truth was... I just didn't know.

"I bet you had a little rash from the heat, Eden. And as for your toys, I'm not sure. We'll ask her when we get there in a few weeks."

"I can't wait to see her, Momma. I hope she remembers me."

"She will for sure remember you, honey. You're unforget-table!"

Anxious to meet her in person, we'd spent much of this year talking about our visit as a family and corresponding with a Chinese interpreter who went by the Western name "Bruce." Well known in adoption circles, Bruce had managed to con-nect many adoptive families with their child's foster family. Before we'd even left the States, we had Bruce tell Yu Li that we'd be moving there. He told us she was excited we'd be liv-ing in China, and even more excited that we planned to visit her. Bruce would serve as our guide for the weekend visit.

I touched base with Bruce a couple weeks before we left, giving him our exact dates and asking him to confirm with Yu Li. Hearing nothing back, I wrote again. Days passed and I be-gan to worry until the moment I saw a message from him in my inbox. The delay in response was explained as I read the first few lines of the email, my heart sinking. I didn't even need to continue with those following to understand the devastation we were about to wade into.

Hi Johanna,

Hello! At my request, my friend went to Yu Li's home in person this morning. He met her daughter at the foster home. Yu Li's daughter told my friend that her mother recently died. She said that her mother mentioned your daughter Fu Yan Zhu several times before she died. She added that she often helped her mother take care of Yan Zhu. She asked me to let you know that she would be willing to show you around Yan Zhu's original living place when Yan Zhu comes to visit. And if you like, Yu Li's daughter also would be willing to take your family to her tomb to present her with a flower.

- Bruce

I sat on the pink shag carpet that I had added to the giant window seat in our bedroom. I stared at the laptop screen, my hand over my mouth. We were too late. We knew we didn't have long, but to miss her by mere months took my breath away. I called Ernie into the bedroom and gave him the news. He slumped onto the bed across from me.

"How are we going to tell her, Ern?"

"I don't know. It's Eden... she'll take it okay. She's such a fighter."

"She never knew her birth mom. Now this. It's not fair."

I started to cry. The children were at school and I wasn't teaching. Thankfully, this left only the two of us home to process the news.

"Jo, she has us. She has you. You are her mother."

"It's heartbreaking. I feel so bad for her. I don't understand it.

It's just too much loss for one little girl."

"Yes, I know. I know. She deserved more. She deserved to be able to piece her life together a little bit more by meeting her foster mom."

"Do you think we should bail on the trip?" I hoped he'd say no, though I knew he felt wary about this trip even before this news. The thought of plunging into Eden's past quite the way we were about to rattled him for reasons that didn't phase me. I'd been the one who'd pushed us to visit. It had been me who'd done all the legwork and built the excitement for Eden.

The difference in the way we approached Eden's past reflected a conflict that we'd had often. I chided my husband for being typically male in this regard. He shied away from the details of Eden's prior life in the same way he didn't enjoy hearing about my prior boyfriends. I joked that he'd convinced himself that my life started the day I met him.

"I don't know. I mean, what's to see now? There's nobody there who spent time with her."

"It says something about Yu Li's daughter. It says she helped take care of Eden."

I shifted my legs, draping them over the edge of the window seat so I could face Ernie. I began to feel frantic, hoping he'd see the same benefit I saw in proceeding with the trip.

"Yeah, but what does THAT mean? It could mean anything. It could mean that she helped once during the entire year."

"Let's tell Eden first and offer that to her, and see how she takes it."

The day progressed slowly. I ran over and over the way we'd frame the turn of events for Edie. Will's visit to the orphanage had gone so beautifully. I had hoped that her visit with Yu Li would be the same. Damn.

As dinner finished that night, I looked across the table at

Ernie. He gave me a nod, the way he did when he wanted me to kick off difficult conversations. It was forever my job to start those and his job to pick up the pieces if I stumbled or if the children needed a less flowery version. Ernie was all about less flowery.

"Eden, we want to talk to you about some sad news we got today, honey."

"What is it?" She looked up from her plate of noodles and vegetables. The kid-sized chopsticks we'd bought her had finally been replaced with an adult version, which she used masterfully at age five.

"It's about your foster mom. You know we've been planning to go visit her. And we'd told you that she was sometimes sick."

Eden nodded and I could tell that she was seeing right through me. She had that same dead stare that she'd mastered since the day we received her.

The one that said, *You're. Not. Fooling. Me.*

"Well, sweetie, we just learned that she died."

"She died?!" Will responded first, and was incredulous. His voice resonated the same frustration and disbelief that Ernie and I had held a few hours ago.

"Yes, well... she was so old and she probably had a great life, and it was time for her life to be over."

"But we didn't see her yet." Eden looked confused, and I braced for the sad part. I struggled to stay seated, feeling angry at myself and at China for having pulled my family into yet another unfathomable challenge.

"The message we got today said she talked about you a lot. Many times. Right before she died. Edie, she was thinking about you all the time."

"So her heart just stopped?" Eden's five-year-old preoccupation with the death part rose to the surface.

"That's right."

"And her blood stopped?"

"Yes, that's what happens when someone dies, Eden. Duh," Will added. An unhelpful comment, though unintended to hurt his sister.

"I still want to go." Eden's tiny voice held certainty. Strength was something she had no shortage of, and I could feel it rise as our conversation continued.

Ernie spoke up with the counterproposal. "We can still go visit your hometown, if you want. We could meet your foster mom's daughter. We learned she also took care of you."

"I wanna go."

"Okay. We'll go. We'll see where you lived and meet your foster sister and it'll be great. And Eden, Mom and I are so sorry that she died, honey. So sorry."

"You're sorry? What do you mean?"

The adult habit of offering apology upon death was unknown to Eden. The only other context she'd known death had been our family dog a year prior. That, like any other death we'd go through in the future, would be one we'd experience together. But this death was hers alone.

"It just means that Daddy and I are sad that you lost someone who meant something special to you."

Eden shrugged her shoulders. Her eyes cast to Will, perhaps looking for the proper, age-appropriate response. But at age nine, Will already knew more about death and what it meant than she did. He seemed frozen, not providing his sister any guidance in how to react. Eden looked down at her fingers, still holding chopsticks from the dinner, which was now clearly finished.

"Yeah... I'm sorry, too, Eden," Will whispered.

She looked up and said, "Me, too."

The foster sister, a woman in her 40's, quickly achieved hero worship in our home over the next few weeks. Her name was Chen Song and we talked her up as though she would be an equally important piece in Eden's puzzle. Having never known she existed until recently, we had few details on her real role and found it impossible to answer Eden's questions about her. We fought the battle that all adoptive families face at some point... Do you tell your child the truth, which, so often, is a version of "I don't know." Or, do you spare them the difficulty of living with the "I don't know" and instead make something up to suit their childlike mind. We usually opted for the former, but in this case, our tactic had been radically different.

For example, our standard response when the children asked us why their parents gave them up was, "We don't know the circumstances. But we know they loved you very much and found a safe place to leave you so that you'd be found and given a new home."

It sounded sugary, but we believed it. After all, if a woman in China were pregnant and knew that she wouldn't be able to keep the baby, why in the world would she carry the baby to term? There were plenty of options for back alley abortions. If she chose to deliver the baby, there was the whole matter of hiding the actual pregnancy. And the agony of abandoning a newborn. There was only one reason any woman would do that, in our minds, and it was clear. Love.

It seemed simple enough, and it sure felt good to believe this, but the truth was, we didn't know if even THAT was fact. Perhaps the birth parents had been too poor to afford an ultrasound to determine gender or an abortion if the fetus was female. Perhaps they had been young and scared, unaware of their options.

And yet, we persisted with this narrative. Taking things even further, we had talked up her foster mother and now her foster sister, hoping to create a bond for Eden in some way. We knew nothing of these people aside from what we'd heard from Bruce. China herself had proven to us a thousand times over that we had little control over our lives here. Yet I felt fiercely determined to salvage the trip for my daughter.

As we walked into the JinFeng Hotel in Nanchang in north-central China three weeks later, I could see with clarity all the details from four years ago. This was the same hotel where Eden had been given to us by government officials in charge of adoptions. The restaurant remained – the one I stumbled into with her in my arms, unsure where to walk next. The lobby where she had toddled around. Narration accompanied our walk around the hotel, Eden's eyes widening as we recounted each piece of our adoption trip.

A fountain in the lobby of the hotel housed koi, presumably the same ones she had squealed at in my arms years ago. I showed her the workout room where I'd escaped for an hour each day to run and stretch. The pool, which was cold, but was surely her first swim and therefore special for that fact alone.

Will proved a distraction. He couldn't seem to grasp the importance of this weekend for his younger sister.

"Mom, tell me again about the Cultural Revolution. What was that all about?"

Good God, he had asked me the same question four hours

earlier as we stood, of all places, in front of the security line at the airport with Chinese immigration officials staring down at us. I'd postponed the question then, and I did so again.

Our day ended with a trip to a nearby shopping district. We stopped at the same scroll painter's shop we had years ago, investing more money into treasures to line our suitcases when we left China. The scroll painter knew his target audience. The location of his shop near the hotel proved effective in drawing in adoptive parents year after year, he boasted. The painter smoked like a chimney, but his bubbly personality and remarkable artwork captivated us just as it had years ago.

The next morning we awoke to gray skies and rain. Bruce met us in the lobby for the drive to Fuzhou, the city where Eden was from. We planned to drive there in a rented van with a driver Bruce had arranged. We'd meet with the foster sister and stay the night. We hoped, of course, to see her again the next day before we headed home to Kunming.

The city of Fuzhou was often called a "village," though its population was over three million. Our hotel in Fuzhou was the nicest in town, but easily the most rundown we'd stayed at since arriving in Asia. Two double beds for the four of us. A tiny, dirty bathroom. A smell that was a cross between garbage and smoke. Knowing we had to stay only one night, we smiled politely and thanked Bruce.

"So when will we get to see Chen Song?" Eden was ready. I was anxious. Bruce had evaded similar questions on the drive here, and I was starting to get nervous.

"After lunch. Eat and rest. Then we will go to her."

I resigned myself to the fact that we were clearly on Bruce's timetable. We rested in the dank room as it rained outside. The beds felt hard and the rain from outside began to seep through the windowsills. I found myself digging through our suitcases to see if I'd packed extra layers for all of us.

A knock on the door an hour later signaled that it was time. I opened the door and Bruce stepped in. I could tell immediately that something wasn't right.

"There's been a change of plans."

Holy crap, China! I don't think I can take much more. You've tormented us for decades. What do you have in store now? Just don't hurt my daughter. Please don't hurt my baby!

"I've learned that Chen Song is very ill. Bedridden, actually. And she is unable to see you today."

The four of us froze. Ernie let out a sigh. I felt myself trying to formulate words, emotions, but nothing came out. I wanted to scream and weep all at the same time. I hated this place. This was our daughter's day, and it was being taken from her. I wanted to take her away from this rainy, cold, gray city as fast as I could. But then I looked down and Eden looked up at me. Trying to gauge how she should react, I assumed. I took her hand and stared at Bruce.

"Well, that is really sad news, Bruce. But surely there is someone else who we can visit with, right?" I suspected that in order to avoid losing face completely, Bruce had a backup plan. Chinese custom required individuals to escape from difficult situations with the least amount of embarrassment possible. I was banking on it.

"Yes. The foster mother also had three sons and they have offered to take you to the home where your daughter lived."

Bingo.

The talk of the foster sister melted away as I grasped at this last chance for Eden.

"Honey, it sounds like Chen Song is pretty sick and can't see us. But we can still see the place where you lived. How does that sound?"

Eden nodded. Resilient. Or perhaps not feeling the same devastation that I was. The two of us had always approached things differently. Eden was like her father in this regard, easygoing and able to adapt easily if plans changed. My personality matched Will's. We thrived on routine, predictability, and advance planning.

My brain felt at maximum capacity with this latest turn, though Eden appeared unphased.

"Very well. If you're ready to go, the van is waiting."

Rain came in sheets as we drove through the narrow alleys of Fuzhou. This section of town had been described to us by Bruce as a slum. Since the information we were receiving was new, I felt my brain trying to take it in quickly, process it, and be prepared for what might be ahead.

He says the area the foster mother lived in is a poor part of town. Much poverty. Okay. We can handle that. I can hang with a little poverty. I've slept in a mud hut in Mali before. This is gonna be a piece of cake.

Two three-story buildings were crammed together, each one showing signs of decay. We'd heard about the rapid destruction of older parts of towns all over China. Making way for bigger, taller apartment complexes with more modern amenities. The picture didn't look all that different than life in our neighborhood in northwest Denver where the same movement was afoot.

"The complex where she lived will be torn down soon," Bruce reported. "Nobody has been living in her home since she died." I felt a sense of deja vu, having just been told a few weeks prior that Will's living quarters were meeting the same fate.

"Can you tell us if these are apartments or... ?" We turned yet another corner and the alley became narrower. Our small van barely scraping by on either side.

"No. Not exactly apartments. It's an area where elderly people live. Together."

It had always seemed odd to me that an elderly woman would foster a baby. One at a time she took them in, we were told. As the roads began to narrow, it became obvious to me that one of the reasons for this was pure survival. The stipend she received to care for the babies likely covered her own expenses.

Okay, so there weren't any other children for Eden to play with. Only 75-year-olds. Okay.

"This is it." Bruce leaned forward, looking through the glass as the windshield wipers worked overtime. The van stopped.

I couldn't see anything that might constitute "it." There were some concrete buildings, but nothing resembling a home. However, as we emerged from the van, it was clear that we were indeed in the right place. The rain continued and we popped open umbrellas as we stepped outside. A middle-aged man approached us, first greeting Bruce warmly and then us, reaching to shake our hands as Bruce translated.

"This is Yu Li's oldest son. He's come to show you where his mother lived."

We shook hands, providing condolences for his loss. Eden and Will remained silent, but their eyes were wide as they took short steps up into the entryway of the concrete structure. Sitting in chairs just inside was a group of elderly men and women who were laughing as they played a game of mah-jong. We were a spectacle as usual, a tall Western man and his wife, holding the hands of two Chinese children. The group stopped its game and chatter. As words were exchanged with

Yu Li's son, a few of them pointed at Eden. I looked for sparks of recognition. Anything to let us know that they remembered our daughter. Instead, Bruce shuffled us further into the building.

The place felt familiar, but not in a way that called out "home" to me. It called out something different, from my childhood years in Wisconsin living on a farm. Barn. It was like a barn. This wasn't a house, but a series of stalls. As we walked deeper inside, I noted that each stall was roughly the size of a large walk-in closet in any suburban American home. At the back there was a small area not entirely closed off from the front. With a hole in the ground. Where, I presumed, the residents went to the bathroom.

Bruce had been right in describing the place as one of poverty. But now that we were inside, I knew that it was decidedly more than that. This was third world poverty, complete with a single string of lights, no indoor plumbing, and dirt floors.

Hoping that perhaps we'd get to a nicer section of the complex, we took steps forward. Our feet kicked up dust. Ernie and I held tight to the children as we walked. The lighting was minimal. Just a few bare bulbs hung from the ceiling. Eden and Will were silent as we walked through the hallways.

In the 30 minutes since we'd left the hotel, I'd prepared myself for a possibly half-torn down home and a place that was populated by only elderly people. Yet nothing could prepare me for the sight of Eden's first home as we were pushed through a small door off the hallway.

"This is where your daughter lived."

"Oh my God!" I said it out loud, then immediately wished I could take it back.

"Mommy, don't say 'Oh my God,'" Eden peeped.

The rosy picture I usually painted for the children even in

times of darkness wasn't going to happen here. The place was stunning. A dirt floor. Small. Dirty. No light. No windows. Unheated. The smell of musty rags. Trash strewn everywhere. It was clear nobody had lived here for a long time. It almost seemed as if the place had been ransacked for valuables.

There were no words. Literally. None. The four of us were silent. Not wanting to offend Yu Li's son, I heard my grandmother's voice ringing in my mind, urging me to say something like, "It's marvelous! Absolutely charming!" But nothing came out. Bruce and Yu Li's son stood in the doorway.

Finally, I bent down to Eden's level and spoke.

"Eden, honey. This is where you lived when you were a baby. What do you think?"

I left a clean slate for her as the question left my lips. She'd always astounded us in the past. I held my breath for it now.

"It's small."

"Yes. That it is, honey. It's small."

"What's this, Momma?"

She picked up a blue and white fabric wallet from the dirt floor. It was covered with cartoon characters. It was surely something the foster mother had owned and left behind. Something. It was something. My focus shifted to the items on the ground. As I looked closer, I noticed they were mostly baby-related. Old cans of formula. A single baby shoe. A nipple for a baby bottle. A child's immunization record. It wasn't much, but it was all that was left.

"It looks like a wallet. Bruce, can you ask the son if we can take a few things with us?"

The children began scouring the floor for treasures, as we confirmed that yes, it would be fine to take some things with us. I spotted a baby's chair that I recognized from photos we'd received from the orphanage of Eden and Yu Li. *How could we bring that home*, I wondered?

Ernie had stepped to the back of the room, into the area with the hole in the ground. I joined him, allowing us a tiny bit of privacy as the children continued to search the dirt floor, picking up pieces of trash and trying to identify each one.

"It's terrible, Jo. Unbelievable."

"I know. It's worse than I imagined. He said poverty, but I wasn't expecting... this. Oh my God, Ernie! Is this all there is? Is there more?"

"There's nothing else. This is what she'll have to remember. She won't know anything else."

"But we do. We know that this isn't how her American friends grew up. They had running water and a carpet to crawl on. And now we're here, and Ernie..." My whispered voice trailed off and I felt a lump in my throat. "There's nothing left."

I turned around in a circle, looking up and down. My shoes grinding into the dirt. Outstretching my arms as I tried to grasp what we were looking at.

"It's rubble, Ern. Eden's history. There's nothing. It's dust. All she has is dust." Tears fell onto my cheeks. "Is there more? Ernie, is there anything more? Isn't there anything more for our daughter?"

"Johanna, this is it. This is it. And us. She has us. We are it."

Ernie stepped into me and held me as I cried softly. Will and Eden had now found a porcelain cup, an ID card, and an English lesson book. They took no note of their heartbroken parents, standing just steps away. Instead they were shouting with glee at the dirty trinkets each of them clutched.

"Pull it together, Johanna. Don't fall apart on me now." Ernie knew the children would notice our moods any second. As always, he was right. It didn't serve any purpose for me to crumble right now. I turned my attention toward the children.

"Momma! Look at all the treasures we found!"

A pile of items was placed in front of us. A garbage bag appeared. Slowly filled with "treasures" from Eden's past. I found several baby outfits. A quilted jacket for a baby in traditional Chinese style. Booties. A knit hat and mittens. A pink, silk dress. They all went into the bag. I looked at the child's chair. Ernie cut me off mid-thought.

"Jo, we can't bring the chair. We have no way to bring it home."

I argued for a moment, then realized he was the voice of practicality as usual. The chair stayed. Our bag overflowed with Eden's past as we stepped out into the hallway. When she was placed in our arms, she'd come with nothing more than the clothes on her back. A green sweat suit. A pair of plastic shoes. A diaper tied with a bungee cord. In five minutes, we'd effectively quadrupled the number of items we had from her first year of life. To anyone else, it was garbage. To us, the items were priceless.

Making our way past the old people playing mahjong, one of them gestured to Eden.

"Maybe he remembers you, Eden." Will encouraged Eden to step closer to the old man.

"Bruce, what's he saying?" I couldn't understand the man as he laughed and spoke quickly to his friends.

"He says he remembers your daughter. He says she liked to be held. He says, 'That baby liked to be held.'"

We left her home with a garbage bag and this nugget. Eden had always been a cuddler. Starting here.

Yu Li's son had nicely offered to take us to his home, which he shared with his younger brother. The skies hadn't let up as we arrived at their home, not far from where their mother had lived. Yu Li's son picked up Eden in his arms and began to carry her towards the front door. She gave me a confused look as he walked with her, but I simply smiled at his gesture and then saw her relax into his arms. His dark pant legs soaked with water as he splashed through puddles to get inside. His younger brother beamed as we approached, reaching to shake our hands. He looked in his mid-20's, had spiked hair, and sport clothes on.

The middle class home was typically Chinese and located in a densely populated area. It spilled out over one level and had several small bedrooms as well as a shrine to their deceased parents. The concrete floors carried a draft from outside. Underneath the shrine sat burning candles and a pile of envelopes. The ambiance felt nothing like home to me, but it radiated warmth and love, nonetheless.

The younger son reached for the pile and handed it to us. The envelopes were addressed in English. I immediately recognized one with my handwriting and reached inside, pulling out the photos I had sent Yu Li of Eden at age 2, age 3, age 4. Her skin was clear, her clothes Western. I wondered if looking at these pictures of her had made Yu Li giggle the way we giggled seeing photos of Eden before we got her. The child the same in both worlds, just dressed in slightly different clothing. Held by different mothers.

We'd been told the name of both sons, but I'd already forgotten them and instead focused on their words. The two babbled back and forth, occasionally pointing at Eden. Between discussions with each other, they spoke rapidly to Bruce, who translated as much as he could.

"They say that their mother loved all the babies she cared for."

"How many did she have?" I inquired.

Bruce turned back to the sons who conferred, coming to agreement on a number.

"Ten. They say she had ten. She was given the sickest babies because she was able to bring them back to life. She cried for many days after each of the babies left."

Eden hadn't been one of the sick babies, but somehow had still ended up with this miraculous caregiver. My heart ached for Edie and for the missed opportunity to meet this devoted woman. Our daughter's second mother. Bruce continued his translation, each piece seeming urgent.

"Her sons say that she knew you were coming. They say that it took her two days to die and in those two days she talked about your daughter and how sad she was that she wouldn't get to see her again."

I couldn't process what I was hearing. On her deathbed, our daughter's foster mom had talked about... Eden? A little baby who she'd only cared for over the course of a year? I was incredulous, unable to look at Ernie for fear that if I looked away from Bruce, I'd lose the moment when I'd heard this beautiful story.

We sat on a bed looking through letters and photos from other adoptive families. Yu Li had kept everything. Her sons offered the children apples, which they took and munched on as we spoke. More words were swapped back and forth, with Bruce seeming to translate only half of what was being said.

"They would like to take you to dinner." Bruce nodded at us, and I could tell by his expression that it would be rude to refuse the offer.

Our group expanded to include more relatives, all descending with us into a restaurant in town. We were served a typical Chinese meal of vegetables, eggs, chicken, rice and soup. The dishes filled a big, round table. At our max there were twelve of us... seven members of Yu Li's family, Bruce and the 4 of us. Laughing, staring at Eden, telling stories of their mother and how kind she was. *The Mother Teresa of foster mothers*, I imagined.

Eden glowed with the attention, paying no mind to the fact that all of us were only picking up a small portion of the conversations. While the stories that were told weren't necessarily about her, I sensed that she knew she was the reason we were here enjoying turtle soup on a rainy Saturday in rural China.

"Momma, I just really love people," she whispered as we finished our meal with a final round of toasts.

"People are pretty nifty, aren't they, Edie? Especially these people. This is your family, too. They're pretty awesome."

Will overheard me talking to his sister, leaned over and said under his breath, "I think Eden had it better than me."

Better than him? I paused for a moment, thinking perhaps Will was joking. My brain flashed back to the scene in the barn just a few hours ago with the rubble, the squalor. Hard to believe that this constituted "better." Will gazed at me, waiting for a response, and I realized the authenticity in his comment. The meaning behind his assessment was focused on the people in her early life, and not the objects.

"She had it pretty good, honey. So did you. We saw that a few weeks ago. Both of you had it pretty darn good."

A half smile crossed his face as Will soaked in the validation he needed on his own experience.

We drove back to the hotel, thanking Bruce for salvaging our day in a big way. Tucking the kids in that night, my ears still rang with words Bruce had translated from Yu Li's sons as we had departed them.

"They say that their mother and your daughter needed each

other."

I remembered the day we met Eden and how happy she'd been. She smiled more than any of the other babies. She'd been loved. I focused on the things that would not matter a year from now, five years from now, twenty years from now. The number of toys she'd had while an infant. The hours she had spent crawling in dirt while American babies were in expensive infant music classes. The fact that she had pooped into a hole and not into a fancy cloth diaper. The insect bites she arrived with. The shady vaccinations she'd been given. None of these things mattered because Eden had been loved fiercely. She'd been held close. Cuddled. Fed. Spoken to. She'd been spoiled in all the right ways. The ways that mattered. Her foster mother had been paid $40 a month to care for her, but the money wasn't the greatest reward. The babies she'd cared for, including Eden, had brought her joy in her last years.

We'd always told the children we loved them and wanted them because they were adopted. Because of the fact that they had lived without us for a year. Because they were Chinese. Not in spite of that. Other people would ask us if we were sad we didn't get them at a younger age. Or said, not intending to be hurtful, of course, "Oh I can't IMAGINE missing my child's first smile, first bath, the first few steps." But we never mourned our loss in not being with them for the first year of their lives. It made them who they were.

I tasted blood as we tucked Will and Eden into bed, and realized I'd been biting the inside of my lip the entire day in an effort not to cry. I waited until Ernie and the kids were asleep. Then, entering the dingy bathroom, I closed the door, sat on the toilet and unpacked my tears into the soft folds of the hotel bed pillow. The tears, both happy and sad, came for a long time until I stumbled back to bed and into an exhausted sleep.

Without rain the next morning, we were able to walk to Eden's finding spot. Which, much like Will's, had been a mystery to us until this very moment. The name of a location had been written on her paperwork. It meant nothing to us, but everything to Bruce, who'd walked the streets of Fuzhou for years.

"It's an office complex. There were other babies abandoned here."

Abandonment really was the only option, as far as we understood. The rules against having more than one child were strict, leaving this the only viable option for many. Further, abandonment was itself a crime, and thus it was most often done in the shadows so it wouldn't be discovered. The Western concept of turning over a baby for formal adoption just didn't exist.

"How many have been abandoned in Fuzhou?" I asked the question, though wasn't sure I wanted the answer.

"Four thousand in Jiangxi Province in the past ten years. Mostly girls."

Staggering. An entire generation of lost girls. I pressed for details, as I knew that Bruce himself had adopted a baby, inspired by his work with adoptive parents from Western countries. As it turned out, Bruce had undertaken a search for his daughter's birth parents and, after searching in fifty different villages, had found the mother. She was 25 years old and had birthed six consecutive girls, abandoning all of them in a desperate plight for a boy. Did she love each one of her baby girls, I wondered? Dizzy at the thought, I asked what became of her.

"The last I heard, she was still trying for a boy," Bruce said.

The strong preference for a boy continued to amaze us. The need for a boy was tied most directly to the Chinese custom of boys providing for aged parents. Were the only child a girl, this might mean that in their old age, parents would be uncared for. The custom was changing, but it still existed enough that a mother abandoning six baby girls was not unheard of.

We arrived at the seven-story office building. Located on a busy street, its gray color blended in with every other structure on the block. Eden looked up at it, unimpressed. We'd gotten such a strong reaction from Will during the visit to his finding spot. In contrast, Eden seemed to be completely uninspired. Nonetheless, Ernie and I knew that someday, the trip would be important. In this moment, we needed to do all we could. Even if she was five and cared more about the next ice cream cone and not this monumental moment. I snapped photos. Ernie took a short video.

"Edie! Do you want a rock?" Eden nodded and Will began trolling for rocks on the side of the building. He had done the same thing at his finding spot, coming home with a rock that was palm-sized and would make the trip home to America with us in a few weeks.

"You are good parents for bringing the children back to China. They are lucky."

In the coming decade, I knew that hundreds of families would return with their adopted children. Mostly to visit, but perhaps in some cases to live as we had lived. Beyond the coming decade, I knew the influx of adult adoptees returning to China would be enormous. At this minute, I knew both Will and Eden would rather be in the United States than anywhere else on earth, but come twenty years from now, one or both of them would want to return. With this in mind, I knew that all the barriers we'd pushed through to be here this year had been worthwhile. Their return would be easier having done it once with us by their sides.

Meanwhile, Bruce had come through for us. The path to this point had been cluttered with misfortune, but he'd salvaged our weekend. Our daughter had more than when we'd arrived. Her story... more complete. I smiled and repeated the refrain of so many other adoptive parents. "Oh Bruce, I know you've heard it a thousand times, but WE are the lucky ones. Lucky to have them."

Our trip from Fuzhou to Kunming that day ended at 1:30 in the morning, after we'd endured yet another long delay. The weekend had gone not at all how we'd expected it to. Yet inexplicably we'd ended up with more than we'd hoped for. The feeling of uncertainty that greeted us at every turn here in China had become familiar. Almost comforting. I'd arrived here as a woman with a vast inability to be flexible. Any deviation from "the plan" rattled me. Somewhere in the past few months, that part of me had softened. Making room for the unexpected.

Outside the Kunming airport, the taxi line looked tame. After loading our luggage into the trunk, I took the front passenger seat as I always did. My job to get us to our destinations had been challenging the past ten months. Taxi drivers looked at me with everything from extreme amusement to full-on irritation. This time the task proved simple. I understood the entire conversation, never asking for help from Will. I joked with the driver as I loved to do, making fun of myself and providing material for the conversations he'd surely have later with his fellow taxi drivers. Ten months in-country speaking Mandarin was finally starting to pay off.

I'd brought our family so far and silently hoped the benefits in this endeavor would shine through as we prepared to leave. I'd exposed them to so much darkness. Would we step out into the light at the end of the year?

I remembered the first time we'd taken this drive from the airport into the city. Piled in Mr. Zhang's van, we'd stared out the windows and felt overwhelmed entering our new life. Tonight, as our taxi sped along, the lights of Kunming approached as we entered the city limits. We were headed to our own beds. We were home.

chapter forty seven

Will sat on our bed, his head resting on my lap, as we watched a documentary on my laptop called *Somewhere Between* about adoptive teens returning to China to meet their birth parents. After our return from visiting Eden's foster family, I felt a sense of urgency about what else we could do to capture the benefits of being in the land of the children's birth. Will had seemed at peace after our visit to his orphanage, yet I felt like digging just a bit more. Was there anything else I could do, I wondered? Anything else to make him feel more connected? Anything else that he wanted from this place?

I'd tracked down the film and billed our evening cuddled in bed as a "movie night" so that it would sound to Will something more exciting than what it really was – a full-on adoption workshop, hosted by his mother. In the United States we had access to multitudes of such opportunities, and they were almost always shunned by Will. Here in Kunming, my efforts took on special meaning and I held a captive audience.

The movie featured moments both difficult and heartwarming as the teens searched for their birth parents. Will watched with curiosity, and I felt my attention drawn equally to the movie, as well as his reactions to it.

"Mom. Pause for a second." Will sat up and looked at me. We'd gotten about halfway through the film, and I felt anxious with the hope that he might have had a revelation. I hit the pause button.

"Mom, this is totally NOT a movie night. This is you trying to talk about my adoption stuff again, Mom."

Crap. I'd been caught.

"Is that bad?"

"What the heck, Mom? We already went to the orphanage."

"I know, but I'm just wondering if there's anything else you want while we're here."

"Anything else? Like what?"

"Well, more conversations. Maybe putting up a sign?"

We'd talked about this when we'd gone to visit the orphanage. We'd heard of adoptive families putting up posters at the spot where their baby was abandoned. The content of the posters typically stated that this was the location where their child had been found. It included photos of their child as a baby and another as they appeared now, grown and healthy. In the words contained on the posters, the adoptees talked about their desire to find their birth parents. An email or a temporary phone number was listed in case anyone saw the poster and had information to share. Secretly, of course.

I'd never heard of anything coming from such an act, though wanted to leave our options open. Will had no interest a few months ago. Our sweet visit to his finding spot remained one of my favorite memories from the year, poster or no poster.

"I'm just not interested in that, Mom. I saw the orphanage and my finding spot. I wrote in my journal about it like you told me to. That's all I need. For now. I'm not ready for more."

"That's all you need now or ever, you think?"

"Now. That's all I need now. I wanna watch the rest of the movie, but I don't want to do that poster thing, Mom. No way."

But what if you're ready in six months and we're not here?! It will be so much harder to get the information you might want. I felt frantic inside. We lived ten minutes from the orphanage. *Oh God! We should have been going there every week. We should have befriended the nannies and invited them for din-*

ner. *What if they knew something about Will's birth parents and
we could have gotten that information?*

The instant felt like so many others that came in the course
of parenting. Your child picks the Happy Meal at McDonald's
instead of the fresh salad with apple slices. She decides to
invite the really sassy girl to her birthday party and not the
sweet, quiet girl from down the street. You suggest he check
out *Charlotte's Web* from the library and instead he picks a
graphic novel with all sorts of potty words.

I'd done all I could do for both kids. There might be more
that I could do for other families while we were here, but my
attempts to get more for both children had come to an end for
the moment. I just had to let go. I nodded and flipped the movie
back on. It ran to the end, leaving me with only one question.

"Buddy, do you think you'd be interested in sharing your journal entry with me? The one from the day we visited the orphanage?"

"I could do that. But don't read the other stuff. That's private."

"Deal."

Will slipped off the bed and into the bedroom he shared with
his sister. Ernie was reading with Eden and I heard her stop him
to ask Will how the movie was.

"It was okay. Don't worry. Mom will totally make you watch it
someday, but you don't need it yet."

*The orphanage was very exciting/interesting/sad. It was
filled with babies that were disabled and healthy. It gave me
small flashbacks from when I was a baby. In the orphanage we
met my caretaker, Miss Zhao, who is now director, Miss Tong,
a nanny, and Dr. Liang. At first I was not that interested in going, but after awhile it started getting better, and I started liking
it. We had a helper named Susan, who was a very fast Eng-*

lish/Chinese speaker. Our van was a very nice one, and we had lunch at a place called Slice of Heaven, which is near my finding spot. To me this is AMAZING! We left a toy there and also let a balloon go with a map with X-marks-the-spot and ten yuan on it.

- Will

chapter forty eight

Our children had received all the benefits that we could give them through living here. So I set out to help other adoptive families in our remaining days. *There must be a way, I thought, to give other families a chance to experience a piece of what we've been able to experience through living here.* Not knowing exactly what that meant, I sent out a message to one of the listserves that I visited from time to time. This one devoted to American families who had adopted babies from Kunming. It contained the basics: Hey, we're an American family living in Kunming. Leaving in a month. Is there anything we can do for you, adoptive families living in America?

After a few days, there was a nibble. A woman named Laura, with a daughter adopted from Kunming within the year, had received word that she'd been left with a note when she was abandoned. At the time of her adoption, she and her husband hadn't been given the note, but now that they were home, they desperately wanted it. Or at least some knowledge as to what it contained. Did it give their child a name, or a date and time of birth? Laura and I chatted by email for a few days as I made sure I could help. She had the same demeanor as mine. She understood that the task might be difficult, but was anxious to get whatever information she could so that she could fill in her daughter Emma's story. The only other sliver of information she had was the location of the police station where their daughter had been taken, and the officer who had filed the police report. *I could run with this,* I thought. I had no illusions that the task would be easy, but I recruited Helen to help me translate and we set aside time to visit the station.

"You're really going to do this? A police station? For these people you don't even know? You're a glutton for punishment, Johanna. Haven't you had enough of the Chinese police for a lifetime?"

The morning of our visit to the police station had risen. Ernie poked fun at me as I pulled together a backpack full of toys and snacks for Eden, who I was taking with me. With only a month left in China, laughter came more easily. The thought of showing up unannounced at a police station seemed more palatable and less terrifying than it had a year ago.

"It's totally whackadoodle. I get that, Ern. It can't hurt, though, and it will mean the world to this family if we get something for them."

"Yeah, I get that. Do you have to bring Eden? Can you just leave her here with us?"

"I could, but look at how cute she looks. She's going to totally melt those communist police hearts!" Eden twirled in the front hall, her hair braided and tied with a bright ribbon.

"Wait. You're using our daughter as bait?"

"Totally, honey. Totes. See ya!"

I threw the backpack over my shoulder and grabbed Eden's hand, leaving Ernie laughing in our wake. Helen met us in the front hall of our apartment. She was chatting with the people who lived across the hall from us. As usual, the woman carried a chicken in her arms. I'd taken note of what I assumed was their pet the past few months, and always thought it weird that he lived inside. Every time I saw the chicken, he looked a little different, and this particular chicken was no different. Didn't he have black tail feathers last week? Eden and I approached to say hello.

"What a cutie! How old is he? What's his name?"

My neighbor looked at me with confusion. *Maybe she hadn't understood me,* I thought. So I asked again, "What's his name?"

"Jī," she answered.

Chicken? Huh? That means chicken. He doesn't have a name? I was totally baffled.

"I think he's dinner, Johanna. Dinner," said Helen, making sure she was out of earshot from Eden. *Oh my God! He wasn't a pet. He was dinner. How could I not know this?* My naivety looked as though it would follow me all the way to our final days here.

The taxi ride dropped us at the main gate of the police station we'd been directed to. The compact, brick building was a single room, holding only two chairs for the officers who sat behind a single desk. Walking inside, conversation stopped as it was clear that whatever we had to say was far more interesting than what the officers were talking about. Western women didn't just show up in Chinese police stations every day. We were ushered inside and given two folding chairs. Eden's presence created a stir as it usually did when she opened her mouth and fluent English came out.

The police, both middle-aged men, wore dark blue uniforms. Their jackets hung off their shoulders, appearing two sizes too big. Being stationed at such a small location, I could tell that they'd likely never seen anything like the combination of the three of us. I pulled a granola bar out of my backpack and gave it to Eden, who was now sitting on my lap.

"What's the deal with that little girl? Is she your daughter?" The officer in charge directed the question at Helen, and he wanted an explanation immediately.

"No, I babysit her. This is her mom, here."

"Her mother is a Westerner? Does she speak any Chinese?"

"Yes, I do." My answer in Mandarin caused laughter in the room. I smiled and confidently explained to them what we were looking for. As I spoke, I slipped my hand into my backpack and turned on the record button on my iPhone voice memo function, just as I'd done during the visit to Will's orphanage. The implications if caught could include deportation, I thought, though if I managed to get a complete recording, I knew it would be priceless for Laura's family. *Hell, I thought, we're only a few weeks from leaving. What's the worst that can happen?*

As expected, we made very little headway. Helen pitched our pre-planned story of my being Laura's "cousin" here to seek the note or its contents. The officers asked if we'd been to the orphanage to ask for the note. I lied and told them we already had. I held in my hands Emma's "finding ad" which every abandoned child has. It was a very small photo accompanied by bare bones details about her finding. The photo of the tiny baby peaked the curiosity of one of the officers, who read the ad several times. I'd rarely seen interest at this level from the Chinese police. The officer seemed to hold compassion as he read and reread the article, staring up at Eden and then back at me.

"He's going to call the officer who found Emma and the note." Helen leaned over, mumbling the translation of the ongoing conversation.

My heart raced as the officer picked up the phone, dialed, offered his greetings when the call was answered on the other end, and began to carry on a conversation.

I strained to understand the Chinese. The tone of the officer's voice sounded flat.

"I don't think it's good news," Helen reported as he began to close the call.

The conversation ended. The officer looked up and spoke to Helen.

"The other guy doesn't remember the note or what it said, does he?" I asked.

"No. At least that's what they're telling us," Helen answered.

I smiled and nodded at the officers, thanking them for trying. In a way I hadn't experienced this year, the mood in the room was deflated, not defensive. The officers seemed invested in our situation for reasons that weren't clear. Maybe it was Eden. Maybe it was my bad Chinese. Maybe Helen had flirted a little bit. It escaped me, but became clear as the two of them conferred back and forth, placing several more calls on our behalf, trying to get us to the right authorities. Finally, they spoke to Helen one last time.

"We're not going to get any further on this, are we, Helen?"

"I don't think so. They tell me that they will take my name and number and will call me."

"In English we call that 'Don't call me, I'll call you.' We'll never hear from them again."

As we walked away, I recalled a conversation I'd had with a Chinese friend a few days prior. I'd expressed frustration at an inability to get something accomplished. Whatever it was had seemed so simple, but the roadblocks that we often faced in China stood in front of me again. When I pressed for the reason why, my friend had stated simply, "Foreigners see Point A and Point B and only a straight line between the two points. Chinese people see many different paths between two points. Find a different way, Johanna."

I loved her comment, which resonated with me as it only could after a year here. If the obvious path didn't work, try another one. I knew that Laura had tried to no avail to get the note through the most obvious channels: her adoption agency, the orphanage. My attempts at going directly to the police were another path. The question was, would this path work?

I returned home, emailing Laura the details of our day. I'd hoped for so much more, I said, apologizing for not coming home with the note or its contents. She wrote back, grateful at the story alone of our visit with the Chinese police. Ernie worked on the contents of the recording I'd captured, sending it to Laura so that she could have it translated in its entirety.

Days passed. I took Helen to dinner as a thank you for all she'd done to help us. Multiple trips to various Chinese police stations had been above and beyond our request so many months ago for her to simply tutor Will.

About one week after our visit, Helen called.

"You won't believe this, Johanna! Someone heard about all those calls the police made that day we were there last week."

My heart skipped, fearful that the sweet officers had gotten in trouble. I inquired, but Helen quickly dismissed my concern.

"No, this isn't bad news. It's GOOD news. I don't know how it happened, but the local newspaper printed a story about our search for the note."

"What? Oh my gosh, really? What does it say?"

"I'll send it to you, though it's all in Chinese. It has the facts right, though. American family adopted a baby and she was left with a note. They're trying to find the note."

I clicked the button to refresh my email as we spoke and the message from Helen with the story appeared. I gasped when I saw the article, which had photos attached to it of Emma, now a toddler, and of Laura and her family. They were a well-dressed family of six. Laura with blond hair, her arm around her husband who held Emma in his arms.

In front were their other three children, two girls and a boy.

The buzz that we'd started had been enough to gather steam, and surely someone in a position of authority would read the article and provide the happy ending the family needed. I popped off a message to Laura who replied right away, elated at the momentum. The two of us conversed several times a day, holding our breath as we hoped to hear more news.

Helen received news first. Her phone number, scratched onto a piece of notebook paper in the police station, had found its way to an official at the provincial level. Within a day, Laura began email correspondence with the authorities, confirming Emma's adoption dates and details. At last, the finding note came. Likely pulled from a file in some dusty office building in Kunming, it had been scanned and traveled via email directly into Laura's inbox thousands of miles away. The characters on the note were simple, but unknown to Laura, so she immediately emailed it back across the ocean to me.

"What does it say?!?!?!?!" she frantically asked across 10,000 miles. I'd functioned fine all year long only speaking Chinese, but in this moment, I kicked myself for not working harder on learning characters. I had no idea what it said. The hour was late. I thought of waking Will to provide the translation, but the solution wasn't my nine-year-old. There was only one person who I could ask. Desperate for the translation, I texted and then emailed Helen a copy of the note. "What does it say?! "

In China, the name of a child conveys hope, love, and dreams for the future. Little Emma's note contained a name given to her by her birth parents. Meng Yu. Meaning "dreaming of excellence." It contained the time and date of her birth, a simple fact, but one unknown by the majority of parents who adopted from China. It also contained one phrase, which conveyed everything. Reading it brought me to my knees. I spent a moment absorbing it, breathing it in. My heart breaking for the birth mother, the birth father and all those before and after them. Then, with shaking fingers, I hit the forward button and sent the entire translation to Laura. It was the middle of the night in the United States, but she knew we were in a race to translate the note, and was undoubtedly awake, breathlessly waiting for any details to add to Emma's history. When Emma grew up, she would always have the phrase that was written on a scrap of paper and left with her as an infant. Just two characters, when translated said:

I'm sorry...

My correspondence with Laura continued after the contents of the note had been delivered to her. Long after we arrived back in Denver, she and I chatted by email again about the gift we'd uncovered for Emma.

Johanna,

While the note did not say much, I think it said enough. It said that she had a beginning that was marked in time, a name that was given with great meaning, and that her parent(s) had regret about letting her go. That's really quite a lot. We are so thankful for your tireless effort to help a complete stranger! It was such a gift to our daughter, Emma Meng Yu, and to us. We continue to search for her birth parents. We realize it's a long shot, but maybe one day they will be at her finding spot and see the posters with her pictures that say she is happy and well. I hope so.

- Laurie

chapter forty nine

"We're sooooo putting them in life jackets, Ernie." I pulled a wrinkled sundress over my head as I felt the gentle movements of the boat rock us. With only a few weeks left in our year, we'd decided to squeeze in one last trip. I'd pulled the kids from school once again and we carved out a week in Vietnam and Laos.

After a few days in Hanoi, we traveled to Halong Bay, boarding a *junk*, an Asian sailing vessel. The ship carried a dozen guests, taking us on a three-night cruise through the Bay. Limestone islands dotted the Bay, each one covered with small rainforests. We'd spent our days going for kayak rides and our nights eating the delicious seafood dishes prepared by the crew. The children were the only kids on board and so well-behaved that the other guests fawned over them.

On our last night, the crew had scheduled a special dinner for the ten adult passengers. We anchored just off shore from one of the small islands. A multi-course meal was prepared on board and the crew planned to bring it ashore and set up a private dinner for us in a cave. The number of times Ernie and I had actually eaten a meal alone in the past year was pathetically small. The four of us had been inseparable for nearly every moment of our year. A date night was long overdue.

It wasn't until I began preparing for dinner that I realized the implications. The kids would be asleep. Fine. The only adult on board our ship would be the captain. Also fine. I didn't feel the need to ask him any important childcare questions. The kids would be zonked, after all.

Then there was the matter of the boat. They'd be sleeping on a boat that would be floating in the middle of Halong Bay. I felt my anxiety rise as I imagined one of them wandering around the ship in the dark. *We need to put them to sleep in life jackets. It's the only alternative.*

I paced between the two rooms that we were sharing, each holding a double bed and a small bathroom. The children jumped on the beds, mimicking the rock of the boat.

"Johanna, you've lost it for real this time. They don't need to sleep in life jackets."

"What if they sleepwalk and wander up on deck and fall overboard? I can see the headline now: American Child Dies in Halong Bay as Parents Dine on Lobster in Nearby Cave."

Eden stopped jumping momentarily to inquire, "Mom, what's sleepwalking?"

"Jo, they'll be fine. We'll have the captain radio us on shore a few times just to let us know that they're okay."

"More than once. I want a radio report more than once, Ern. And don't you ever tell my mother about this. Good God! She'd be mortified. She'd die at half the things we've done this year."

"I'd agree with that. The crazy taxi rides we've taken? The fact that we nearly got deported in October? Wading through a parasite-invested river in Nepal on top of an elephant? How about the fact that we're all about five pounds lighter than when we arrived because all we've eaten is fruits and vegetables all year?" I chuckled and continued getting ready, satisfied that the children would be okay for a few hours with regular checks. My attention turned to my mother and her potential horror at how we'd carried on our lives here.

"How about taking Will to the Chinese medicine clinic instead of a Western doctor for most of the year? Or walking through a river of chicken blood in the meat markets during the bird flu scare in the winter? Riding our bike without a helmet? Watching pirated movies all year long?" Ernie let out a snicker, then jumped in.

"What about when you told Eden that she could be the next Dalai Lama? That was classic." Will came into the room, momentarily leaving his sister bouncing alone.

"Eden's never going to be the Dalai Lama, Mom. Why did you tell her that?"

"It just seemed like the right thing to do at the time, buddy."

"Anything else to say about little lies like that, Mom?"

"What lies?"

"You know. The whole Santa thing."

I glanced at Ernie and saw a crooked smile on his face. My heart began to race as I tried to remember the talking points we'd gathered for the Santa-isn't-real conversation we intended to have before we went home. I'd even pegged June 25 as the day to have the conversation, as it was the furthest point from Christmas that we could possibly be.

"Uh, yes, well. Your dad and I want you to know that you can always believe in Santa. He represents the spirit of giving."

"But it's really you, right? You and Dad?"

"Well, yes it is. Actually that's true."

I searched into Will's eyes to see if I saw a look of devastation. Instead, he looked at me and commented, "I knew it, Mom. I've known it for years. Seriously? A guy coming down a chimney? Give me a break."

I felt a mix of relief and surprise at the revelation that we weren't breaking bad news. I assured Will that we'd continue the tradition for Eden, then checked that TO DO item off my mental checklist.

Ernie and I finished getting ready, kissed the children good night and made our way to the cave for dinner. The venue didn't disappoint. A gorgeous table surrounded by ten chairs and backlit with candles. We found our seats, chatting briefly with the other people from the boat, then turning our attention to each other.

The thread we'd started on the boat continued as we sipped wine and dined by candlelight. The topic veered from things we'd done that were positively crazy this year, to the things we weren't looking forward to returning to. The list included:

1. School politics and drama
2. A bigger house. Somehow we'd grown accustomed to living in a 500-square-foot space.
3. Television
4. Driving a car and related traffic jams
5. Overscheduled children
6. Junk mail

"I think we're gonna make it, don't you?" Ernie wondered out loud.

"I feel safe in answering YES to that question, Ern."

"Was it what you thought it would be? The year, I mean?"

"Well, yes and no. So much harder than I thought it would be. For all of us, you know? For the two of us. For the kids."

"I'd agree with that. I just hope that they look back on it with fond memories and don't remember all the crappy parts."

"Time will tell. I'd like to think we'll know right away that they got something out of the year, but right now they seem pretty anxious to go home."

"Aren't you?"

"In a way. I'm ready to be more comfortable in our daily life. But I'll miss the chaos a bit."

"I will, too. Chaos might not be the right word. But the twists and turns. The humor. The unknowns. I'll miss that."

"You impressed me, honey, this year. You handled it like a champ. I seriously thought I'd be running the show here, but we both know that I sorta fell apart before I pulled myself back together."

"Wait, did you just admit what I think you did? That I was actually in charge for a little while?"

I laughed, knowing I had admitted just that.

"I did, but it was a temporary state. I plan to be fully in control again once we hit U.S. soil."

"That's fine, Jo. You've always said I'm just along for the ride, but this has been a pretty good one."

At the end of our trip, I was certain that we'd hit our travel quota for the year. My regular jokes weren't working.

"Will, look at this backpack! One million Vietnamese dong!"

"So?"

"Doesn't it just sound cool to say that? ONE MILLION dong? Don't you think everyone should have a chance to say that in their lifetime?"

"Mom, you're weird. I just want to go home. America home."

"We're nearly there, Will. Just a quick stop in Laos and then it's back to Kunming to pack." *Oh my gosh, did I really just say "a quick stop in Laos" like it was a run to 7-11 for Gatorade?*

With only 24 hours in Laos, I was once again on my own. My travel-weary family enjoyed our day of walking through the capital, though crashed at the end of the day, leaving me to explore the night market solo.

The next morning I let Ernie and Will sleep, but woke Eden at dawn so we could peek out our hotel room window. On the street below was a line of monks who gathered each morning for alms giving. The monks were wrapped in orange robes and were barefoot. Their shaved heads helped disguise their ages, though it appeared they ranged from teenage to well past sixty. They chanted as they walked, stopping in front of the hotel holding out silver bowls for a woman on the street to fill with rice and vegetables.

Eden rubbed the sleep from her eyes and asked, "Why is that woman giving them food, Mom?"

"She feels it's a good thing to do, sweetie. That it will help her on the path to Nirvana."

"What's Nirvana?" At 5:30 AM, this answer was a stretch.

"It's a place that Buddhists think of as freedom. A happy place."

"Like heaven?"

"Not exactly, but you've got the right idea, Eden. Let's go back to bed now. I'll explain it in a little while."

Eden crawled into bed between Ernie and me, a place she often found comfort during the early morning hours. I shut my eyes and tried to imagine what we'd be doing a month from now. It would be summer in Wisconsin. All the regular summer activities would swallow us. Swimming. Ice cream. Movies. As the litany of Americana scrolled in my mind, I listened to the sounds of the monks chanting their way down the street.

As we boarded the plane to leave Laos, Eden had an announcement. "Everyone! Everyone listen! For the next two weeks, we'll only speak Chinese at home."

"Well, that IS going to be a challenge!" Ernie chuckled, realizing he was the most likely to fail at the task.

"Daddy, you have to at least TRY."

"I'll try, Eden. I'll try anything after this kooky year."

We lifted off into the skies for the short flight to Kunming. Our final two weeks lay just ahead.

chapter fifty

The menu at The Lost Garden remained the same. We'd come so often that I'd memorized the selections, the prices, and the way the cooks prepared our eggs. We were here one more time with Nina and Alex as all the children scampered about. It was June and their children were due to be released from the international school they attended in a few days. As was common among the expatriate crowd in Kunming, their family would leave China and spend summer in their home country. A summer in Finland with Nina's family broke up their year, followed by an annual trip to Australia over the winter holiday to be with Alex's.

"So, how's it feeling?" Nina asked. "Are you feeling ready?"

"I kind of feel like I'm trying to put the brakes on," I replied. I sipped on the latte I'd been served.

"It feels like you JUST got here, doesn't it?"

"That's so true. I remember our first breakfast here with you guys. The children were overtired and didn't want to play with your kids."

"And now look at them! The girls are like two peas in a pod."

I glanced over at Sofia and Eden who were drawing and giggling in the corner. The two of them couldn't look more different, Sofia's Scandinavian blond hair contrasting with Eden's black hair. Together, they were a force. Their personalities identically strong-willed and creative. The previous weekend, I'd heard them arguing endlessly about their game of make believe, eventually finding them in the bedroom dressed up as ninjas.

"You know why I remember that first brunch here?" Nina inquired, a silly grin on her face.

"You're scaring me. Why?"

"Because you absolutely couldn't sit still. Like you had somewhere else to be. More to do. You were so very... American. Needing to keep busy. It took months before you could settle in for more than an hour here."

Her assessment rang true. Ernie and I had already chatted about the need to slow down once we got back to the States. We planned to build an outdoor patio in the front yard so we could replicate our Lost Garden oasis. Our weekends wouldn't be overloaded with activities, we vowed. The way we'd previously emerged tired from our American weekends seemed... backwards.

As we recapped the year, we began a game of What We Will Miss in China. The woman who sells papaya at the university... watching her core it, cut it up, put it in a bag and add little toothpicks so it can be eaten immediately. The tailor who fixes lost buttons or tears in our jeans for just a few yuan per job. The beauty salon where I can get my hair washed and blown out for only $3.

Will rushed up the stairs, hearing our conversation and added, "The five friends I wouldn't have made. I'm thankful for my friends."

"Asian pears!" Eden screamed from across the patio.

"I'm really going to miss the looks we got from the Chinese parents at the apartment complex," Ernie piped. Our impact at the complex had been unmistakable. It had started when I allowed Will to climb the trees that lined the gardens. With only one child per family, each one was typically attended to by four grandparents. Any activity which could cause bodily harm was strictly forbidden. Will climbing trees caused pandemonium amongst the adults. They scolded him, begging him to climb down, until I came into the yard and reassured them.

"It's no problem. Children need to climb trees. He's very athletic," I had said in Chinese.

I felt them ease up, but sensed their agitation as their own children and grandchildren looked longingly up at Will in the tree, aching to climb themselves.

To make matters worse, there was the skateboard that Will rode constantly through the complex. Though not as mystifying as the tree climbing, it was equally compelling to the other children. For months the children and their parents had watched Will skillfully scoot around on his board, never falling.

I recounted the story as we sat eating our last bites of brunch.

"But here's the kicker," I said. "Last week I went out into the courtyard and there were like ten kids on skateboards! And apparently their parents had finally broken down and they'd all bought them at the same time." Nina and Alex roared with laughter as I followed up with how I'd told Will that he'd left his legacy here in Kunming in some small way.

As we left The Lost Garden one last time, Nina leaned over and whispered, "I'm proud of you. You didn't try to leave early. You made it a full three hours here without going all crazy American on us."

Our official good bye to Nina and Alex came days later. It felt familiar to say goodbye, and in a split second, I realized why. We'd just gone through this whole teary-goodbye-thing a year ago when we'd left the United States. The difference then was that we knew we'd return. As for a return to Kunming, it remained a mystery.

chapter fifty one

With only a week left, we busied ourselves tying up loose ends. On the work front, Ernie merely had to pack up his home office and turn off the power. His work during the year had been fruitful, if somewhat lonely. He'd return to the same company in a similar position. His work had completely changed the dynamic of our year, and for that we were grateful.

Then there were the school goodbyes. I told Teacher Che we wanted to visit Will's classroom to say thank you in person. With open arms, she welcomed us. His experience in Chinese public school had started bumpy, but smoothed as the year passed. Teacher Che had done everything in her power to make Will comfortable. As for his friends – they'd been a godsend. I'd embarrassed him endlessly on the streets outside school, but his friends seemed to secretly love it, and by the end of the year, he was at the top of the school popularity list.

Teacher Che greeted us as we entered. I asked for a few minutes to speak to the students.

"I want to say thank you to all of you for being such good friends to Zhi Yong this year," I said. I looked out at the sea of 44 classmates. Each attentive. Smiling. Listening. Supportive.

"We are returning to America and Zhi Yong would like you to sign his journal."

In the back row, a hand shot up. "Are you coming back?"

"We're going home to America, and hope to come back to visit someday."

Silence. I wasn't sure what the students had been told prior to this. The children looked upset. My heart sank. Slowly, each student began to approach Will. They unloaded their pencil cases to give him their possessions. Correction tape, pencils, sticky notes. Will was surrounded, and I could tell it would take some effort to extract ourselves from the classroom.

Turning to Teacher Che, I thanked her. My Mandarin lacked the depth needed to convey my gratitude. I hoped she could tell by my body language and the glistening in my eyes.

"Thank you so much, Teacher Che. You've been a wonderful teacher and friend to Zhi Yong. We are so grateful."

"He's a good boy, and so very lucky."

As we prepared to leave, I noticed a crowd in the back of the room. The students were chattering quickly and lovingly to Will's best friend, Chu Guo, who was sitting in his seat positively, entirely, and fully awash in tears. And not the sniffly kind. The big, loud, sobbing version. Crestfallen to lose his best friend, he was being rescued by his classmates.

"Don't worry, Chu Guo. It'll be okay. You still have us."

"Chu Guo, you can write a letter to Zhi Yong."

"Chu Guo, do you want my nice pen?"

As I watched, I realized it would never play out in quite the same way in the U.S. A crying third grader might be ostracized or bullied. In communist China, students clung to a pack mentality, lifting each other up in times of trouble. The goal of teamwork overrode almost everything else. It started here in elementary school. Eventually, the importance placed on relationships made its path through the years and played out in other ways, as children became adults. On this day, it was helping Chu Guo mourn the loss of his friend. Will approached Chu Guo, giving him an awkward hug. Then he stepped back, the students closing in on Chu Guo as we slipped out of the room and headed home.

chapter fifty two

The handheld, digital luggage scale groaned its disapproval as I hoisted it and read the number. I felt the bedroom floor creak as I plunked it down again. We'd vowed to return to the States with less than we'd brought over, but it looked like we were failing that task. When we'd left, I'd purposely packed clothes that I thought we would wear out and leave. While it was true that we'd leave most of our clothes, the number of gifts we'd accumulated in Asia didn't equate to an even trade. As I began to dig through the back corners of my closet, out came all of the treasures that marked our travels:

- A dozen scarves from Nepal
- Twenty kid purses from Cambodia
- Ten pairs of gorgeous, hand-embroidered shoes
- Fifty traditional Chinese porcelain necklaces
- Four hundred hand-painted chopsticks
- Eight tea sets
- A fancy rice cooker
- Three bags of oversized, plastic straws I just HAD to have

I set to the task of reshuffling items from one bag to another. As I worked, I made a mental note of the items we'd leave for our housekeeper Xiaocui. Over the past month, we'd sold some items to other expats, but it became clear that Xiao would be a much better candidate. The gift of her time had been enormously helpful to us. Not only had she cleaned our apartment and washed our clothes, but she'd fed us and cared for the children.

All year long, I'd watched her scurry around the apartment, her bare toes sticking out of the holes in her socks. It only made sense to give her our pots and pans, our set of fancy knives, the table linens. The last major item we struggled over was the bunk bed. The children had slept in it all year long, but it seemed silly to offer it to Xiao, as she had the usual one child. I persisted, offering anyway. The reaction I got took me off guard. I hadn't known the real level of poverty that Xiao lived in. With tears in her eyes, Xiao explained that she would very much like the bunk bed. It would allow her family of three to not have to sleep side-by-side on mats laid directly on their dirt floor, but instead be raised off the floor. They'd be warmer and save precious floor space. It would be a tight squeeze for Xiao and her husband on the bottom bunk, which was slightly larger than a twin size. No matter. Her home had been upgraded.

Back in our bedroom, I set down the luggage scale and pulled together my backpack. My final classes called me on this day, my last day of teaching. I'd told the students in each of my three classes that we'd celebrate with a party. In part, I did want to celebrate with them. In part, I wanted to celebrate my birthday. I knew beyond a shadow of a doubt that with all the prep going into leaving Kunming, nobody in my family would remember that today was also my 43rd birthday. I'd told Walt, who'd surely remember. That would have to be enough.

The front of our apartment looked barren. Pulling a scarf around my neck, I called to the kids and Ernie as they scampered around getting ready for what was also Eden's last day at school.

"Okay, I'm outta here! Last day of classes, here I come!"

"All right, bye hon! Hope it goes well."

"It's gonna go great. Anything else to say?"

I let a moment pass, and then heard, "I love you!"

I smiled to myself. "I love you" was more important to hear than "Happy Birthday," though both would've been nice. I briefly flashed ahead to the moment Ernie would realize he'd forgotten, feeling sorry for him. It had happened once before on my 40th birthday and was amended with a stunning diamond ring of apology a few weeks later. I called it my "Oops ring" and though it was beautiful, I didn't need another one, especially after a year surrounded by poverty and the knowledge that Xiao would still be living that life. Going home to America would be enough.

A few hours later, I stood at the front of my classroom handing out grades. I'd given the students an oral final exam during which I asked them questions that required their opinions. They'd clearly shared the half dozen questions over time with the other classes I taught because as the classes progressed, the answers had become more and more…canned. Nonetheless, the answers were interesting. An equal division between students who approved of the college entrance exams and those who didn't. Ditto the One Child Policy, which some embraced and some didn't. The single fact that most of the students were willing to give voice to their opinions about controversial subjects elevated my spirits.

I'd left the party planning up to each class individually. At first they'd been perplexed. The concept of a party in school seemed foreign. And then I realized…it was. Once they understood the opportunity to entertain freely, they defined a party as a chance to teach me everything I needed to know before I left China. There were demonstrations in kung fu, paper cutting, and Tibetan dance. There were tea ceremonies and calligraphy lessons. Karaoke, tai chi, and endless tables of food. In short, the students melted my heart with their kindness.

My first day of classes I'd stepped to the podium and looked out over a sea of terrified faces. Many of the students had never seen a Westerner in person, much less been taught by one. It had taken every tool in my toolbox to teach them that mistakes were okay and that it wouldn't be possible to expand their English without them. It had taken them months to warm to my laughter and the casual manner with which I conducted class. In most cases, they'd heard my advice and I'd seen improvement. With the hope that they'd listen one more time, I gave advice to all of my classes before saying goodbye. It was unlike advice they'd received before.

I told them to ask questions, though I knew that often times questions took a back seat to accepting the status quo. I told them to practice creativity. The creativity that I recognized in many of them would be harder to practice in China than the West, but I wanted them to know that it was valued. I told them to see the world. Though travel outside China was nearly impossible, I hoped my constant reminders about how close they were to other countries would resonate. Finally, I told them to be themselves. Tough in a society that valued teamwork and group thought.

The words were completely contrary to everything they'd heard from former teachers, yet I could see many of them breathe in the advice. Some began to cry. Whether it was because they were inspired or felt unable to practice what I hoped for them, I didn't know. *They all have so much potential. I want so much for all of them. I wish I could have given them... more.*

As the students streamed out of the classroom, I stood at the door giving each of them handshakes and hugs. I could see Walt waiting just outside. He had a small box, which he tried to hide behind his back. We stepped into the classroom and I looked up at him, asking in Chinese,

"Hi there! Do we have one more lunch date today?"

"We do! And I brought lunch to you today!" He pulled the box around and placed it on one of the desks, then opened it with a flourish. A gorgeous, frosted cake sat inside. It looked Western, but I knew from experience that its taste would be nothing like the cakes at home. More sweet and less filling, its symbolism more important than its flavor.

"Happy Birthday!" Walt smiled, clapping his hands as I screamed.

"Oh my gosh! You remembered!"

"Of course. It would be terribly unlucky if I forgot."

I put my backpack down and pulled up a chair. There would be no visiting the crazy cafeteria today. All I needed was right here. With two forks, we dug into my cake, he preferring the cake and me the icing. Walt grinned at his accomplishment as I lavished compliments on the cake's beauty and meaning.

"Walt, it's just so sweet. Thank you so much. I've learned so much from you. I can't even tell you how much I hate to say goodbye to you today."

"I will see you again, Johanna. You'll come back. Or I'll come there. We will make it happen. We're….adventurous. We'll find a way."

Our final conversation that day focused on Walt's hope to leave China and obtain a master's degree in a Western country.

"I don't really understand the point of the essay part of the application," he complained. "What is it supposed to do?"

"It's really just to give the universities a good idea about what motivates you. What inspires you."

"Some event?"

"Well sure. It can be an event or it could be a person. Something that happened to you that changed your direction. Some person you met who gave you focus or inspiration."

As the words tumbled out of my mouth, Walt's eyes lit up with a moment of recognition. After all the hours we'd spent together, I knew him well enough to know where he might be going. I held my breath, hoping that the strife of the year might wash away in the next few seconds with his words. And it did.

"I have that, Johanna. I have that person. It's you. You will be my essay."

chapter fifty three

Will and Eden raced their little rolling carry on bags around our empty apartment. A series of photos I'd taken in various Southeast Asian airports featured these bags. They'd become so adept in foreign airports that all we needed to do was tell them the gate number and off they went, typically ahead of us. And often reaching out for each other's inside hand, their outside hand rolling the bag. The handholding, suitcase-dragging moments were picture perfect.

True to form, our last day in Kunming had been unpredictable. Ernie had developed a rotten sore throat. I'd gone to school to pick up Eden, bringing treats to celebrate the last day with her classmates. Instead of finding her bouncing off the walls, I discovered her clothes hanging on the railing outside the classroom. Stepping inside, her teacher told me that she'd vomited all over herself, no doubt the victim of a final bout of food poisoning. I'd plopped her on the bike seat, brought her home and put her to bed for a few hours.

My final day was marked by a call from a university official who was calling to verify where to send the standard letter of recommendation for all departing professors. While on the phone, the official told me that though I had been an excellent teacher, Mr. Zhang had found our family "not very independent." I suspected this arose from the mass of challenges we'd experienced early on in our year. The ones not attended to or even acknowledged by the university.

"Not very independent? What the hell?" I muttered as I stepped out of the way of Will and Eden's suitcase race. We'd come without the backing of a multinational company, without a stipend. Little help finding an apartment and even less help getting the kids into school.

Then there was Will. The anxiety he'd experienced prior to coming to China had resurfaced. This time, in response to leaving China. I'd found him in the bedroom that morning looking out the big, picture window. On the street there were several elderly men walking along the sidewalk. One of them had a baby expertly strapped to his back in an embroidered sling.

"That's something we're not going to see in a few days, is it, buddy?"

"No. And I think I'll miss it. I know we're all packed, Mom, but I sorta wish we could stay another year."

His comment caught me as off guard as I'd been all year. In part, I knew he felt safe saying this because he knew we were actually leaving. Still, it was a long way from where we'd been. We'd peeled away all the layers of one another, getting to know our children and ourselves in ways that would never have been possible without this experience. It had been dark. It had been raw. We'd hit rock bottom. We'd had days when I was convinced we'd never climb out of the hole we'd dug. Somehow we'd managed to find our way out. We weren't exactly the triumphant quartet I'd envisioned, but we'd…grown. The long-term benefits of our year might blossom in the years ahead, but at the moment, I felt myself counting the minutes until we boarded the plane to Shanghai. I retold the story to Ernie as I heated him a cup of tea. How Will had asked for another year here.

"And if we can't provide that, he says he'd, at minimum, like to make it an annual trip."

"Unbelievable. Is this the same child we brought over here?"

"It's crazy town. And it's not as though we're all leaving on a high. Look at all of us. You and Eden are sick, Will's mourning the fact that we have to leave, and I've just been told that I'm needy."

"China knows we're leaving. And she's kicking us where it hurts, Jo."

I chuckled, preferring to think of his comment as an expression of China's love for our family. It's all I'd ever wanted. For her to love us as we loved her.

The morning of our departure arrived. The rooms of our apartment echoed from the weight of their contents being lifted during the previous week. We moved silently getting dressed, brushing teeth, and snapping buckles on suitcases. Seven monster bags, each tied with a brightly colored fabric ribbon with the name of its destination in bold, black handwriting. One labeled "Shanghai," where we'd start our trip home. One labeled "Hawaii," our second stop. Two labeled "Wisconsin," where we'd spend two months. Two that said "Denver" where our journey had started, and where we'd return at the end of summer.

The buzzer on the door rang, indicating that Helen and her mother had arrived. We'd called a van to take our luggage, but planned to ride with Helen to the airport. Our goodbyes to her had stretched out over a week. A goodbye dinner. Goodbye movie. Goodbye presents. Every conversation for the past few months had been laced with the promise that she would find a way to get to America. She would nanny or enter grad school. Possibly studying to become a teacher. Somehow, she'd find a way.

As we moved to step outside, I stopped and locked hands with the children. The empty foyer of the small apartment we called home was the one spot I wanted us to remember the most. Not a beach in Thailand or sitting on the Great Wall. Not riding on the back of an elephant or drinking fruity cocktails on a boat in Vietnam. While those places had been our lifeline, they weren't really what our year was all about. I knew we'd return to America and be swept back into our lives there, going in four different directions.

"I just want one more moment," I whispered. The children looked at me wide-eyed.

"You and your 'moments' Johanna," Ernie laughed. And then, "Thanks for the year, honey."

"Yeah, Mom, thanks for the awesome year," added Will.

"I'm so proud of all of you. It wasn't easy, but you totally did it. WE did it." My voice cracked, full of every emotion…relief, joy, gratitude.

"Don't cry, Momma. We're gonna go to Shanghai now, and they probably have cheese and jelly beans for you," Eden whispered to me.

As we pushed open our door, Helen folded the children into her arms. Our departure marked the end of an experience for her that was bigger than I'd imagined. Her face showed such sorrow that I couldn't make eye contact, walking ahead to confirm with the guards at our gate that the van to take our luggage had arrived.

"Where are you going today?" asked the Happy Guard.

"Home!" I piped.

"But you're home now," he replied, confused.

"America home," I added.

Happy Guard burst out in laughter, responding, "Lucky! You're so lucky! I'd like to come with you. Can you take me with you?"

I laughed with him, but inside a voice spoke softly to me.

You will come with us. ALL of you will be with us. Always.

chapter fifty four

"Mom, where are we going today?"

The three days in Shanghai had sealed our conviction that our year had been genuinely Chinese. The clothes and food options tilted Western here. People didn't stare at us, nor was there the same sense of chaos that prevailed in Kunming. Things felt oddly... organized. The mish mash life of Kunming had been more difficult to manage but had felt so much more... authentic.

Our suitcases sat piled on a luggage cart as we paced the lobby of our hotel. To Eden, it was just another day in transit. The destination not nearly as important as the journey.

"Ah, honey, we're heading back home today. We're stopping in Hawaii for a week. Then we'll go to Wisconsin. Elkhart. Re-member? Where Aunt Nano reads books at story hour every week."

"Hawaii? What country is that in? Is there a pool there?"

What the...? We'd made such an effort to provide lessons on all things Asia that apparently we'd forgotten to fill her in on our last stop. I calmly told her that Hawaii was in America and it did indeed have a pool, as well as, uh...an ocean. She perked up.

"When are we coming back to China, Mom?"

"Someday, Eden. Someday we'll come back."

"I wanna come back. I love it here. This is where I was born. I wish I could have been in your tummy, Mom. But I love China."

We'd always described the things we didn't know because of their adoptions as "beautiful mysteries." I'd grown accus-tomed to marking the medical history boxes on pediatrician paperwork "NA" and found peace knowing that we'd watch some of those mysteries become answered little by little. Tiny treasures sprinkled throughout our lives. The year we were leaving behind had gifted us with many such answers. Many treasures.

"I love China, too, honey."

All that lay between the life we'd embraced here and the familiar life of America was a ten-hour flight. I looked out the window and bit my lip. My poor lip had taken a beating this year. The plane gained speed, taking flight at last. Up and out of Asia. An image settled over me. Thirty-five giddy Syracuse students buckled in their seats as I was now, heading home to their families. Their lives had ended over Lockerbie, but mine had continued for 25 years. I would never be exactly what they might have been, but I had tried to build a life that they would have admired.

I heard a voice next to me. The same one that had spoken to me a year ago as we lifted off from O'Hare. Will's feet curled under him, the airsickness bag being used as a canvas for a series of cartoons he'd started working on.

"Mom, are you sad because our adventure is over, or happy because we're going home?" Will looked only slightly concerned, having seen me in a similar, emotional state at many points in the past couple years. Only one answer fit the question. "Both… both."

The cabin doors opened and a rush of warm, humid air greeted us. And skies. Blue skies. I swelled with joy, relief, sadness, closure. The children raced down the stairwell brought to the edge of the plane and we joined other travelers in the baggage area. It hit me as we stood there, waiting for our seven suitcases. I could understand. Every word of every conversation happening around me. It felt like a violation at first. Then made me laugh a little bit.

"What's up, Jo?"

"Oh my God, everyone is speaking English. I just heard that father chew out his son. And I fully understood it."

"It feels weird, doesn't it? We can't talk about anyone behind their backs anymore."

We'd decided to stay at a large resort after realizing our stay could be paid for entirely by the hotel points we'd accumulated in our Asian travels. Though we'd been spoiled many times in Asia, it was nothing compared to Western standards of luxury. Everywhere we turned...excess. A moat surrounding the resort stocked with small sharks and stingrays. An endless supply of beach towels. Women wearing lots of jewelry. Clean drinking water poolside with lemons in it. Children with piles of beach toys. The houses surrounding the resort looked palatial. The cars parked in the driveways were ridiculously large.

We settled into our ocean view suite. Its square footage nearly matched the size of our apartment in China. Once un-packed, we decided to go to the grocery store to stock up on drinks and snacks. The automatic doors of the grocery store slid open, welcoming us into its temperature-controlled luxury. For a moment, all of us froze. Five seconds later, both children ran. Down every aisle, totally out of view from me. I could hear them screaming, completely oblivious to the fact that other customers could hear and understand them.

"Cereal! Chips! Eden, look at all the chips!"

"Will! Will! I found juice boxes!"

I found myself standing in front of the cookies. Row after row of choices. Sugar free. Extra chocolate chips. Gluten-free. Various frosting flavors. I'd heard from other expats about the first time back in a grocery store. At the time it seemed a myth. How could having 65 choices of breakfast cereal feel anything but pleasurable? Now, standing here deciding between Chips Ahoy and Oreos…I got it.

I called a cease-fire and we walked out without purchasing anything, finding Ernie, who was next door at an AT&T store re-activating our cell phones. The children gawked at the latest technology while I pulled Ernie away from the conversation he was having with the salesperson.

"I can't do it. I'm freaking out, Ern," I hissed.

"What do you mean?"

"The grocery store is so…indulgent. Nobody needs that many choices."

"Oh my God, Johanna. It's just a grocery store. You can do it. We just need bottled water."

"I can't do this. It's too soon. I'm not ready."

"Just get the things we really need and be done."

"Honey, I don't think we need bottled water. Can't we just drink from the tap here? We don't need anything. I gotta get out of here."

I escaped to the rental car, turning on the engine and thus the air conditioning. Overcome by options everywhere, I looked at yet another one staring up at me from the dashboard. Did I want it to be 72 or 73 degrees? I put my head in my hands and breathed.

The solution came in the form of laughter. Because really…

the contrasts were just plain outlandish. I realized in short order that it did no good for any of us if I wallowed in culture shock for too long. So we laughed.

About the fact that three days ago I'd bought an American newspaper for ten U.S. dollars in Shanghai, but now they were laying around for free everywhere I looked. About the fact that Ernie and the kids had forgotten my birthday, but by simply picking up the phone and calling the hotel concierge they had managed to get an "oops" birthday cake delivered to our suite by a waiter dressed in a tuxedo. About that fact that one week ago I'd been standing in the local market negotiating the price of mangoes while freshly slaughtered pigs dripped blood from meat hooks next to me. While now we sat on the balcony of our suite and watched a private Fourth of July fireworks display over the ocean. And perhaps the most staggering contradiction, about the fact that last week our neighbors had been a Chinese family of five and a chicken they intended to slaughter and eat for dinner. While now we were located in a suite just above... celebrities.

On our second morning, I noticed a photographer nearby. He held a long angled lens and was set up in a cabana taking pictures as Eden and I played in the shallow end with another mom and her adorable son. We chatted about silly kid stuff and the crabs that lined the rocky alcove.

Good God... is that... paparazzi? Why would he want pictures of me and Eden? The mom I'm talking to has a knockout body and her husband is a total hunk. I wonder if it's about... them?

Though it had been a year since I'd diligently read American magazines, I proudly retained some body of knowledge on Hollywood celebrities. I soon realized that the paparazzi wasn't after us, but was after our new beach playmates, who I finally recognized as former Playboy model Kendra Wilkinson, her former NFL wide receiver husband, Hank Baskett, and their son. I couldn't decide if the photographer was a nuisance or a blessing to this adorably sweet family, who'd soon have their own set of sunny, frolicking beach photos splashed over the tabloids.

It all felt... bizarre. That I could be living a simple life in Asia one day, and the next day be worrying about whether my bikini body would show up alongside Kendra's in the online version of People magazine. Our reality had gone from an ill-fated chicken to a Playboy model overnight. I giggled to myself and ordered a fruity drink with an umbrella. Just like in China, I realized that laughter was more valuable than angst.

You've just gotta go with it, Johanna.

chapter fifty five

Our flight into O'Hare descended, and I heard Eden jabbering in Mandarin. It was nonsensical, though her tones looped properly up and down. I was trying to focus on the next few hours which I knew would be a flood of questions and love from my parents and sister who were meeting us at the airport. A man sitting behind us tapped me on the shoulder, nodding to the children who were seated on either side.

"Are they twins?"

I paused, unsure I had heard the question correctly. Eden had just turned five and Will was about to turn ten. Though this nice gentleman would have no idea, the two of them could not be more different. It stood to reason that any given set of twins in the world might be like night and day also, but in that moment, I savored this question and all that was wrapped up in it. Different biological parents. Different hometowns. Different ages, genders, interests. Yet closer than any siblings I knew.

The reunion with our family at O'Hare and then our extended clan in Wisconsin erased the struggles of the year and brought forth the good. Perhaps more than anything, it was the overwhelming kindness all around us that took the most getting used to. Kindness had surrounded us in China, but the Wisconsin version was unparalleled. Near stifling at times. My uncle Rob described it aptly one afternoon, telling me that the kindness of a man was directly proportional to the distance he lived from his neighbor. Ernie affirmed the sentiment, telling me,

"You've just come from China, Johanna. A country of a billion people. And now you're in a small town in Wisconsin with a population of 967. Give yourself a break. It's gonna take some time. It's gonna take some getting used to again."

Within days of eating nothing but cheese and ice cream, I'd gained back the five pounds lost over the course of the year. Laughter filled our days and nights as we sat on the beach at the lake unloading story after story from our experiences. After six weeks, I felt faint from a stream of family parties, swimming and endless piles of presents exploding from our suitcases. We loved Wisconsin, though the place we truly called home lay just ahead.

Nighttime was closing in as our car pulled up in front of our home in Denver. Melissa and Dan had fallen in love with our neighborhood and moved into their own home just ten blocks away.

I had thought of this moment all year. In my mind it was un-realistically romantic. I could practically hear the year being tied up with a bow as the children would fall out of the car and marvel at their home. With the addition of a sports bar on our corner, the street was full of parked cars. *How inconsiderate of people to not leave a spot in front of our house for such a momentous occasion*, I thought to myself.

I turned to Ernie, saying, "Ern, just pull up here and double park. You gotta get out so we can have a family hug." He gave me the look that I'd seen so many times before. It was a cross between "You've gotta be kidding" and "This is why I married you."

At that moment the children of course didn't share my desire for long recaps of all that we had accomplished. They simply wanted to run in and tear through the house, jumping up and down without fear of waking a neighbor through a shared wall. So my comments were brief as we huddled on the front stoop.

"We're so proud of both of you. You showed a lot of courage this year, and we got through good times and bad. We're a good team now, and we always will be. We've all been through a lot this year, but we always promised we'd bring you home. So here we are guys. Welcome home."

The front door opened into a familiar space of comfort and warmth. I couldn't see the lessons we'd learned in flashing lights. It would be months or years before the impact of what we'd undertaken would sink in. For now, I would settle for the screams of the children as they raced around our home, discovering all they'd left behind. And now returned to.

epilogue

The significance of the year took hold in small ways. As we returned to life in America, I received short notes from my students, updating me on their new English teacher and their progress with the language. My favorite read:

Merry Thanksgiven Day! I still remember the lessons you give us, Be yourself, be creative, be curious, go to travel. I am so happy to be your student, i never feel boring or stressful in your class, what you teach us is that life not just a life, it's an attitude, how to choose a life you want to live with. it's alway chanllenging for me, i want to chase after a life i want, but the truth is life drive me move forward with my unconciousness. how terrible it is. sometimes i feel anxious and i can not sleep well, for worrying my future, althoug i know worry is useless and it does not work at all. as if i am far away from my ideal life. i always keep trying to practice my spoken English, and i found that the funny and important truth is that i have no need to be inferior any more, i just need bring my mouth, my smlie, keeping an open mind to communicate with others. life always has things needed my finding. mayby a surprise, hope you and your family are happy for your life.

The message stirred me in the ways that all teachers are stirred by small gestures from their students. Somehow the trials of our year in Asia were washed away with one small reminder that I had been valued.

Will and Eden returned to school, Eden in kindergarten and Will in fifth grade. Photos of Will's best friend Chu Guo, Helen, and Sofia hung alongside those of their cousins and American buddies, reminders that friendships could span thousands of miles and many languages.

I corresponded with Helen, who continued her quest to come to the United States. Walt enrolled in graduate school in Sweden, while Nina and Alex and their children began their final months in Kunming, with plans to move back to Finland.

I read news of China with enlightened eyes, my attention always drawn to the slow changes with the One Child Policy, which was now loosening in some parts of the country to allow more families to have multiple children. It meant fewer families would ultimately adopt from China, a fact that made my heart swell for the babies who wouldn't be separated from their country of birth. At the same time, a small part of me wondered how families like ours would be created, with one option taken off the table.

We'd been home about a year when Will pulled me aside one night. Ernie had taken Eden upstairs to bed, leaving the two of us alone in my office, a place we often found ourselves parked for deep conversation as the day drew to a close.

"Mom, you know how you said that we would someday think back on our year in China and would appreciate it? I think I'm there now."

"Oh really?"

"Yeah...you told us not to waste our time being miserable, because it would go so fast, and then we'd regret that we spent all that time whining. I know I whined a lot, but I think I just didn't want to let myself enjoy it, cause I was worried I wouldn't want to come home." Will stepped further into my office. My hands reached out for his and he took them.

"And also Mom, I've been feeling a little guilty and happy and sad and confused and lucky. All at the same time. I can't really explain it. I don't have the right words. It's kind of like how I feel when you ask me to describe my adoption."

"I'm listening. You mean how you feel like your brain doesn't have the words yet?"

"That, yeah. I feel kind of pulled apart. Kind of like this isn't my life, but I don't know why. I get really sad for no reason. And then happy the next second." His voice seemed concerned, almost unsure of where the words would lead him next.

"We saw a video at school about people who are poor and how they live. I think that's when all these feelings came up. Most of the other kids said it was disgusting. They didn't want to watch. But I just felt sad. I remember seeing people like that in China. And so now I'm feeling lucky. That I'm here."

"Well yes. We've got a good life here, buddy."

I thought about the conversations I'd had with Ernie since being home. The children recalled their time in Asia with joy, but we often wondered if the lessons they learned there would ever be apparent. It took a bit of looking, but perhaps this was one of those instances.

"Those kids in the videos didn't have any toys. They looked like the kids we saw in Nepal. The ones playing with the tires."

I lowered my voice, a tactic used by my father when I was a child. It required complete attention, as I'd strained to hear his words. Will moved closer to me.

"And how did that make you feel?"

"Well, I felt guilty, because I have an iPad that I play with a lot."

"And didn't those kids look pretty happy? With just the tire?"

"Yeah."

"Do you remember visiting Eden's foster mom's home? And the dirt floor?"

"I remember all the old people sitting outside playing mah-jong. They seemed really happy and they remembered Eden."

"That's right. And they told us how happy Eden was. That her foster mom loved her. And her sons told us she and Eden need-ed each other."

"Why? Her foster mom was 75 years old. Why did she need Eden?"

"Well for one thing, she didn't have a lot of money. She got money from the government to pay for Eden's food. And she probably bought food for herself, too."

Will nodded, then looked down. I continued. I could tell that it was a moment when my words would make a difference. I didn't want a throwaway conversation. Will needed the real deal.

"But more important than that, she needed love. Everyone needs love, buddy. Whether you're a baby or 75 years old. Eden and her foster mom were meant to be together for that year. They didn't need money to love each other."

"I still feel sad about all those people who don't have a good life like us."

"It's okay to feel sad. And I'm not saying it's okay to not have money. It must be hard to not have enough money to feed your family. You've seen people who are too poor to buy food. You walked over homeless people on your way to school in Kun-ming last year."

"I remember. And I think I'm starting to get it, Mom. I'm lucky."

"That you've got a good life, you mean?"

"Well, yes. But more than that. I could have ended up there

and been one of those people on the streets if you and Dad hadn't adopted me."

I felt that familiar lump in my throat.

"We feel lucky, too. Dad and I feel lucky that we got you. And you know we didn't adopt you because we wanted to rescue you."

Will looked at me as I repeated the same words I'd said 100 times before. He'd always heard me, but this time, he was listening, not just hearing. His eyes radiated knowledge in a way I hadn't quite seen before.

"I know. You wanted a baby."

"Not just any baby. We wanted you. There are just certain people in this world who are… meant to be together. Sometimes they aren't together from the moment that they want to be. But eventually, they find their way to each other. They just…find a way."

"And that's how it was with us?"

"That's how it was with us."

I held my breath awaiting a response from my wise son. Instead, I got a shrug of his shoulders. An adolescent half-smile, which signaled that our conversation was ending, but also… continuing.

"Okay, that's cool. Wǎn ān, Mom."

"Good night to you, too, Will."

"Wǒ ài nǐ, Mom."

"I love you, too, buddy."

acknowledgements

The only place to begin is with my husband Ernie, who's been the perfect partner on my path. I'm overjoyed that it's been you by my side for nearly all the chapters of this story.

Will and Eden... thank you for tolerating months of a distracted mother as I stepped through the journey to write every word. I hope you can see now that I was with you all along and always will be.

Anjuli, Carolyn, Carrie, Laura, Lisa, MC, Missy... The women of my writing group who guided me from the very beginning. The mantra they planted in me is perfect for writing and for life: "Just keep going." I shall.

Liz, you answered untold questions of every shape and oddity. You are so very wise and I hope your wisdom has rubbed off on me in these pages.

To Nina and Alex, whose friendship kept our spirits lifted as we swam together through the hilarity of our lives in Asia.

Alice, without your perseverance and sense of humor as we navigated choppy waters, our adventure would have started and ended in Denver. Thank you.

Trish and Kat saw something meaningful in my story. I'm grateful to have crossed paths with you at just the right time.

Ann and Jenn, thank you for running every mile with me since age 18.

Heidi, Ellen, Nicole, Jean, Pam and Jamie... My stable of dear friends who are each smart, witty and add so much to my life.

Megan, you have held me up and made me laugh. Your

New England sensibilities balance my craziness and I can't wait for more travels of all sorts together.

Chris, Julie, Steph and Sam have known me since we were all in diapers together on the Toyland Beach. You are all so much more than cousins to me.

To my parents Tony and Jane and my sister Britt, whose love and patience grounded me from the start and allowed me to seek more. I love you so.

And to The One who launched my journey so long ago... thank you for our Moment and all the moments since. We will find a way.

about the author

When not crafting adventures near and far, Johanna Garton fills her days as the owner of Missionworks Consulting, a non-profit management consulting firm in Denver. By night, she teaches advocacy at Regis University. In her spare time, she enjoys using her journalism and law degrees so she can justify the fact that she's still paying her student loans. Prior to her year in China, Johanna created *Kids Yoga Speak*, an on-line tutorial to teach Mandarin Chinese to children through the use of yoga and storytelling. To keep pace with Will and Eden, Johanna tries to get upside down at least once a day and find stories in every corner of life. *Awakening East* is her first book.

Visit Johanna online at www.facebook.com/awakening east.

Other adoption-related books published by Marcinson Press:

Are You Ready to Adopt? An Adoption Insider's View from the Other Side of the Desk

The New Crunch-Time Guide to Parenting Language for Chinese Adoption

Geezer Dad: How I Survived Infertility Clinics, Fatherhood Jitters, Adoption Wait Limbo, and Things That Go "Waaa" in the Night

Jazzy's Quest: Adopted and Amazing!

Ladybug Love: 100 Chinese Adoption Match Day Stories

The New Crunch-Time Guide to Parenting Language for Haitian Adoption

Additional copies of this book
may be purchased through
most online book retailers and
by request through major and
independent bookstores.

To purchase this book for your
library, bookstore, or university,
please contact the publisher at
www.marcinsonpress.com.

MARCINSON PRESS

Made in the USA
Charleston, SC
02 December 2015